OZU

OZU

DONALD
RICHIE

UNIVERSITY OF
CALIFORNIA
PRESS
Berkeley, Los Angeles, London

University of California Press
Berkeley and Los Angeles, California
University of California Press, Ltd.
London, England
Copyright © 1974, by
The Regents of the University of California
Paperback Edition 1977
ISBN: 978-0-520-03277-4
Library of Congress Catalog Card Number: 73-76109
Printed in the United States of America

Portions of this book originally
appeared in *Film Quarterly,*
Film Comment and *Eiga Hyoron,* as well as
Shochiku and New Yorker
Films catalogs, and program
notes for The Museum of Modern
Art, New York, Cinema 16, and The Boston Museum
of Fine Arts

15   14   13   12   11   10   09   08
16   15   14   13   12   11   10   9

Itsumo yu koto da ga—
ore ni ichiban taisetsu na mono wa ore da.
Ore no naka no ichiban kamiza ni suerarete iru
mono wa shigoto da.

It's something I always say—
most important thing for me is me.
And in that me the most important position
is that of work.

From Ton Satomi's
SHIKARU, *quoted by Ozu*
in his diary entry of
April 6, 1935

CONTENTS

PREFACE

INTRODUCTION

SCRIPT

SHOOTING

EDITING

CONCLUSION

Yasujiro Ozu. *Ca. 1936.*

PREFACE

THE JAPANESE continue, ten years after his death, to think of Yasujiro Ozu as the most Japanese of all their directors. This does not mean he is their favorite, though he has been given more official honor than any other. It means that he is regarded as a kind of spokesman; Ozu, one is told, "had the real Japanese flavor." This "Japanese flavor" has a more definite meaning than, say, "the American way" or "the French touch" if only because Japan remains so intensely conscious of its own Japaneseness. Modern civilization, only a century old, remains a Western veneer over an Asian culture that has endured for two millenia.

The uneasy juxtaposition of the two cultures has created the familiar contrasts of the country, and has given the Japanese his often near-schizoid intensity and made him extremely conscious of his differences from the Westerner. The careers of many men of letters, and some not so lettered (politicians, for example), show a familiar pattern: a period of early exploration among things Western followed by a slow and gradual return to things purely Japanese. The career of Ozu followed this pattern. After an early enthusiasm for American films, particularly the works of Ernst Lubitsch, he consolidated these influences into his mature and fully "Japanese" style—and indeed this pattern is one of the things celebrated in the Ozu films. Their tension derives from confrontations between men and women who are in different sections of the pattern, between, for example, parents who have returned to Japaneseness and children who are on their way out.

There is never any doubt where Ozu's essential sympathies lie in these confrontations, though as a moralist he is scrupulously fair, and for this reason some young Japanese have disliked his work, calling him old-fashioned, bourgeois, reactionary. And so he would appear, since he so continually celebrates those very qualities, the traditional virtues of their country, against which young Japanese must revolt. That these virtues are mainly theoretical in no way falsifies Ozu's position. Though everyday Japan is not a country noted for its restraint, simplicity, or near-Buddhist serenity, these qualities remain ideals, and Ozu's insistence upon them and the public feeling for or against them make these ideals more than empty hypotheses.

Take, for example, the quality of restraint. In even a strictly technical sense, Ozu's films are among the most restrained, the most limited, controlled, and restricted. From early in his career, for example, Ozu used only one kind of shot: a shot taken from the level of a person seated in traditional fashion on the tatami. Whether indoors or out, the Ozu camera is always about three feet above the ground, and is rarely moved. In the early films, though there were numerous dolly shots, there were few pan shots. Likewise there were some fades in and out, but dissolves were rare. In the later films the camera is almost invariably immobile, and the only punctuation is the straight cut.

This traditional view is the view in repose, commanding a very limited field of vision. It is the attitude for listening, for watching. It is the same as the position from which one watches the Noh or the rising moon, from which one partakes of the tea ceremony or a cup of hot sake. It is the aesthetic attitude; it is the passive attitude. Less poetically, it also represents the viewpoint of a then-majority of Japanese. They spent their life on the floor and "any attempt to view such a life through a camera high up on a tripod was nonsense; the eye level of Japanese sitting on the tatami becomes, of necessity, the eye-level through which they view what is going on around them." [1]

Finally, it also resembles the attitude of the haiku master who sits in silence and observes, reaching essence through an extreme simplification. Inextricable from Buddhist precepts, it puts the world at a distance and leaves the spectator physically uninvolved.[2]

Ozu's method, like all poetic methods, is oblique. He does not confront emotion, he surprises it. Precisely, he restricts his vision in order to see more; he limits his world in order to transcend these limitations. His cinema is formal and the formality is that of poetry, the creation of an ordered context that destroys habit and familiarity, returning to each word, to each image, its original freshness and urgency. In all of this Ozu is close to the *sumi-e* ink drawing masters of Japan, to the masters of the haiku and the *waka*. It is this quality to which the Japanese refer when they speak of Ozu as being "most Japanese," when they speak of his "real Japanese flavor."

More is implied in this description, however, than restraint in the service of art. The unique art of Ozu is very evident, but so is his common humanity. The Ozu character is among the most lifelike in cinema. Since character for its own sake is always a major subject in the Ozu film and since it is but rarely that a character must work to forward the ends of the story the director is determined to tell us, we are often given that rare spectacle of a character existing for himself alone. This we observe with the delight that precise verisimilitude always brings, and with a heightened awareness of the beauty and fragility of human beings.

The unexpected humanity of the Ozu film is made possible by the rigor of its construction. In an Ozu film, as in Japanese architecture, one sees all the supports, and all of them are equally essential. Like the carpenter, the director uses neither paint nor wallpaper; he uses, as it were, natural wood. The finished object one may measure, one may inspect, one may compare. But within this object, this film, as within the house, lives the human, the immeasurable, the nonfunctional. It is this combination of the static and the living, of the expected and the surprising, that makes the films of Ozu the memorable emotional experiences they are. Without the rigorous frame that is

xiii

the director's technique, the intense humanity of the character could not be so completely revealed. Without the useless and lovable humanity of the Ozu character, the film's structure would degenerate (as indeed it sometimes does) into mere formalism.

A similar duality occurs with respect to the sense of time in an Ozu film. His pictures are longer than most and at the same time have less "story" than most. What story there is, moreover, often seems more anecdote (which is why a précis of an Ozu film fails even more completely than usual to convey what the picture is like as an experience). Since the story is presented over a long period of time, and since there is little overt action to sustain the time values, unsympathetic critics complain about a pace that to them seems slow. They would have real grounds for complaint if this pace existed by and for itself. Yet Ozu's films are not slow. They create their own time and for the audience, drawn into Ozu's world, into a realm of purely psychological time, clock time ceases to exist. And what at first seems a world of stillness, of total inaction, is revealed as appearance. Beneath this seeming stillness one finds the potential violence present in any Japanese family, and also the quiet heroism of the Japanese faced with his own family. One finds drama enough to justify the length of the Ozu picture, but the point is that one *finds* it, it is not deployed before one. It is their potential for action that gives Ozu's films their vigor, and that makes his use of time meaningful.

Thus, just as technique restricted comes to make us see more, so tempo slowed comes to make us feel more. The effect of both is the same: characters come alive in a manner rare in film. And both means are the same: the spectator is led into the film, is invited to infer and to deduce. He gives of himself and of his time, and in so doing he learns to appreciate. What remains after an Ozu film is the feeling that, if only for an hour or two, you have seen the goodness and beauty of everyday things and everyday people; you have had experiences you cannot describe because only film, not words, can describe them; you have seen a few small, unforgettable actions, beautiful because real. You are left with a feeling of sadness, too, because you will see them no more. They are already gone. In the feeling of transience, of the mutability and beauty of all life, Ozu joins the greatest Japanese artists. It is here that we taste, undiluted and authentic, the Japanese flavor.

Ozu's method of creation was as idiosyncratic as his films are unique. Ozu had but a small store of themes and a limited roster of character types. He and the scriptwriter with whom he collaborated would decide the kind of character and theme they wanted to make a film about. Then together they would write a complete dialogue script. The theme was dramatized and the character amplified at first only through dialogue; only later was the continuity script written. Already, however, the stock character had come alive and become a particular person; already the general theme had become a particular series of events. Only when the script was considered satisfactory did Ozu turn his attention to the shooting of the film. Here, too, his methods were unique, as was the way he eventually cut his picture.

In the hope of revealing the coherence of the Ozu film, I have decided to approximate in the structure of this book Ozu's method of creation. I begin, therefore, with a discussion of Ozu's themes, since that is where he himself would have begun, and go directly into the dialogue, trying to approximate his working method in my own presentation. Later I discuss the way in which he shot and edited his picture, and the effect of the finished film itself. Those readers who would prefer the more usual chronological rendering of a director and his work should perhaps read first the Biographical Filmography. I believe, however, that both Ozu's biography and the chronology of his films make more sense in the context of the way he worked, of his style, for this was the man himself.

Ozu's films are referred to throughout by their English titles. Despite the failure of many of the accepted English titles to capture the nuances and distinctive quality of the original Japanese, the films are known abroad mainly by their English titles and any other form of reference would be confusing. Readers who wish the Japanese titles may refer to the Biographical Filmography or to the Index.

The major documents necessary for writing this book were the two issues of *Kinema Jumpo* devoted to Ozu (June, 1958, and February, 1964) and the monumental *Ozu Yasujiro— Hito to Shigoto* (1972). Also essential was Tadao Sato's *Ozu Yasujiro no Geijutsu* (1971), and I remain indebted to Paul Schrader's *Transcendental Style in Film* (1972). The numbering of the script extracts, given after each dialogue example, is taken from the English title list for each film, though my translation often departs from the one used in the subtitled version of the film itself. The subtitle scripts were obtained largely through the courtesy of Shochiku; those for *The End of Summer* and *Floating Weeds* were from Toho and Daiei, respectively.

ACKNOWLEDGMENTS

I N WRITING this book I am most indebted to Eric Klestadt, without whose help it would have been difficult to write at all. I am also very grateful to Tadao Sato whose monograph on Yasujiro Ozu is the finest in the Japanese language and who kindly made his materials available to me. Access to the original Ozu scripts and drawings was given me by Akira Shimizu of the Japan Film Library Council; to the letters and diaries by Shizuo Yamauchi, one of the editors of the definitive *Ozu Yasujiro—Hito to Shigoto,* who also gave me a number of the stills. For the printed scripts, many of the stills, and a number of private screenings I am indebted to Toshinori Fukuma of the National Film Center, the Japan Film Library Council, Daiei, Toho and, in particular, Tetsuo Yanai of Shochiku. I am also grateful to Hisao Kanaseki, Sheelagh Lebovich, and John Nathan for their readings of the manuscript and for their ideas and, especially, I am indebted to Muriel Bell, my editor, whose care, understanding, and good sense have made this a better book.

Finally, I want to thank the many people—cameramen, actors, assistant directors, friends—who knew Ozu, who had worked with him, and who shared with me their experiences and their memories.

DONALD RICHIE
Tokyo, 1974

INTRODUCTION

Y ASUJIRO OZU, the man whom his kinsmen consider the most Japanese of all film directors, had but one major subject, the Japanese family, and but one major theme, its dissolution. The Japanese family in dissolution figures in every one of his fifty-three feature films. In his later pictures, the whole world exists in one family, the characters are family members rather than members of a society, and the ends of the earth seem no more distant than the outside of the house.

The Japanese family, in the films of Ozu as in life, has two main extensions: the school and the office. Both are almost foster homes, traditionally far less impersonal than their analogues elsewhere. The Japanese student finds a second home in his school and keeps close contact with his classmates throughout his life; the Japanese white-collar worker finds in the office a third home, and will identify himself with his company in a way rare in the West. The Ozu character, like the Japanese himself, tends to move among the three: the house, the schoolroom, the office.[1]

Thus Ozu's films are a kind of home drama, a genre that in the West rarely attains the standard of art and that even now is generally perceived as somehow second-rate. In Asia, however, where the family remains the social unit, the home drama has been refined far beyond the examples found, say, on American radio or television. Ozu's home drama, however, is of a special sort. He

I

The Life of An Office Worker. *1929.*
Mitsuko Yoshikawa, Tatsuo Saito

College Is a Nice Place. *1936.*
Sanae Takasugi, Choko Iida

neither affirms the family as, for example, Keisuke Kinoshita does in his later films, nor condemns it, as Mikio Naruse does in many of his pictures. Rather, though Ozu creates a world that is the family in one or another of its varied aspects, his focus is on its dissolution. There are few happy families in Ozu's films.[2] Though

2

Tokyo Story. *1953.*
So Yamamura, Kuniko Miyake, Chishu Ryu, Setsuko
Hara, Haruko Sugimura, Chieko Higashiyama

An Autumn Afternoon. *1962.*
Shinichiro Mikami, Shima Iwashita,
Keiji Sada, Chishu Ryu

the earlier pictures sometimes show difficulties overcome, almost
all the mature films show the family members moving apart. Most
of Ozu's characters are noticeably content with their lives, but
there are always indications that the family will shortly cease to
be what it has been. The daughter gets married and leaves the fa-

3

ther or mother alone; [3] the parents go off to live with one of the children; [4] a mother or father dies, etc.[5]

The dissolution of the family is a catastrophe because in Japan —as contrasted with the United States, where leaving the family is considered proof of maturity—one's sense of self depends to an important extent upon those with whom one lives, studies, or works. An identification with family (or with clan, nation, school, or company) is necessary for a complete identification of self. Even in the West the remnants of such a need are strong enough for us to regard the plight of the Ozu character, and the predicament of the contemporary Japanese, with sympathy. The father or mother sitting alone in the now empty house is an image common enough in Ozu's films to serve as an epitome. These people are no

Tokyo Story. *1953.*
So Yamamura, Setsuko Hara, Haruko Sugimura, Kyoko Kagawa, Chieko Higashiyama

Late Autumn. *1960.*
Setsuko Hara, Yoko Tsukasa, Nobuo Nakamura, Chishu Ry

4

longer themselves. We know they will somehow survive, but we also know at what cost. They are not bitter, they know this is the way of their world, but they are bereft. The reason they impel our sympathy is that they are neither victims of their own flaws, nor the prey of a badly organized society; they are the casualties of things as they are, the way that life is. And here we are, all of us, similar casualties.

Though the majority of all Ozu's films are about the dissolution of the family (as are a large number of Japanese novels and of Western novels too, for that matter) his emphasis changed during his nearly forty years of film-making. In his first important films the director emphasized the external social conditions impinging upon his characters: the strain in a family occasioned by the father's joblessness in difficult times, the children's inability to understand that their father must be subservient to his employer to keep his job, etc. It was only in later films that the director found more important the constraints on the human condition imposed from within.

This change has been held against the director: "Ozu used to have an open-minded view of society; he tried to capture the complicated aspects of its day-to-day existence. . . . He always had a burning fury against social injustice, but his realism began to degenerate and to decay. . . . I remember that when *Passing Fancy* and *A Story of Floating Weeds* were released, many of us were deeply disappointed to find that Ozu had abandoned serious social themes." Though Ozu's "pioneering achievements" in creating a realism new to the Japanese cinema are credited, and though *I Was Born, But . . .* is found to be "the first work of social realism in Japanese film," the pictures after 1933 are found wanting: "Young critics who have seen only Ozu's postwar films know but one side of the director. . . . His craftsmanship and taste are, of course, impeccable; and his deep, mature understanding of the life that scintillates within is profound. Nonetheless, the sorry truth is that Ozu's greatest virtues those which made him what he was in his earliest days, can no longer be found." [6]

The criticism is cogent and one may argue only with its basic assumptions: that realism must be social, and that proletarian reality is somehow more real than bourgeois reality. Ozu did not, of course, abandon realism. He did, however, abandon the idea that unhappiness is caused solely by social wrongs; he came to recognize that unhappiness is caused by our being human and consequently aspiring to a state impossible to attain.[7] He also abandoned the naturalism of his earlier pictures. This was in part due to his changing families, as it were. The struggling middle-class or lower-class family, prey to every social current, disappears from his films.[8] From the mid-1930s on the family was, with exceptions, of the professional class, and in the postwar years it became, again with exceptions, upper-middle-class. Ozu's sense of reality, however, did not change.[9] One still hears the complaint that the interiors in the later Ozu pictures are too pretty, too neat. But an attempt at neatness and prettiness is, after all, one of the attributes of bourgeois life everywhere. Bourgeois life is no less real for being more pleasant than proletarian life—a fact that Ozu's critics, quite unfairly, hold against him.

If anything, Ozu's later films gain in a feeling of reality, and, more important to his art, transcend it. He is concerned not with quintessential family. He achieves the transcendental from a base in the mundane, in the bourgeois family—undisturbed by social upheavals, undismayed by financial misfortunes—where a sense of the dailiness of life is perhaps most readily to be discovered. It is precisely "day-to-day existence" that Ozu so realistically and hence so movingly captured.

The life with which Ozu is concerned in so many of his films, then, is traditional Japanese bourgeois life. It is a life singularly lacking in the more dramatic heights and depths found in a society less conspicuously restrained. This does not imply, however, that such a traditional life is less affected by the universal human verities; on the contrary, birth, love, marriage, companionship, loneliness, death, all loom particularly large in a traditional society because so much else is ruled out.

A traditional life also means a life based upon an assumed continuum. As Chesterton somewhere remarks: "Tradition means giving votes to that obscurest of classes, our ancestors. It is the democracy of the dead. Tradition refuses to surrender to the arrogant oligarchy of those who merely happen to be walking around." Traditional life assumes that one is a part of something

Tokyo Chorus. *1931.*
Hideko Takamine, Emiko Yagumo,
Hideo Sugawara, Tokihiko Okada

The Munekata Sisters. *1950.*
Chishu Ryu, Hideko Takamine

The Only Son. *1936.*
Yoshiko Tsubouchi, Shinichi Himori

Early Summer. *1951.*
Kuniko Miyake, Kan Nihonyanagi,
Setsuko Hara

larger: a community in time encompassing the dead and the yet unborn. It assumes one is a part of all kinds of nature, including human nature.

Traditional life gives rise to an attitude that is as common in Japanese daily life as it is in the films of Ozu. Though there is a useful Japanese phrase for it, *mono no aware,* a term that will be examined later, the attitude was best described in English by W. H. Auden, when (in another context) he wrote: "There is joy in the fact that we are all in the same boat, that there are no exceptions made. On the other hand, we cannot help wishing that we had no problems—let us say, that either we were in a way unthinking like the animals or that we were disembodied angels. But this is impossible; so we laugh because we simultaneously protest and

7

accept." [10] Perhaps the Japanese, in accepting the conflicts of being human, would sigh rather than laugh, would celebrate this transient and unsatisfactory world rather than merely find it absurd. But the underlying, profoundly conservative attitude remains the same, and it animates all but the very young in the Ozu family.

If the family is Ozu's almost invariable subject, the situations in which we see it are surprisingly few.[11] The majority of the films are about relations between generations. Often a parent is missing, dead or absconded,[12] and the one remaining must rear the children. The dissolution of the family, already begun, is completed by the marriage of the only or the eldest child or the death of the remaining parent. In other films the family members move away from one another; the children attempt, sometimes with success, to reconcile themselves to their married state.[13] Or again, the child finds the restrictions of traditional family life stifling and must, albeit against his will, defy them.[14] There are perhaps a few more variations on the theme, but not many.

I Was Born, But . . . *1932.*
Hideo Sugawara, Shoichi Kofujita,
Tokkankozo

Good Morning. *19*
Masahiro Shimazu, Koji Shida
Yoshiko Ka

Just as Ozu's illustrations of his theme are few, so his stories, compared to the majority of those found in full-length films, are slight. A précis of an Ozu film (e.g., daughter lives with father and does not want to marry; she later discovers that his plan to marry again was but a ruse, accomplished for the sake of her future happiness) sounds like too little upon which to base a two-hour film. Any Ozu story, however, is in a way a pretext. It is not the story that Ozu wants to show so much as the way his characters react to what happens in the story, and what patterns these relations create. Ozu used progressively simpler stories with each succeeding film, and he rarely availed himself of plot.[15] In the later films the story is little more than anecdote. Some of the reasons for this will be discussed later. For the present it suffices to observe that Ozu was perhaps primarily interested in pattern, in the design that Henry James called "the figure in the carpet."

Ozu's patterns are reflected in his stories. A character moves from security to insecurity; he moves from being with many to being alone; or, a group shifts, loses members, accommodates; or, conversely, a younger character moves into a new sphere with mixed emotions; or a person moves from his accustomed sphere and then returns with a new understanding. These patterns are stacked, as it were, one upon the other; it is the rare Ozu film that has only one pattern and one story. Through the similarities and differences of the patterns and stories with their parallels and perpendiculars, Ozu constructs his film, the sum of his thoughts on the world and the people living in it.

Ozu's pictures, then, are made of very little. One theme, several stories, a few patterns. The technique, too, as mentioned earlier, is highly restricted: invariable camera angle, no camera movement, a restricted use of cinematic punctuation. Similarly, the structure of the film (to be examined later) is nearly invariable. Given the determined limitations of the Ozu style, it is not surprising that his films should all resemble one another. Indeed, there can have been few artists whose *oeuvre* is so completely consistent. In film, Ozu is unique. Some of the noteworthy recurrences in his pictures are described below.

Many of the titles are similar (*Early Spring, Late Spring, Early Summer, Late Autumn,* etc.), and the general structure is, in the later films at any rate, invariable. The titles remind one of the novels of Henry Green, and both the titles and the general structure of the novels of Ivy Compton-Burnett. Ozu was obviously not the kind of director who said all he wanted on one subject and then turned to another. He never said all he had to say about the

Japanese family. He was like a close contemporary, Giorgio Morandi, the artist who spent his life drawing, etching, and painting mainly vases, glasses, and bottles. As Ozu himself said, during the publicity campaign for his last film, *An Autumn Afternoon,* "I always tell people that I don't make anything besides *tofu* (white bean curd, a common and essential ingredient in Japanese food), and that is because I am strictly a *tofu*-dealer." [16]

Not only did Ozu often use the same actor in the same kind of role, playing, generally, the same kind of character (Setsuko Hara and Chishu Ryu are notable examples), he also used the same story line in various films. *A Story of Floating Weeds* is the same as *Floating Weeds, Late Spring* is very similar to *Late Autumn,* which in turn resembles *An Autumn Afternoon.* The secondary story of

The Story of Floating Weeds.
1934. Emiko Yagumo,
Yoshiko Tsubouchi

Floating Weeds. *1959.*
Machiko Kyo, Ayako Wakao

Early Summer (children running away from home) becomes the main story of *Good Morning,* etc.

Character, too, is recurrent. The daughters in *Late Spring, Early Summer, Equinox Flower, Late Autumn,* and *An Autumn Afternoon* are, though played by different actresses, essentially the same character involved with the same problem—whether or not to get married and leave home. Minor characters, too, are often

te Spring. *1949.*
ishu Ryu, Setsuko Hara

Late Autumn. *1960.*
Yoko Tsukasa, Setsuko Hara

near-identical. The unfeeling sister of *The Brothers and Sisters of the Toda Family* becomes the unfeeling sister of *Tokyo Story,* and shows her insensitivity in the same way (asking for something after her parent's funeral). There is often (*Late Spring, The Flavor of Green Tea over Rice, Tokyo Story, Early Spring, Good Morning*) an old salaried man due to retire who, drunk, thinks back over his life and questions it. There is, from *The Brothers*

Tokyo Story. *1953.*
Hisao Towake, Chishu Ryu,
Eijiro Tono, Mitsuko Sakura

and Sisters of the Toda Family on (including *Equinox Flower, Late Autumn, Tokyo Story, An Autumn Afternoon*) the gently ridiculed lady proprietor of a Japanese-style restaurant. Characters also tend to keep the same names. In some cases they are as invariable as the burlap backing that Ozu consistently used for the main titles of all his sound films. The father is usually named Shu something-or-other, a favorite being Shukichi, with Shuhei a close second. The traditional daughter is often named Noriko (as in *Late Spring, Early Summer, Tokyo Story, The End of Summer*), whereas the more modern friend or sister is named Mariko (*The Munekata Sisters, Late Autumn*). The younger brother is usually named Isamu (*The Brothers and Sisters of the Toda Family, Early Summer, Good Morning*), and so on. This is not primarily because the names carry special connotations (though Shukichi sounds old-fashioned and Mariko rather modern to the Japanese), but rather because Ozu was arbitrarily consistent with what he had already created.

The activities of Ozu's characters are also consistent. They almost all admire the civilized nature that they view in their gardens or in Kyoto or Nikko, they all are acutely aware of the weather and mention it more often than any other characters in films, and they all like to talk. They also like bars and coffeehouses. The former, in film after film, are named Wakamatsu or Luna, the latter Bow and Aoi and Bar Accacia. Here Ozu characters sometimes get drunk, though they are more likely to do so in nameless small Japanese restaurants and drinking stalls. More usually they sit and enjoy the slightly foreign flavor so gratifying to city Japanese. (There are many foreign references in Ozu's pictures, mostly from the movies: characters speak of Gary Cooper in *Late Spring*, of Jean Marais in *The Flavor of Green Tea over Rice*, of Audrey Hepburn in *Early Summer*. In the background of *That Night's Wife* is a large poster for *Broadway Scandals;* Marlene Dietrich has a poster in *What Did the Lady Forget?*, as does Joan Crawford in *The Only Son* and Shirley Temple in *A Hen in the Wind.*) They also eat, more often than most film characters, and seem to favor Japanese food, though they handle knives and forks as easily as chopsticks, just as they are equally at home on chairs and tatami matting. This ease, how-

The Flavor of Green Tea over Rice. *1952.*
Koji Tsuruta, Chishu Ryu, Shin Saburi

Autumn Afternoon. *1962.*
Chishu Ryu, Daisuke Kato

ever, is one they share with other Japanese film characters and
with most Japanese themselves. Western critics who believe that
Ozu is commenting on Western influence in his country are mistaken; he is simply reflecting Japanese life as it now is.

The father or brother in an Ozu film is typically shown sitting
in his office (we almost never see him doing any actual work),
and the mother or sister doing the housework (hanging out towels
to dry is a favorite occupation, but there are others; *The Brothers
and Sisters of the Toda Family* and *Early Summer* have identical
scenes in which the women fix the *futon* bedding) or serving tea to
guests who are always appearing in the Ozu household. The children often study English (*What Did the Lady Forget?*, *There Was a*

13

Father, Tokyo Story, Good Morning), and the daughter of the house can type in English (*Late Spring, Early Summer*). The family (and its extension in the office) likes games (go in *A Story of Floating Weeds* and *Floating Weeds*, mah-jongg in *A Hen in the Wind* and *Early Spring*), riddles (*I Was Born, But . . ., Passing Fancy*), puzzles, and jokes. Another pastime to which the Ozu family is addicted is toenail cutting, an activity worth mentioning because it occurs possibly more often in Ozu's pictures (*Late Spring, Early Summer, Late Autumn*) than in Japanese life.

Outdoor activities are also few, including only hiking or bicycling (*Late Spring, Early Spring, Late Autumn*), fishing (*A Story of Floating Weeds, There Was a Father, Floating Weeds*), and golfing (*What Did the Lady Forget?, An Autumn Afternoon*). The outdoor activity, though no sport, most often depicted is train-riding. To be sure, movies have from their inception featured trains, and Lumière, Gance Kinoshita, Hitchcock, and Kurosawa have all been fascinated by them. Ozu, however, probably holds the record. Almost all his films include scenes with trains, and in many of them the final sequence is either in or near a train. *A Story of Floating Weeds, There Was a Father, Equinox Flower, Floating Weeds,* and others all end in trains; *Tokyo Story, Early Spring,* and others all have trains in their final scenes. One reason for all the trains is simply Ozu's liking for them.[17] Another is that for the Japanese, if no longer for us, the train remains a vehicle of mystery and change. The mournful sound of a train in the distance, the idea of all those people being carried away to begin life anew elsewhere, the longing or nostalgia for travel—all these are still emotionally potent for the Japanese.

In some Ozu films the nostalgia for a once visited place is stated directly. In *The Munekata Sisters* there is a scene in which the two sisters sit on the steps of Yakushiji. The elder is very subdued. Later she returns with the man she loves, and we learn that they had met there before when their love was new. Her feelings during the scene with her sister are thus explained without our seeing the event that prompted them. Sometimes an occurrence in one film is mentioned in another, even though all the characters are different. In *Late Autumn* the mother is reminded while traveling of a pond of carp at Shuzenji; these are the same carp that appear in *The*

Flavor of Green Tea over Rice, a film made eight years before. The same line of dialogue expressing a sense of life passing will recur in a number of films. One such recurring line is *"Owari-ka?"* (Is this the end?), an utterance typical of Ozu in its simplicity, clarity, and use of familiar vernacular. It is used by the father in *Tokyo Story* when he learns his wife is dying; it was used, we are told, by the father as he lay dying in *The End of Summer,* and it is also used by the father when he learns that the girls will have to close the Bar Accacia coffeehouse in *The Munekata Sisters.*

Ozu's most potent device for nostalgia, however, is the photograph. Even though family pictures, class pictures, company pictures, remain in Japan something of the institution they once were in the West, there is a surprising amount of formal portrait-taking going on in Ozu's films. There is the group picture, of students and teacher, for example, in front of the Kamakura Buddha in *There Was a Father;* there is the wedding portrait, as in *Late Autumn;* there is the family portrait, as in *The Brothers and Sisters of the Toda Family, Early Summer, The Record of a Tenement Gentleman.* Except in the first example cited above, we do not see the finished picture. No one drags out the portrait of his dead mother and gazes fondly at it. Rather, we see the family gathered (invariably for the last time), smiling bravely into an uncertain future. Nostalgia lies not in later reflections, but in the very effort to preserve the image itself. Although Ozu's characters occasionally lament that they have no photos of a missing loved one, the actual use of photos is restricted to prospective brides and grooms. Death, in the films of Ozu as in life, is simple absence.

All these similarities (and there are many more) among the films of Ozu came about partly because he saw each film as either a continuation of the preceding picture or a reaction to it.[18] The notes written by Kogo Noda, the well-known scenarist and collaborator in more than half (twenty-seven) of Ozu's films, in the joint diary the two men kept at Tateshina are indicative: "FEB. 1, 1962. As preparation for our work [on *An Autumn Afternoon*] we read some of our old scenarios. FEB. 3. We talk [about the new film]; . . . it will be in the genre of *Equinox Flower* and *Late Autumn.* We consider some story about a [widowed] man and his child, and a woman trying to find a bride for him. . . .

JUNE 10. For reference we reread *Late Autumn. . . . JUNE 11. For reference we reread *Equinox Flower.*" [19] Such a method of construction (more common for the later pictures than the earlier ones) inevitably meant strong similarities from picture to picture, particularly since Ozu and Noda apparently defined genres in terms of their own earlier work.

Similarities, then, are many, and differences few in the extraordinarily limited world of the Ozu film. It is a small world, closed, governed by rules apparently inflexible, controlled by laws that are only to be deduced. Yet, unlike Naruse's narrow family-centered world, Ozu's does not provoke claustrophobia, nor do its apparently inflexible governing rules give rise to the romantic idea of destiny seen in the apparently wider world of Mizoguchi. What keeps Ozu's films from these extremes are Ozu's characters, the kind of people they are and the way they react to their life. The simple and real humanity of these characters, their individuality within their similarity, makes it difficult and ultimately misleading to categorize as I have been doing for these past several pages.[20]

The End of Summer. *1961. Setsuko Hara, Yoko Tsukasa, Ganjiro Nakamura, Keiju Kobayashi, Michio Aratama*

16

Although Ozu's stories certainly are few, the pictures do not seem repetitious; though a précis of the anecdote is thin, the film never is; though the roles are similar, the characters are not.

Human nature in all its diversity and variation—this is what the Ozu film is essentially about. It must be added, however, that as a traditional and conservative Asian, Ozu did not believe in any such essence as the term "human nature" may suggest to us. Each of his characters is unique and individual, based on known types though they all may be; one never finds "representative types" in his films. Just as there is no such thing as Nature, only individual trees, rocks, streams, etc., so there is no such thing as Human Nature, only individual men and women. This is something that Asians know better than Occidentals, or at least act as if they do, and this knowledge is responsible, in part, for the individuality of the Ozu character; his entity is never sacrificed to a presumed essence. By so restricting our view and confining our interest, Ozu allows us to comprehend the greatest single aesthetic paradox: less always means more. To put it another way, the several invariably indicates the many; restriction results in amplification; endless variety is found within the single entity.

Ozu never said this, and for all I know never thought it. He did not question his interest in character or his ability to create it. Yet that interest never failed. When he sat down to write a script, his store of themes firmly in the back of his mind, he rarely asked what the story was to be about. He asked, rather, what kind of people were to be in his film.

SCRIPT

"I N MAKING FILMS," Ozu once said, "the most difficult part is writing the script." [1] One reason for the difficulty was Ozu's very Japanese need to turn his material—remembered family life, a story told him, something he had observed about people—into something personal. As with most of his countrymen, Ozu's originality lay not in the material itself—it was always of the most mundane—but in the angle from which the material was viewed, the personal, even idiosyncratic way it was reassembled on film. Like most Japanese artists, Ozu was in this sense a formalist, and the pattern of events in a film was as important to him as the events themselves. Unlike many artists, however, Ozu was rarely formalistic, rarely contented with just a pleasing pattern. It was from the conjunction of the elements of his film, the harmony and occasional incongruity of the patterns, that the meaning of his cinema emerged. Ozu took more pains with the ultimate placing of a scene or a line of dialogue in the growing script than with any of the other aspects of film-making—shooting, editing, etc. On more than one occasion he observed that a good script meant a good film; in this, he was like the architect with his fully detailed blueprint, the carpenter with his precise working plan.

Of course any competent film director recognizes the ultimate importance of the scenario. What was distinctive about Ozu was the way his scripts got written. Ordinarily scripts are written as stories are written: they are begun at some hopefully propitious juncture, and character is observed to form. The story or plot rises from this character, or (and this is perhaps more common in traditional Western cinema) the story or plot forces the character to evolve in a certain way, and when an action is over and a change observed, the script is considered finished. Ozu had little use for the latter method, feeling that it distorted character and destroyed verisimilitude, and not much more use for the former method. "Plot bores me," he would occasionally say,[2] and certainly there is in his films rarely anything resembling it. Rather, there is the lightest of story lines, its slightness rendered even slighter by its conventionality.

The conventionality of the events in the Ozu film is even by Japanese standards extreme. Marriage and death are the only conclusions permitted in many of the later pictures, and the appreciations or misunderstandings that mark the progress toward the conclusion are usually unexceptional. Truisms abound, as do both coincidence and the obvious, and Ozu's manner and method match his material. He never attempts to unsettle.

We have seen that Ozu thought of his script as a blueprint, to be followed as scrupulously as possible. Though it was he who (with an originality remarked upon by Japanese critics) brought the methods of the architect to the Japanese film, he was also, like any Japanese carpenter, working with modules. As the Japanese carpenter builds a house using tatami and *fusuma* doors of invariable size and identical lintels and frames in every building he constructs, so Ozu, constructing films of emotional modules, as it were, knew the size and shape of many of the scenes he would use, so thay recur with little or no variation in picture after picture. Carpenter-like, Ozu proceeded to fill in his film, connecting one scene to the other with a series of architectonic stresses and balances, creating an entire dwelling for the viewer to wander in. The traditional Japanese carpenter uses wood for this purpose; Ozu used dialogue.

Ozu did not use what became his characteristic working method for his early films. The notebooks for *I Was Born, But . . .* , and *There Was a Father* indicate that the scripts were written chronologically, with the dialogue for each scene nearly completed before the next scene was begun. Place was indicated by either a line or, more usually, a picture. The later films were all made in a somewhat different manner. Although Noda does not chronicle the complete cycle of creation in the diary he kept jointly with Ozu, he does indicate the method from the middle of one late film (*The End of Summer*) through the beginnings of two others (*An Autumn Afternoon* and the unfinished *Radishes and Carrots*).

The original idea could come from anyplace. Sometimes, as with the original conception of *The Only Son,* it came from Ozu's own life.[3] Some ideas came from stories he had heard; the germ of *The End of Summer* lies in a story a woman friend told him about a man whom everyone thought was dying until he suddenly sat up and got well. Some came from personal experiences people told him about; back from the Chinese war, Ozu visited the survivors of friends who had been killed (one widow in particular impressed him; her husband had been a notable coward, and she wanted only to hear how brave he had been), and "years later, in *Early Spring,* he said he was using a lot about what these people had shown him." [4] Most often the ideas came from a combination of such sources.[5] One uncharacteristically clear-cut example, however, is the genesis of *Radishes and Carrots:* "MARCH *15, 1963.* Tadao Ikeda [one of Ozu's earliest collaborators] came. Mentioned something about Goethe's saying someplace something about the meanest thing being someone who fouls another's happiness. From this we go on to outline the story and the disposition of the characters." [6] The main idea of *An Autumn Afternoon* came on January 31, 1962, from an article in *PHP,* a militant moral rearmament journal that Ozu and Noda happened to read.

Once the two men had decided in a general way what the film was going to be about, the talking (if not the writing) began:

MAY 3, 1962. We more or less decide [for *An Autumn Afternoon*] on a man who has a friendship with a woman who resembles his dead wife [a lead not followed up by the finished film]. MAY 15. We decide on the disposition of the characters and the scenes. MAY 16. We discuss various episodes for about an hour and a half. MAY 19. We consider various episodes and take various notes. MAY 20. We consider the relations within the household, with the feelings of the daughter as the focal point [a lead that does appear in the finished film] and gradually our thoughts get firmer. MAY 26. At long last, work is beginning. Another push, and we'll have somehow or other gotten the form together.

By work Noda means not the dialogue script (that would come later), but a listing of the various scenes they decide they want. The first month in the creation of *An Autumn Afternoon* has been spent in talking. Even then, "work" has not actually begun. "JUNE *13*. Beginning tomorrow we will start making cards. JUNE *14*. Made six cards: the class meeting, the scene with the old teacher, the bar scene, etc." Writing began on June 30, half a year after their original idea, two months after they had begun talking about it. The actual writing, however, took only a month. "JULY *25*. Finished. 233 pages."

From the diary of the year before, one may reconstruct what went on from the time Ozu and Noda began writing cards until the completion of the script. In these later films, at any rate, the two men wrote up details of each scene on a card—one card, one scene—and then shuffled them about on the table. This method of construction, commonly used for animated cartoons, allowed them to keep track of events and the growing form of the film. An example of this working method is found in earlier diary entries chronicling the creation of *The End of Summer*. "MARCH *10,1961*. The total number of scenes is thirty-two, of which twenty-four are in fairly good shape. MARCH *12*. We are discussing the scenes from various angles and it looks as though we can begin writing day after tomorrow. MARCH *15*. Started, but decided some large comic incident is lacking. MARCH *16*. We've constructed something or other, but something is missing. Work not going well." During March, 1961, then, one should visualize Ozu and Noda seated at the big table in their Tateshina villa, moving about, as though in some extended game of double solitaire, large and much scribbled-on and sketched-over manila cards. Sometimes the dialogue script was begun as soon as the formal arrangement of scenes was satisfactory; the diary (entry of June 30, 1962) indicates that *An Autumn Afternoon* was written directly from a stack of these now numbered cards—first scene first and right on through to the end.

The writing of *The End of Summer* was less straightforward:
MARCH 17. We start writing from the Kyoto ice-cream parlor scene, about four pages. MARCH 21. We consider the shape of the family after the business has stopped and we have some ideas. MARCH 30. We finish the scene where the old father has a fight with his daughter and her husband. APRIL 3. We finish the evening and dawn scenes (covering the death of the old father) and the office scene next morning. APRIL 9. Finish the hide-and-seek scenes, the scene at the bicycle races, and the Osaka bar scenes. APRIL 10. Finished the big family scene where they hear that the old father is taken ill. Afterward we talked about the following Kyoto scenes. APRIL 11. Finished the scenes at the Sasaki in Kyoto and the field scene [with the two peasants for the end of the film]. APRIL 12. First part of crematorium scene. APRIL 13. Finished creamatorium scene. APRIL 14. Finished the field and road scenes (the funeral procession). Intended to go back to the scene but didn't feel like it and went to bed. APRIL 15. We look once more at what we have so far done, and thought about what was left to do. . . . APRIL 21. Finished. Took twenty-seven days of writing. 208 pages.

It is apparent from Noda's diary entries that whether the two men scripted the scenes in sequence or piecemeal, they were both fully familiar with the characters before they began writing, and that the dialogue script and the balances within the picture had achieved satisfactory form before writing began. To reach this point took time, a vast amount of talk and, as Ozu often said, very hard work.[7] During the writing of the dialogue script, changes sometimes were made. In a diary entry dated May 30, 1960, Noda says that for *Late Autumn* they decided to put the inn scene before the lake scene, reversing the positions they originally had had both in this film and in its model, *Late Spring*. Once the dialogue script was finished, however, no further changes were made. The finished film emerged as though from a blueprint.

One of the key differences between Ozu and other film directors is the autonomy of the single scene in Ozu's films, and the enormous importance assigned to character-revealing dialogue. The conventional film-maker often decides first on location and plot, has a specific place for the scene within the film in mind, and only then tries to think of something for the characters to say that will forward the plot a bit. Ozu's method more closely resembled that of directors of animated films or musical comedies who construct their film around a finished sound track. One result of this method was the creation of characters that in no way depended upon the convolutions of plot or story. Usually Ozu and his collaborator would have only the most general notion of the shape they wanted their picture to have. They would know, for example, that they wanted to make a picture about a daughter who gets married and leaves her parent alone at the end; this was the germ of films as otherwise dissimilar as *The Only Son, The Brothers and Sisters of the Toda Family, Late Spring, Early Summer, Late Autumn,* and *An Autumn Afternoon.* But unlike other film-makers they would not begin by blocking out the action in the hope that a believable set of characters would evolve. Rather, desired result in mind but both vague and far away, they would simply begin a scene. Each character had his own name and a set of general characteristics appropriate to his or her family role (father, daughter, aunt, etc.), but as yet few distinguishing traits. These characters grew—or, rather, the dialogue through which they came to life grew—according to the personality that Ozu and his fellow writer discovered in them. The character became real with no reference to story or plot; he became real because all the words he spoke gave expression to those principles of his character which it was the writers' duty to discover.

The result was the invariable rightness of the Ozu character, a rightness based upon his being given an amount of freedom almost unknown to cinema characters. Since he had no work to do, no story to act out, no plot to advance, he could be contradictory, illogical—and always faithful to himself.

The rightness of the Ozu character was predicated upon the rightness of the Ozu dialogue. Even in Ozu's silent films the dialogue titles, and there are many of them, must be considered as important as the visuals. It is the dialogue, spoken or printed, that supports and creates the character and differentiates one character from another. Though there are many scenes without dialogue in

Ozu's films, these occur only after a character has been established. We know him, initially, through what he says.

In writing the script Ozu did not, of course, completely neglect the visuals. He usually scribbled in some indication of place, and, a skillful amateur artist, he often drew sketches of proposed scenes. The point is, however, that he sketched them; he did not write them. There are only the tersest descriptions of what people do, and there are no descriptions of feelings whatever. The final script, then, is something like a radio play, but one is in the film unaware of it because no radio play was ever as well written. In Japan Ozu's scripts are regarded as literature: the degree of verisimilitude and character delineation achieved is so great, yet the economy so extreme, that the scripts themselves qualify as works of art. Though the many nuances of the dialogue are only appreciable in the film itself, there is even in translation a feeling of rightness to the Ozu dialogue, of inevitability, that is uncommon in any medium and extremely rare in film.

Ozu's mode is one of heightened realism. The characters say just what they would say, yet the dialogue continually surprises because it is always unfolding facets of the character that we were hitherto unaware of. This is like life, but the tempo of the Ozu dialogue (as opposed to the tempo of the Ozu film) is so swift that we learn in seconds what in life takes months. Yet we are taught nothing, we merely observe, with a heightened awareness. As will later become evident, much is demanded of us when we watch an Ozu picture. We are presented with the evidence, as it were, but must put it together for ourselves. To be sure, the skill with which the film is made usually precludes our putting it together in any way but the one Ozu intended.[8] Nonetheless, Ozu asks an amount of trust and goodwill uncommon among directors. Those who do not bring these qualities to his pictures go home as empty-headed as they came.

The apparent indirection of the Ozu film demands our forbearance, particularly during the opening reels. Although there is always lots of dialogue in the opening scenes, it is never, apparently, *about* anything. If we are impatient for the thing to get started, for the story to begin, for some kind of plot to hold onto, we have come to the wrong movie. It is a vindication of Ozu's

24

ethos that in practice one rarely experiences such impatience. The reality of this world is so apparent; its demands are, after all, only those which the daily world habitually makes upon us. And from the beginning we are given sudden illuminations of character, quick glimpses of a pattern, that make us first hope and later believe that there is, after all, a kind of order to life, however mysterious, however incomprehensible.

Ozu was not simply bored by plot. He actively disliked it. Perhaps he felt that it used people and resulted in characters in bondage, characters who failed to reflect the complexity and illogicality of truly human characters. In the same way he would have felt that in conventional screen dialogue the characters are continually sacrificed to what the scriptwriters would have them say. To use is to misuse, Ozu sometimes said. His opinion of human nature was in this sense so high, his curiosity and interest in people so great, that he denied himself the undoubted convenience of story, plot, and conventional dialogue. In this Ozu joins a few, very few, other artists with similar convictions and working methods: Jane Austen, Anton Chekhov, Naoya Shiga, Henry Green, Kafu Nagai, Ivy Compton-Burnett, and perhaps a few others. Ozu, unfamiliar with most of them, echoes them all, because all are animated by a similar concern for human nature as it is, a belief in form as a true revealer of the human state, and a faith in irony as the proper instrument for that revelation. The resultant lovability of the Ozu character, by now well-known, is based upon his perfect freedom and consequent fullness. If we love him it is because we so understand him. And we understand him because Ozu has sacrificed none of him to those considerations—action, continuity of character, plausibility—usually paramount in film.

The creation of a script under such constraints was, of course, a matter of the greatest difficulty. Ozu's only recourse was to work as Chekhov is said to have worked, to write and rewrite, creating single scenes, matching them, trimming them, adding to them, slowly discovering the parallels and ironies in the growing structure. Perhaps for this reason he rarely worked alone. Usually he worked with Kogo Noda, the lifelong friend and companion who died shortly after the director. Ozu always said they got along so well because they were so much alike. "When a director works with a scriptwriter they must have some habits in common. Otherwise they wouldn't get along at all. With Noda and me, we see alike about staying up late and drinking, and things like that. That is the most important thing." [9]

Their method of work was always the same: to go someplace and stay up late drinking until the ideas began to come. Noda later remembered the various places they worked: "We used to sometimes work in a bar named Fledermaus in Nishi-Ginza, or we'd go down to an inn called Nakanishi in Yugawara. We locked ourselves in an inn in Chigasaki and wrote *Late Spring*." Later Ozu bought a mountain house in Tateshina, and there they wrote all the films from *Early Spring* on. According to Noda:

> One scenario usually took us from three to four months, that is, if we weren't adapting something [as they did in the case of *The Munekata Sisters, Floating Weeds,* and others] but were working from scratch. That's how long *Tokyo Story* took. We did it at this inn in Chigasaki.
>
> It was more a boarding house [*yadoya*] than an inn [*ryokan*]. We had this eight-tatami room which looked out on the east and south to a long garden and had good sunshine. The buds came out, then the flowers, then the fruit, and we still weren't finished. Whenever we went for a walk we'd do the shopping. Ozu used to buy meat and make hamburgers. And we drank a lot, too. By the time we'd finish a script we'd sometimes have over a hundred big empty sake bottles—though our guests would help drink them up, too. Ozu used to number all the bottles. Then he'd count them and say: "Here we are up to number eighty already and we haven't finished the script yet." [10]

There is a note of triumph in the diary at the conclusion of *Tokyo Story:* "Finished. 103 days; 43 bottles of sake." [11]

Ozu not only drank more than perhaps any other major film director, he saw in this habit a source of his artistic strength.[12] Usually Ozu's comments in the diary that he and Noda (and anyone else who happened to be there) kept were confined to poetical remarks about the weather (in the most arcane of *kanji*) and an accounting of how much of which kind of alcohol he had drunk

26

that day (he preferred scotch, but he also drank sake and relatively inexpensive Japanese whiskeys). In an entry of July 7, 1959, however, written in elegant imitation of classical forms, he observed, "If the number of cups you drink be small, there can be no masterpiece; the masterpiece arises from the number of brimming cups you quaff." He descends from these heights in the following line: "It's no coincidence that this film [*Floating Weeds*] is masterpiece—just look in the kitchen at the row of empty bottles." [13]

Ozu usually found himself in accord with all his scriptwriters, but with Noda agreement was so complete that Ozu was sometimes surprised: "When I work with Noda, we agree even on short bits of dialogue. And though we never discuss the details of the sets or the costumes, his image of these things is always in accord with mine. Our ideas never contradict each other. We even agree on whether a line should end with a *wa* or a *yo* [a particle indicative of degree]. Of course, sometimes we have a difference of opinion. And we don't compromise easily since we are both stubborn." [14] After Ozu's death and shortly before his own, Noda recalled several such differences of opinion: "If we didn't agree we would sometimes scarcely speak to each other for two or three days in a row except for remarks like, 'Well, the birch leaves have finally started to fall,' or, 'Last night there was a bird singing down in the valley.' After some days of this kind of thing there would come, strangely enough, either from me or from him an idea quite different from anything we had been considering before, and then work would go smoothly again." [15]

The work was, initially, always on the dialogue script. The two men created what was said, and usually decided later on where it would be said and, to a lesser extent, when. Sometimes plans or outlines were made, as in the case of *Good Morning,* because of the number of characters. Usually, however, dialogue was freely written, and from it the characters emerged. The notebook for *There Was a Father* is one of the surviving examples of such an original draft; in this case scene compositions have been added, but it was more usual for place descriptions, etc., to be added to the dialogue script; once it was done, the whole was recopied, and the original thrown away. Character was thus built almost entirely through conversation, but not completely. One of the reasons why

Ozu and Noda were able to make films in such an unorthodox manner is that they were, in a sense, working from models. "It is impossible," Ozu said, "to write a script unless you know who is going to play the part, just as a painter cannot paint unless he knows what colors he is going to use. Name stars have never been of much interest to me. What is important is the character of the actor. It is not a matter of how good an actor is; it is a matter of what he is as a human being. It is not the character he projects. It is what he really is." [16] Thus the first step in the Ozu script was actually casting. He and Noda knew more or less who was to play what. They knew the actors, what they had done, and, perhaps more important since Ozu often cast against type, what they could do. At the same time, however, Ozu never allowed much for an actor's limitations. He firmly believed that if actors followed his directions, they could do what he wanted them to. As he worked, the reality of the actor as a person and the reality of the forming character converged.

There is in the Ozu script no character description beyond the simple indication of age, name, relation to the other characters, etc. No indication of the character's feelings is given. There are instead lines of dialogue so written that they carry their own inflections. As with all expertly written dialogue, it need not be acted; simply to say it or to read it is enough. Like the reader of such novels as Henry James's *The Awkward Age* or Henry Green's *Loving,* for example, the viewer of an Ozu film is expected to infer the characters' feelings, and usually the dialogue is so beautifully written that reasonably attentive viewers do just that, whether consciously or not. In films such a demand is even rarer than it is in literature; in the films of Bresson and the earlier pictures of Antonioni, though, thoughts and feelings are so lightly implied that we must infer most of the motivation. The same is true of the Ozu film; as in the middle novels of Henry James, we are shown everything and told nothing.

The reasons are various. As mentioned earlier, Ozu respected reality too much to put it to ostensible use, that is, to sacrifice its complexity by arbitrarily assigning single emotions when a subtle combination of them would be truer to our experience. Again, Ozu did not want to editorialize, as he would be doing if he said that a character was happy or sad. The film-maker also editorializes when he chooses a special angle from which to take a scene, or decides on an extreme close-up here and a far long shot there. Ozu solved the latter problem by means of invariable camera placement, no angles, and a vocabulary consisting mainly of long shot, medium shot, and close-up.

Another important reason for Ozu's avoidance of emotional description is that he was, among other things, a humorist. Though his films are full of sadness and death, they are also full of jokes, absurdity, and laughter. As a humorist he knew that humor arises almost entirely from personal apprehension. One person leads another to understand a joke by showing him the incongruous ingredients. It is the person not already in on the joke who puts these ingredients together and sees the point. Otherwise there is no joke. Ozu made the assumption of this kind of comprehension central to his style.

Ozu began as a director of comedy; all his films are amusing, some are very funny indeed, and even the most serious are filled with humor. Indeed it is the often incongruous juxtaposition of the sad with the funny that accounts for the distinctive flavor of the Ozu picture. One of Ozu's earliest duties in film-making was to think up jokes for other directors. These he would devise even when he knew little of the film for which they were intended. Independent sequences, they were unconnected with any consideration of story or character. Almost always based on situation, they were usually visual and often contained that element of logical incongruity which was Ozu's hallmark. In one such scene, apparently never used, a hungry tramp is standing in the background. In the foreground some children are tantalizing a dog with pieces of roast chicken. As the dangling chicken swings from left to right, the dog turns first one way, then the other. In back, unperceived by the children, the head of the tramp is doing the same thing.[17] The humor derives from the incongruous juxtaposition of two logical gestures.

There are many gags based on the illogic of logic in Ozu's pictures. In *Tokyo Chorus* a little boy's mother reprimands him for standing on the rice bucket, a grave breach of manners. The child realizes his error at once and jumps off as his disapproving mother turns to other work. Anxious to make amends, he spits on the lid of the rice bucket and begins rubbing away with his sleeve to remove any trace of dirt that his feet might have left. Again, in the same film, the sister takes a piece of candy that the little boy wants. He hits her over the head to make her cry, and when she opens her mouth to do so, he reaches in, grabs the candy, and eats it. Our own logical expectations are tripped up in a later scene, when there appears a close-up of a baby with an enormous tear running down its cheek. The next scene is a close-up of the mother: it is she who is crying, her tears falling on the baby's face. Logic triumphs after a fashion, when one of the characters in *Tokyo Chorus* successfully sharpens his pencil in an electric fan.

Similarly, in *Passing Fancy* the little boy discovers that the milled edges of the fifty-*sen* piece can be used to file nails. In another scene, having destroyed in pique a dwarf *bonsai* tree, the boy defends himself by admitting it, and then, logically but incongruously, citing the example of George Washington. The running riddle in the film is a famous example of Ozu's special logic. Question: Why do humans have five fingers? Answer: So that gloves won't have one finger left over.

Such logical incongruities form the basis of Ozu's humor. They are not only amusing in themselves, they contribute directly to the revelation of character. The people involved are rarely aware that what they have said or done is funny. They have simply been what seems to them logical and what seems to us funny. Their error was either in method or in the degree of application. From this rises irony, and also our own sudden interest in a character capable of such incongruities. Ozu uses such devices because in suggesting the complexity of the human character, he is unwilling to tell us anything. Rather, he would show us everything, and the success of this method depends upon our willingness to be shown. Ozu's invitation, when tendered through humor, is commonly amusing, logical, and questioning of our assumed values. A typical example appears in the diaries: "FEBRUARY 28, 1933. Gravity must have hated Newton . . . just because an apple was carelessly dropped by someone or other and he happened to see it, gravity has been having a hard time of it ever since." In *I Was Born, But . . .* , the two little boys are discussing their problems with the ɔther boys in their new neighborhood. The titles carry the following dialogue: "Father said to ignore them," says the first. "If we ignored them, they'd be sure to beat us up," says the second. The first thinks, then says: "I wish they'd ignore *us*. Then we could beat *them* up." (4, 57.) [18] A perfect reverse syllogism.

This kind of inversion is very common in Ozu's dialogue. There is an elaborate example in *Late Spring*. The girl's aunt, who is attempting to find the girl a husband, describes a recently discovered possibility: "He looks like that that American . . . you know, the one in the baseball picture," she says. "Gary Cooper?" asks her niece. "Yes," answers the aunt, "just like him, especially his mouth, not so much the upper half of his face though." (5, 358.) Five reels later, the girl has met the young man and describes him to her friend, who wants to know if he is good-looking: "My aunt thinks he looks like Gary Cooper," she answers. "Good," says her friend. "You've always like him." The girl does not seem so sure. "I think he looks more like our electrician." "Well," wonders the friend, "does *he* look like Cooper?" "Oh, yes. Exactly." "Well, then, this means that the new one *does* look like Gary Cooper then, doesn't it?" (9, 554.) Despite this amusing display of circular logic, it seems unlikely that anyone involved looks like Gary Cooper.

Sometimes the effect of such inverted observations is not humor, but winning, even childlike simplicity. *Floating Weeds* contains a charming example. The father is remarking to his mistress on the size of their almost grown son, and says: "He's a big boy now. No wonder we're so old." (2, 261.) More often than not, however, inverted logic leads to an amusing chain of mistaken assumptions. In the same film one of the actors is passing out handbills for the coming performance. A small child asks for one. "Do you have a pretty sister?" asks the actor. When the child says he does, the actor plainly anticipates a local conquest. Then he remembers to ask, "How old is she?" "Twelve," answers the child. (1, 65.)

The mistaken assumption in Ozu's dialogue is based upon faulty, inverted, or circular logic. Often the logic of the person speaking stays well within accepted limits while that of the listener strays outside, usually with ludicrous results. A simple example

31

occurs in *Passing Fancy*. The main character gets dressed up to pay a call on a girl. One of his fellow workers asks if he is going to a funeral. The same contrivance recurs in *An Autumn Afternoon*, now deepened by the main character's awareness. After his daughter's wedding he goes to a bar. The mistress, noticing his clothes, asks: "A formal affair? A funeral?" To which he answers: "Yes, more or less." (9, 997.)

In *Early Summer*, the two women are talking about their husbands. One says: "It was the dog again. It ruined his pipe. But it was his fault, too. He was careless with it. Still, it was from London. And in any event he blamed me. So, just for spite, I served him only carrots that evening." To which the other woman responds in apparent surprise: "The dog?" (3, 224.) In *Late Autumn* two entirely different trains of thought are simultaneously followed to their logical conclusions with amusing effect. The father is now convinced that he is going to marry. The girl who has been helping arrange a match has taken him and his friends to her father's *sushi* shop, making it clear that the bill will be large. At the same time she has made him promise repeatedly to be a good and faithful husband to the woman she finds for him, now and forever. Toward the end of the scene she adds, "Remember, you promised." He replies, "Surely. It is now and forever." "No, no, not that," cries the young lady, "I meant about paying the bill." (9, 175.) Another amusing example of mistaken assumptions relentlessly pursued occurs in *Equinox Flower*. The exchange is funny because the faulty logic is so rigid, so willful that it overrides all concepts of good manners. The talkative old lady from Kyoto arrives at the Tokyo residence of her friend. As is customary, she brings a gift for her hostess, giving it, as is usual, to the maid. She hands over the present and says, "And I brought this present." The maid properly accepts it with thanks. "It's for the family," insists the Kyoto lady, having interpreted the maid's traditional and rhetorical thanks literally. "It's not for you, you know." "Yes, I know that," says the maid with unruffled dignity. (4, 371.)

Such unwonted extensions of logic, or concern, interest, or comprehension, often come from characters who are completely unaware of what they are doing. Sometimes, however, Ozu's characters knowingly break conventions. In *Early Spring* the wife is serving her friend tea and asks if she will not have more sugar. The friend replies with a smile, "No thanks. It's too sweet already." (4, 320.) In *Late Autumn* one of the guests arrives late at the funeral. One of his friends asks, "How come so late?" Another friend interjects reassuringly, "It's just started." The late guest answers, "Then I'm too early." (1, 52.)

The aware Ozu character is often led by his observation of the ways other minds work into the personal remark, of varying degrees of asperity. In *Early Spring,* the main character and several friends are talking with an acquaintance who knows where to get washing machines at a discount. One asks, "And I can buy it at a discount?" On being assured that he can, he reflects and says, "Well, we do need a washing machine." The main character, who knows his friend well, asks, "Are you buying one?" "No," says the friend, "I was just asking." The main character, confirmed in his opinion of his friend, says, "I thought so." (4, 365.) In *Late Spring* the men at the funeral are talking about food. One of them observes, "As one grows older, one begins to appreciate such things more—seaweed, mushrooms, dried radish, bean curd—" To which the main character, interrupting, adds, "Beefsteak, pork chops, . . ." (1, 43.) Though they all laugh at this, the main character's bland continuation of the list with Western foods presumably liked only by the young contains a personal thrust at a notorious example of Japanese cant. In fact, everyone in Japan eats everything.

When the talk turns to someone not present, the personal remarks become both freer and funnier. At the same time, because they are not responses to anything said by the person in question, they rarely exemplify misapplied logic or misapprehension. In *Late Spring,* the daughter and her friend are talking about the class reunion the friend has just attended. She is asked: "And Professor Murase—was he foaming as usual?" "Oh, yes," replies her friend. "Spit flying all over the place. Even in our tea. None of us touched our cups." (5, 310.) In *Early Summer,* the two women are speaking of a similar social occasion. "And what happened after that?" asks one of them. "Oh, it was bad," says the other, "Mr. Yoda sang again." "What a shame," says the first. (2, 88.) In

The Flavor of Green Tea over Rice, the wives have gone off on an outing by themselves. At the inn they are staying at there is a pool filled with large carp. The women, happy away from their husbands, begin talking to the fish, pretending that today, as on most other days, they are seeing their husbands off to work. One woman looks at a carp and says, "Aren't you forgetting your briefcase, dear?" Another says to another fish, "Oh, your tie's crooked again, dear." The third addresses another with, "And you simply must go to the barber's today." (4, 410.)

Sometimes this kind of direct and personal remark becomes innuendo. A conversation occurs the subject of which is only ostensible. The real meaning, enjoyed greatly by the others, remains unperceived by the listening third person, about whom they are really talking. Logical, rational, the conversation is completely misinterpreted. The later films in particular contain some elaborate examples of this.

In *Late Autumn* the men are discussing the beautiful widow and her lovely daughter, who have just departed. "Well, it must be true," says one of them, "that saying about men with beautiful wives not living long." At this point the fat and unprepossessing mistress of the establishment appears. One of the men, seeing her, says, "Ah, madam, I trust your husband is well." She thanks him, and the first man says: "Of course, he must be—he will undoubtedly live to a ripe old age." After she has smiled and left them, the men underline the meaning of their remarks. "She's as good as life insurance," says one. "A wife like that could kill you, though," says the other. (2, 119.)

In *Equinox Flower* some of the men are talking together and one says, "There is this theory that if the husband is stronger, then they'll be boys." (1, 55.) Later, the mistress of the place appears and one of the men asks innocently how many children she has. When she answers that she has three, he looks at his friends and says, "All girls, aren't they?" (2, 72.) The men all laugh at their joke, and the uncomprehending mistress is discomfited. Later, toward the end of the picture, the men meet one of their old friends, a weak-looking man, at a reunion. It transpires that he has seven children. One of the men asks ironically, "All girls, I presume?" (11, 1101.)

In *An Autumn Afternoon,* the men are pretending that young wives are so demanding their older husbands often succumb, and that such a fate has just befallen one of their number. Told that Horie's funeral is the next day, the mistress of the restaurant asks about the cause of death. "High blood pressure," says one man. "You see," explains another, "his wife was too much for him. Just you be careful and don't overdo it." She is shaking her head at the news when Horie himself comes in and wants to know what is happening. (3, 339.) This little joke leads to another. Hirayama, one of the friends in the earlier scene, has an eligible daughter and his friend Horie has been helping him find a suitor for her. When Hirayama visits Horie to find out how things are going, Horie tells him that the young man he had in mind is already spoken for. Hirayama is very disappointed. "I see," he says, "then it's more or less definite." Horie nods. "Yes, certainly. And it should work out. Both sides seem pleased at their prospects. You were just a little late. Terribly sorry." Horie's wife has been looking on. She smiles and tells her husband not to be so cruel. They both laugh, and Hirayama wants to know why. Then it comes out: his daughter's prospect is still available. This little joke was revenge for the premature announcement of Horie's death. (8, 897.)

When one joke leads to another, or when a single joke is repeated or referred to throughout a film, as above, a motif is formed. Ozu and his fellow scriptwriter observed and then wove such motifs into the fabric of the scenario, and they thus contributed both to the creation of character and to the form of the film itself. It is doubtful that Ozu would describe what he was doing this way, and it is most unlikely that formal considerations entered this early into the writing of a script. Still, the way he wrote the scenario—repeating jokes, repeating character traits, referring again and again to a characteristic or an event—led naturally to the formation of character, led spontaneously to the form of the finished film.

Good Morning, in some ways Ozu's most schematic film, certainly one of his least complicated formally, is an example of a film constructed around motifs. There are a number of motifs in the film, all easily recognized because they are underlined, as it were, in a manner one associates with the earlier rather than the later Ozu. We will examine two of them: the first is the breaking wind or farting motif, the second the one that gives the film its title.

It should surprise no one that farting has a place in Ozu's "world of stillness." Characters run off to the toilet on many occasions, children finger themselves, ladies pick their teeth and express themselves with occasional earthy vulgarity, sex is openly acknowledged. His reason for such earthy touches is always the same: it is at these moments that a person is often most human. A man who farts, a man having sex, is—among other things—acknowledging his similarity to all other men. Etiquette, a concept which suggests that we are more than merely human, obscures what is common to all human beings. Although Ozu admired breeding and manners if they reflected concern for others, he had no use for social cant, and some of his funniest scenes completely shatter it. This is, of course, very Japanese of him, for his are a people who manage, despite repressions, to remain whole and to express their wholeness. More important, however, such moments in an Ozu picture serve to suggest not just "human," but also "only human." There is a living pathos in the sight of an old man (in *Late Autumn*) running off to the bathroom in excitement over the prospect of marrying; there is a graceful acknowledgment of being only human (as well as wry humor) in the wife who leaves her guest upon the latter's arrival (in *Equinox Flower*), and returns explaining that she has been to the toilet because she knows the guest will be staying a long time. Ozu's world is one of supreme loveliness, of art, of aesthetics, but its major beauty is the natural beauty of human nature.

This said, one may examine the fart motif in *Good Morning*. It begins, like so many of Ozu's motifs, as a joke. The two little boys on their way to school are playing a game with their friends. They take turns pushing one another's foreheads. When one pushes, the other farts. When they push the forehead of one boy, however, he tries too hard, soils his pants, and has to return home. (1, 2.) Later, in the home of one of the boys, the father is reading the evening paper, the mother is in the kitchen. He farts loudly; she comes in and asks, "Did you call me?" (2, 22.) Shortly after, the boys are shown playing again (2, 84), and this time all break wind successfully. Back at the house the husband again farts and again the wife asks if she is wanted. He ignores her and farts again. This time, sure she heard something, she bustles in and asks, "What is it?" (2, 91.) Later, the boys and their father are exercising. Each time the father deep-knee-bends, he farts. The boys much admire this. "He's really good at it," says one. "Naturally," says the other, "father works at the gas company." (5, 62.) Later, toward the end of the film, the boys are playing again as at the beginning. Again, the same boy tries too hard (7, 131). He goes home and asks for clean shorts. This time he doesn't get them, and must stay there with his complaining mother. The last shot in the film shows his shorts drying on the line (7, 157).

There is also a submotif on the same subject, involving pumice stone, the consumption of which is supposed by the children to increase one's prowess. Although in this film this is perhaps too much of a good thing (Ozu's characteristic jokes do sometimes go on too long; another example is Hideko Takamine's endless *kodan* [old-time storyteller] imitations in *The Munekata Sisters*), there is in the course of a ninety-minute film less than the above recapitulation suggests. Moreover, the fart motif is experienced only in conjunction with the film's second principal motif.

The boys in this picture have decided to go on a hunger strike. The ostensible reason is that their father refuses to buy a television set. The real reason, however, is that they are at an age to be bored with themselves and those around them. Particularly they resent the sameness of their daily existence. As a focus for their discontent they pick on those meaningless phrases, such as "Good morning," that adults habitually use. One reason the boys are so taken with breaking wind, then, is that a fart is a spontaneous utterance pleasantly devoid of just that kind of predictable meaninglessness found in the everyday phrases they have decided to dislike. Specifically, they call such phrases unnecessary.

The adults understand their feeling. A teacher, talking to their aunt, says: "Well, what they say is true enough. But then everyone has to use words like that. And perhaps they aren't really so unnecessary after all. The world would be rather dreary otherwise." The aunt says: "You're right, but these children are too young to understand that." "Probably so," agrees the teacher. "But, still, the world needs lots of unnecessary things, you know." (5, 96.) The teacher's voice is Ozu's. He does not share youth's fierce criticism of the world; he accepts the world as it is, imperfections, unnecessary things, and all. Again, the teacher's mother speaks for the director when she says, "You might call phrases like this a kind of lubrication that helps make living together possible at all." (7, 16.) At the end of the picture, after the children get their television set and have forgotten the real reason for their revolt, after they are happily saying "good morning" to the neighboring wives (and thus repair the omission that gave rise to the slender story of the film; the neighbors think the boy's mother is angry at them and decide to retaliate), Ozu includes a scene between the aunt and the boys' teacher, whom she likes, which is so silly as to be in every way a vindication of the children's rebellion. The aunt and the teacher are waiting for the train. He says "Good morning," and she replies with the same words, adding several polite comments. After a pause he says that it is a nice day. She quickly and smilingly agrees, a very nice day. Another, longer pause. "It certainly is a fine day," he says. (7, 152.)

Just as a character is never all bad or all good in an Ozu film, so never is an idea all right or all wrong. There are no absolutes in these films, only immutables. One is born, but . . . the rest of life is not certain in the slightest. Ozu's characters all have to make their own sense out of their lives. So, in *Good Morning* neither the boys nor the adults are wholly right. In the Ozu film we rarely if ever experience the fierce joy of certainty. The world of the Ozu film is a flowing world, in which little is ordained. The life we see in these films nonetheless makes more sense because one event visibly leads to another, parallels another, or presages another. In the Ozu film there is often a minor motif running parallel to the main theme or story and, to an extent, both presaging and sustaining it. We have seen how the breaking of wind and the uttering of commonplaces are arranged in *Good Morning*. We will now look at several more serious examples.

One of the minor motifs of *Late Autumn* is a contrasting parallel to the main story. Three of the older men are talking about a mutual acquaintance, the still attractive widow and her beautiful daughter. One of them says: "A long time ago when we were still in college there was this drugstore in Hongo where this pretty girl worked, and this fellow here was going all the time. He bought bandaids." "I like that," says the man referred to. "And who was it, then, that kept on buying cold pills until he had whole piles of them?" (2, 132.) Later, the second man is discussing the handsome widow with his wife. "Yes," she says, "and there was that drugstore in Hongo and the bandaids." "That wasn't me, that was Mamiya." "And what did you buy then?" she asks. "Just a cold pill or two." "Fibber. It was you who had all those bandaids." "And who told you?" he asks. "You did." "When?" "Just after the child was born," she answers. "You don't say—I must have been an honest young man." She smiles and says, "Yes, compared to now." (2, 219.) A scene between the two wives who have long known about the drugstore and made jokes about it follows, and is succeeded by a scene between Mamiya and his wife. "And what did you buy?" she asks, "Bandaids, cold pills?" "Who could have told you such a story?" wonders Mamiya virtuously. "Now I know why you don't catch cold," she says. "You're still doped." (3, 386.)

This minor motif of light romantic attachment parallels a major theme of the film, one also concerning love and marriage: a girl's marrying and leaving her widowed mother, who allows her to think that she herself may remarry so the girl will feel free to go. Ozu, as always, resists all temptation to plot—having the widow turn out to be the girl in the drugstore, for example. For his purposes it is quite enough to have two strains (and others) showing variations on a theme. The variations may be presented as contrasting with each other, e.g., romantic love versus conventional marriage. Or one variation may continue another, e.g., romantic love followed by conventional marriage. The canvas of the Ozu picture is filled with mutually supporting lines.

An unusually close parallel, which may be interpreted in at least several ways, appears in the structure of *Late Spring,* in which a father wishes his daughter to marry and consequently allows her to believe that he is thinking of remarriage himself. Very early in the film her aversion to a widower's remarrying is established. She is talking to an old friend of her father's, a man named Onodera who has recently remarried, and says: "Well, I feel sorry for your daughter. It's not—well, it's just not natural and I find it distasteful." He asks, "You find my new wife distasteful?" The girl smiles. "No, you. It seems so—well, so unclean." He smiles in return. "Unclean? I think you mean indecent. Is that any better?" (2, 101.) Later Onodera meets her father and says in front of the girl, "Nori-chan says that I'm unclean, that I'm base, that I'm indecent. Isn't that right, Noriko?" (3, 138.) Later Noriko, thinking her father intends to remarry, says, "Then you intend to do what Mr. Onodera did. You're going to get married again." (8, 519.) Toward the end of the film Noriko and her father go for their last trip together before her marriage. They meet Onodera, his wife, and daughter. Her father asks them to dinner and Onodera, turning to Noriko, says: "And may the unclean one come too? Noriko, do I still look so unclean?" Noriko is embarrassed and the daughter innocently asks who is unclean. "Well," says Onodera, "perhaps not unclean—more like indecent, eh, Noriko?" (10, 665.) Finally, in a later scene Noriko and her father talk openly about what she has said: "I didn't know what I was doing but I was very rude to Mr. Onodera. His wife is so nice and they make such a good couple and there is nothing unclean about that at all." "Don't let it worry you," says her father. "But I shouldn't have said it." "Well, it never bothered him so don't let it bother you." There is a silence and then she says, "Father . . . even with you—well, I found it distasteful." (11, 225.)

Finally, in this last line, near the end of the film, the two are joined, story and parallel motif. Noriko has at last attached her feelings of distaste to their proper object, her father, and thus dissipated them. The untroubled serenity of the conclusion follows. Actually, her father is not going to marry and she now knows it; at the same time her former objection (for he and not Onodera was always the object) has disappeared. But it contributed (along with many more subtle motifs) to support the line of the film.

More often in an Ozu film, however, the parallels running side by side do not meet; they stretch into infinity, and if they do meet we are not shown the event. This is the position that best ensures their commenting upon each other without Ozu's having to overtly state that they do.

In *I Was Born, But . . .* , as well as many of the earlier films, there are direct visual parallels. A slow tracking shot along the desks of the sleepy pupils in the classroom is cut directly to a similar shot along the desks of the yawning businessmen, their fathers. Here the comment is only partly satiric: it is the parallel that is most important, a demonstration that the two scenes are identical. In the same film a similar point is made with titles. The little boys ask for the protection of the sake-delivery youth. He obligingly chases off most of the other little boys. Then they ask him to chase the single child remaining. "Oh, no," says the sake boy. "He's a good customer. His folks buy a whole lot more than yours do." (5, 80.) This is a parallel to the main story. Again, it is also satiric, but, more important, it presages and supports the main theme, which is a demonstration of inequality in the adult world.

Tokyo Story has a short scene at the beginning of the film in which the children are rude to their visiting grandparents. Though nothing is made of this, either by the grandparents or by Ozu, it stands as a parallel and presage of the much greater rudeness of their own children, the boys' parents, of their selfishness and eventual remorse. Another of the minor parallels in the film (the major ones are self-evident) occurs when the youngest son gets some humorous advice from a friend in the form of an old-fashioned Confucian proverb when he finds that he must visit his sick mother in Onomichi: "Be a good son while your parents are alive; none can serve them beyond the grave." (10, 769.) They both smile at this and the son goes off to Onomichi, where, in fact, his mother has already died. At the funeral service he breaks down and, now in seriousness, repeats the proverb. "I never did anything for her when she was alive. . . . I can't love her now. No one can serve his parents beyond the grave." (12, 915.)

In *Late Autumn,* as in many of the other films, there are scenes of parallel feelings. The son advises his father: "When I marry you'll be all alone, and that means that you'll have to come live with us, and my wife may not like it, and you wouldn't be happy." (6, 175.) Later the daughter's friend advises the mother, "In her place I'd want you to get married again because then I wouldn't have to look after you." (8, 20.) In the same film the daughter and her friend have gone to the roof of their office building to wave a newly married friend off on her honeymoon. The train passes and the girls wave, but there is no answering greeting from the distant window. Disappointed, they speak of the brevity of friendship. Later, the friend and another girl are on the roof, watching a departing train that may contain the daughter and her mother, off for a final trip together. This time, however, there is no talk of brief friendship, but because of the first scene (same place, same time of day), the second is redolent of hope relinquished in the face of the world as it is.

There are many other kinds of parallels in Ozu's films. Sometimes they are playful, as in the pantomime scenes in *The End of Summer*. In the fifth reel the grandfather engages in a game of hide-and-seek with his grandson. He leaves the house and goes off to his Kyoto mistress while the boy is still searching. This repeats a scene in the second reel in which the old man, on his way to his mistress, is followed by a company employee in what is essentially a hide-and-seek game in the side streets of Kyoto. Sometimes Ozu's parallels are purely pictorial. The same scene is shown again and again, its presence supporting the theme of the film. *Early Spring,* for example, has many morning scenes—the street, the houses, the wives taking out the garbage. Each scene differs slightly from the one before, but the effect is a series of almost identical scenes throughout the film, all commenting, in this case, on the boredom and sameness of the life of the office worker. Other repeated parallels are personal traits repeated often enough to suggest more than that. The pipes in *Late Autumn,* for example: they belonged to the dead husband of the widow, and she gives them to the men who are helping her arrange her daughter's marriage. There are many scenes of the men with these pipes— and many scenes of the man who wants to marry her without a pipe, for he never receives one. These scenes constitute a continued parallel to the ingredients of the story, a contrast to the woman's widowed state and to married intimacy.

Certain parallels seem to exist for almost entirely formal reasons. In the ninth reel of *Equinox Flower* there is a beautiful pair of formal scenes, one complementing and commenting upon the other. The mother is listening to *nagauta* on the radio and much enjoying it—the scene of her pleasure is rather long. Her husband comes in angry and turns it off. Later in the film she turns the radio on again and he, in part because he is still angry but more, one suspects, for formal reasons, shouts at her to turn it off, which she does. No reasons for any of this beyond his impatience are given. One is left to infer: she is asserting herself in turning it on again, or her love of the music is strong enough to counter her husband's wrath, or he shouts at her to turn the thing off merely because he wishes to appear consistent, etc. It is not here important what it is in their character that is being shown by these parallel scenes; what is important is that they suggest a complex of emotions to us and also provide a formal frame for the scene.

The most satisfying parallels in Ozu's films, and the few that are readily recognizable as parallels, are those which fit the film and amplify it but whose connection with the main theme remains elusive. They are mysterious; one recognizes a pattern but does not know what it means. Perhaps these are the most satisfying because they are the most lifelike, the most recognizable from our own experience. Perhaps they are the most beautiful because they are the most apparently useless.

One such parallel occurs in *The End of Summer*. The sisters are walking along the banks of a river and pause, continuing their conversation. Still talking, they squat on their heels in that awkward, touching, and graceful way that Japanese women have. Later, at the end of the film, they are walking by a stream. It is after the funeral and they are in formal kimono. Again they pause, again they squat, and again they talk, speaking of matters reminiscent of their earlier conversation. We do not know what the parallel means, but we remember it.

Again, in *An Autumn Afternoon,* an old-time war song is sung (4, 465) as a part of the action in a bar. Later in the film, father and son are in their beds. The father has been drinking and the son says, "And lay off the sake. Can't have you dying yet." The father begins to sing: ". . . In defense or attack, these plates of steel—" "Go to sleep," says the son. ". . . a floating fortress she looms in our eyes." "Stop groaning," says the son, "I'm going to sleep." There is silence, then the father says, to himself: "Yes, all alone at the end . . ." and then continues the song: "Floating fortress . . . pride of the land." (9, 1034.) This is followed by the end credit. It is a beautiful and mysterious scene. We do not know quite what it means. There is an equation of times past and pres-

43

ent, of past companionship and present solitude, but beyond this the scene is as opaque as it is memorable.

In *Equinox Flower* there is a similar experience. At a reunion one of the men sings a long poem by Masashige Kusunoki:

> The precepts of my father remain deep in memory,
> The edict of the Emperor I'll follow faithfully;
> Ten years of patience and now the great day is here.
> Strike a mighty blow, fill the foe with fear.
> For the Emperor's cause we fight once more. (11, 1121.)

The poem is very long and the scene is extraordinarily long. Its length seems to suggest an importance beyond itself, as though it were somehow commenting on the film as a whole. And yet the kind of patriotism the poem suggests is far from the theme of the picture, and even its classical tone contributes little because *Equinox Flower* is one of the few late Ozu films not concerned with nostalgia for time past. The following scene shows the waves at Gamagori, and, as though the two scenes had made some kind of succinct comment, we then move on to other things. And of course the scenes have made a comment, but they have made it emotionally. The scenes in combination are moving, but one looks in vain for a possible parallel with the main themes of the picture. The scenes remain opaque, mysterious, fitting.

It is through such methods, then, that Ozu and his fellow scriptwriter completed their scenario, writing first the dialogue, and then enlarging upon it to include scene, context, etc. As we have seen, the starting point (as it were), often a joke or a single incident, then became through repetition a motif; these motifs sometimes formed the film's main story, and sometimes echoing or contrasting supports for the major theme. Parallelism was the mainstay of Ozu's method of film construction because it enabled him to show what he wanted without telling us what we should be thinking and feeling.

And all the material used to construct these parallels is undramatic in the extreme. It has been so ordinary, so mundane, that if one were not attempting to elucidate the way Ozu constructed a film, there would be little reason to record it. Outside its proper context, i.e. the film, the dialogue quoted in this chapter betrays little of its effect once in proper context, once spoken. There the dialogue becomes properly unnoticeable, and the parallels are so completely natural-seeming that they are often invisible until one notices that they are inevitable. In *Tokyo Twilight,* for example (15, 1079), there is a bit of dialogue in which the daughter decides to return to her husband. The reason she gives is that she does not want her small daughter to grow up as she and her sister did. (Her sister had committed suicide, apparently because their mother had left their father.) From the parallel circumstances of two generations the daughter learns—as do we. And yet her comments and her assumptions are so natural, so much what would occur to anyone, that we feel rather than notice that this parallel has completed, in this case created, the main theme of the picture.

In the completed film these parallels are often balanced, in a way that contributes to the full and finished feeling of an Ozu picture. A partial listing of parallels in *There Was a Father* indicates this balance: (1) The son wanted to go to Tokyo but the father would not let him; later, the father himself goes to Tokyo, and the son does not want him to go. (2) When the father goes to Tokyo the boy turns his back and cries; later, when the father dies and leaves forever, the boy, now grown, turns his back and cries. (3) The boy goes on a train trip with his father and looks out the window with pleasure. Later, the father dead, the boy takes his ashes on the train trip back home; he looks out the window sadly, and then looks at the ashes, recalling to us the former scene. Without any of the usual convolutions of plot ("someone did this so someone did that" is very rare, though "someone did this so someone did *not* do that" is perhaps more common), with none of the ordinary story-line kinks, Ozu completes a picture with scenes that make any other "solution" seem improbable. The delicate balance of parallels is crucial to this sense of rightness, of inevitability. The parallels are perhaps more visible in *Late Autumn* than in any other of the late films; a listing of them will show how they are balanced:

(1) A group of older men, friends to the dead husband, are helping to get the daughter married; she objects because she feels she should be with her mother. At the same time the men think the widow should remarry; she objects because she feels she should be with her daughter.

45

(2) The men arrange for the girl to marry and the mother does not object. They arrange for the mother to marry and the girl does not (at once) object.

(3) They neglect, however, to tell the mother of their plans for her and these plans come to nothing. They neglect also to seriously help the girl to find a husband, and these plans, too, come to nothing.

(4) The girl, however, meets the same man they had in mind through the introduction of another. The mother hears of the man she is supposed to marry through another. The daughter finally marries; the mother finally does not.

Such a list may elucidate Ozu's use of parallels, but it cannot pretend to reproduce the experience of the film itself. There is every evidence that such parallels were foreseen and purposely created: "MARCH 23, 1963. Work. The fight between Saburi and Ryu; the small edition of that, the fight between Oda and Kita; on top of that, the fight between the children." [19] There is also every evidence that the utmost skill and patience were exercised to so humanize such schema that parallel-counting would not occur. Just as to discuss Ozu's humor is largely to destroy it, so any discussion of the structure of his films must obscure its richness and the accidental-seeming way in which it is achieved. It might help, however, to examine the way one parallel, the third in the above list, is presented in the finished film.

The mother has been to see one of the men supposedly helping arrange her daughter's marriage. "Did you notice the boy who bowed to me in front of the elevator?" he asks. "About my height, hair hanging over his forehead." The mother says she didn't. "Well, he's not exactly an eye-catcher, but he's a good boy, works hard," etc. The mother says it sounds like a good choice. (2, 226.) Later, after the girl has said they won't marry, she brings a pipe to the older man and a young man appears in the office. "Wait a minute," says the elder. "This is the girl who jilted you. Aya, this is the boy you brushed off." After the young man has bowed and left, the daughter turns and says, "Well, that wasn't very nice. You embarrassed him." He says, reading her concern as interest, "Well, then, should we reopen the case?" She is firm in her refusal. (3, 437.) In the next reel the daughter has gone off to the mountains with some friends and is talking with one of the boys there. "Aya," he says, "I hear you turned Goto down. He told me." "I never did any such thing." "He's a very nice fellow." "It was all a silly mistake," she says. "Want to see him again?" "Don't bother," says Aya. (4, 531.) Finally, the older man is in a coffee shop and in walk the girl and the young man. Apparently introductions have been properly made and they are out together, though neither the older man nor the audience has been told anything about it. After the boy and his friend leave, Aya comes and sits with her mother's friend. "Well, this is a strange coincidence," he begins. "It was our first meeting, it was arranged by a friend." "I introduced you first, you know." "Sugiyama," says the girl, "the one who introduced us, works in the same place I do and he's a friend of Goto's and —" "I don't want to hear about Sugiyama. How about Goto?" "But I met him for the first time today," she says. "You already said that," he answers. (5, 582.)

The richness, contradictions, apparent indirections, and inconsistencies of character shown even in this small section of the finished script almost completely obscure the parallels that give the film its form and feeling. The supports are hidden by a meticulously mundane dialogue and an avoidance of any expected story complications. Yet it is largely these parallels and our half-awareness of them during the picture that account for the ironies in the Ozu character. These often emerge when a character notices a parallel and comments on it; when he sets for himself one plan of action and then follows another, different but parallel; or when he unknowingly does something completely different from what he stated and intended.

The father in *Equinox Flower* provides a clear example. He expresses himself in good faith, but we shortly understand that actuality is opposite to what he (innocent of any deceptive intention) represents it to be. At the beginning of the picture he gives a liberal-sounding speech at a wedding banquet:

> These two have evidently been in love for a long time. From time to time I've heard "interim reports" about the progress of the romance. And it was pleasant news. But even so I was struck by the contrast with how things were when I was young. And I recall how prosaic and unro-

mantic my own marriage was. [He glances at the woman beside him.] My wife is present and she, too, will remember how everything was arranged between our parents. In that respect newlyweds today are fortunate and I envy them. (1, 22.)

Having delivered himself of these fine thoughts, however, he demonstrates throughout the rest of the film that he believes precisely the opposite. By the next reel he has already forgotten his speech. His youngest daughter has said that she agrees with him, that she would hate the idea of an arranged marriage. "You would?" he asks, surprised. When she reiterates her opinion he says, "You worry me." (2, 109.) At the same time it becomes clear that it is his own daughters he is worrying about, not daughters in general. Despite the fact that he is pushing his own elder girl into an arranged marriage, he tells her Kyoto friend, Yukiko, "There is no need to marry at all. Why should every girl be in such a rush. Why not be an exception?" (3, 304.) This leads to a conversation between the two girls. Yukiko says: "That's why I envy you, Setsuko. Your parents are so different—so understanding." Setsuko, knowing better, smiles and says, "I wouldn't be too sure of that." (4, 342).

This in turn leads to the rather elaborate joke played by Yukiko that marks the climax of the film. She calls on the father and pretends to ask for his advice. "So then I should marry the man I love?" she asks. "Is he a good man? Dependable?" She nods. "Then go ahead, you are responsible for your own life." (8, 880.) He sounds absolutely certain of himself. Having heard this advice, both honestly meant and completely incongruous, she phones Setsuko and says that, finally, her father has agreed: the daughter is free to marry the man of her choice. Yukiko has exposed the double standard exhibited by the father, a very Japanese one, incidentally: one standard for members of his family, quite another for outsiders.

The girl's mother is, of course, well aware of her husband's ways:

MOTHER: I heard you say you wouldn't worry so much if Setsuko had a boy friend, and now that she has you disapprove. Your attitude is inconsistent. FATHER: This is a father's love and you call it inconsistent. MOTHER: I certainly do. If you love her, you'd take full responsibility, one way or the other. But you don't. You're inconsistent. FATHER: Everyone is inconsistent now and then, except god. Life is full of inconsistencies. . . . The sum total of all of the inconsistencies of life is life itself. (9, 954.)

Both parents, of course, are right. In Ozu's films as in life itself the seemingly antithetical live happily side by side. It is inconsistency which creates irony, and which also makes the father seem so human. Perhaps then, as Ozu so often indicates, it behooves us to regard humanity with irony; perhaps that is the only way to live in the world.

In any event, the moment of truth passes. Shortly we find the father giving more contradictory advice to Yukiko:

FATHER: A parent should give in to the child. It is enough that the child is happy. . . . YUKIKO: Now this is very strange. Once you told me not to marry. FATHER: Did I say that? Well, anyway, get married. It is time you did. YUKIKO: You change so often that I get confused. Should I get married or not? FATHER: It is better that you should. YUKIKO: Is this an act? FATHER: I can't act as well as you can. Think it over. Marry if you can find a good man. Be happy and your mother will be happy, too. (12, 1218.)

Obviously it is one thing if Yukiko's mother is the parent and quite another if he himself is. When Setsuko marries he is not at all happy, though she is. He even says he won't go to the wedding, though he is eventually prevailed upon to attend. Like most spectacularly inconsistent people, he has a very poor memory. At the end of the film he is shown on the train, going to Setsuko's for a visit, humming to himself, showing signs of contentment. He has, at the last, quite consistent in his inconsistency, forgotten that he opposed the marriage.

The irony with which we must observe the father in this film is extreme; perhaps no other Ozu character demands so much. The film is, in part, the study of a man deep in self-deception. Yet Ozu's irony is always one of character. There is nowhere in his work a scene of which the real, intended meaning is contrary to the one seemingly expressed. Rather, a character reveals his beliefs to be the contrary of those he expresses, or maintains a belief different from the one reality quite apparently imposes. In Ozu's work, such self-deception is, as the father in *Equinox Flower* plainly states, proof of humanity.

Ozu's films are filled with such proof and this, in turn, is what makes his characters so human and consequently so real. He shows us the gulf between opinion or intent and reality, and then bridges it for us. In *Tokyo Twilight,* the father, Shukichi, is having a conversation with the elder sister about the younger. She says: "Akiko's lonely. I am sure of it. You must be more gentle with her. She grew up without a mother and that's why. It's different without a mother." This is the first time she has spoken to her father directly about this subject, and she is quite aware that her words apply to herself as well. She, too, suffered a motherless childhood. Moreover, she has left her own husband and taken her child away with her, thus depriving it of a father as she was deprived of a mother. Her father's answer reveals his complete unawareness of any alternative meaning. He accepts the simple surface meaning; it never occurs to him that his wife would not have left had he been a different kind of man, that the breakdown of the marriage was at least half his fault. "I've looked after her," he says of Akiko, "paid so much attention to her that I was afraid you'd be jealous. And now look at her. Something's gone wrong." The elder daughter looks at him, perhaps wondering if he does not understand his part in the domestic tragedy. She is certain he does not when he adds a remark painfully banal in the circumstances: "Well, bringing up a child is certainly a difficult thing." (7, 537.) Later in the film Akiko shows herself to be her father's child when she obtusely says to her mother: "I'll never have a baby. Never. But if I do I won't abandon it like you did yours. I'll love it—love it with all my heart." (11, 931.) As it turns out, she does more than abandon her child, she has an abortion.

One of the traditional functions, or perhaps results, of irony is that one keeps one's distance, that one finds a wholesale empathy impossible. Ozu's irony, however, like that of Chekhov or Jane Austen, is there for but one purpose: our detachment reveals a design of which the characters are unaware, and this makes us want to move closer to these warm and very human people. Perhaps it is for this reason that many of the ironies in Ozu's films are neither explained nor exploited. They are simply there—large, inconsistent, moving. When in *Tokyo Story* the mother upon arriving says, "I'm glad I lived to see this day," (2, 115) the irony is at least double: the day she finally came to see her Tokyo children was not worth the waiting for, and this day proves to be one of her last. Later in the film the father is drinking with a friend and talking about his preoccupied children: "I suppose I should be happy. Some young people today would kill their parents without a thought. At least mine wouldn't do that." (8, 628.) He apparently means that other children neglect their parents even more, not that they would literally kill them. Still it is ironic that it was the children who sent the mother off to Atami, where she had her first attack. Touchingly ironic also is the father's little speech to his children at the end of the parent's visit. The irony cuts several ways because first, he believes it, and second, it is prophetic. "You've been very kind to us—all of you. We have enjoyed our trip. You were so nice to us, children. Now that we've seen you all, you need not come down if anything should happen to us—to either of us." (9, 744.) These words, kindly meant, innocently expressed, with no sarcasm or even irony in them, are of course completely at variance with what we have observed: the children were wretched and, in contrast to the widowed daughter-in-law, rarely in the least nice to their parents for whom the trip was rarely enjoyable.

And yet even here Ozu allows his characters no rancor, no bitterness, no expression at all of fallen hopes. It is as though the father, like all of Ozu's fathers, accepts the world as he finds it, and is not surprised by ungrateful children, indeed seems anxious to find excuses for them. And it is true that just as there are no heroes in Ozu's pictures, so there are no villains. One may not approve of the grasping older sisters, say, in *The Brothers and Sisters of the Toda Family, Tokyo Story,* or *The End of Summer,* but one accepts them because everyone else in the film does and because Ozu himself does.

The philosophy of acceptance in the films of Ozu may be called this both because it is so deeply felt and because it has antecedents both in the Buddhist religion and in Japanese aesthetics. In basic

Zen texts one accepts and transcends the world, and in traditional Japanese narrative art one celebrates and relinquishes it. The aesthetic term *mono no aware* is often used nowadays to describe this state of mind. The term has a long history (it appears fourteen times in *The Tale of Genji*), and though its original meaning was more restricted, from the beginning it represented feeling of a special kind: "not a powerful surge of passion, but an emotion containing a balance; . . . on the whole, *aware* tended to be used of deep impressions produced by small things." [20] Now it is used to describe the "sympathetic sadness" (Tamako Niwa's phrase) caused by the contemplation of this world, and is also used to describe a serene acceptance of a transient world, a gentle pleasure found in mundane pursuits soon to vanish, a content created by the knowledge that one is with the world and that leaving it is, after all, in the natural state of things.

Ozu did not, of course, set out self-consciously to capture this quality. To do so would have seemed to him artificial, just as the concept itself would have seemed to him old-fashioned and bookish.[21] Nonetheless, his films are full of it, since he was. The many examples of *mono no aware* in his pictures, homely, mundane, often seemingly trivial, are none the less strong for all that. Perhaps the most celebrated example is Setsuko Hara's smiling concurrence when her young sister-in-law suddenly discovers that life is disappointing, but there are many others in which a less than perfect existence is readily accepted. In *The End of Summer,* the Kyoto mistress's daughter is talking with her mother about the Osaka merchant who is the leading character in the film:

> DAUGHTER: Mother, is he really my father? MOTHER: Why? DAUGHTER: Didn't I have another father when I was little? There was someone and I think I used to call him father, too. MOTHER: Did you? Well, maybe you did. DAUGHTER: Then who is my real father? MOTHER: What difference does it make—it's up to you. DAUGHTER: Don't you know either? Not that it matters. The fact that I got born, that's the most important thing. MOTHER: That's right, think of it that way. (3, 500.)

Not that it matters—and this as answer to the burning question of parentage, the question that has animated Western art since *Oedi-*

pus Rex. The girl, pragmatic to an extreme, represents one possible answer to the problem: the past does not matter. Ozu characters are all without pasts and only very occasionally and indirectly suffer because of some past action or lack of one. But the present matters because it is all we have. One should live in it as fully as possible and not bemoan its gradual disappearance because that is the way things are and, consequently, should be.

Any question of the future in Ozu's films usually is also firmly dragged back to present circumstances. An amusing example of this occurs in *An Autumn Afternoon* when the father meets a man who served under him as sergeant during the war. The man asks: "Sir—how come we lost the war? It sure made things rough. My house got burned down, nothing to eat, prices impossible. . . . Captain, if Japan had won, I wonder how things would be. I bet if we'd won we'd both be in New York now. Yes, New York. No cheap imitation but the real thing—in America." He pauses before continuing and the ex-captain says mildly, "Well, I wonder." The ex-sergeant continues: "It's because we lost that the kids are all shaking their behinds dancing this rockabilly thing. But if we'd won, then all the blue-eyed foreigners would be wearing geisha wigs and chewing gum while plunking out tunes on the samisen." The older man turns, smiles, and says, "Then it's lucky we lost." (4, 427.)

The typical expression of *mono no aware* in the Ozu film is more complex. In the following example from *Early Spring,* the past, the present, the heroic ideal, and all-too-human reality all come together. The wife is talking with her mother about her husband's wartime buddies and says, "And he calls them friends." "But remember," says her mother, "they faced bullets together." "Soldiers like that!" retorts her daughter. "No wonder Japan lost the war." Then, in seeming indignation, she adds, "And he forgot all about our dead son's anniversary, too." To which the mother quietly adds, "I forgot about my husband's death anniversary, too." (8, 813.) One is reminded of Setsuko Hara's smiling assurance to her troubled sister-in-law that she, too, will forget the dead, that she will, to an extent, become like those relatives she has just criticized. She will become like that for life is like that.

The phrase itself is often heard in Ozu's dialogue. The young man's despairing but accepting "Tokyo is like that" in *The Only Son* becomes the daughter-in-law's "life is like that" in *Tokyo Story*. Though occasionally the line "maybe he was the lucky one," referring to someone recently dead (notably in *Early Spring*), is heard, more often death and disappointment are accepted with the phrase *kore de ii no yo* (literally, "It's all right as it is," expressing resigned contentment) or *sonna mon yo* ("that's how things are"). There are many scenes in which the phrase is not heard and for this reason sounds all the louder: the endings of *Late Spring, Tokyo Story, Late Autumn, Tokyo Twilight,* etc.; those many scenes (e.g., the final sequence of *An Autumn Afternoon*) where no one is any longer in rooms where we once saw them; scenes in which a disappointment is quietly assimilated (e.g., the parents at Ueno Park looking at the lost balloon, in *Early Summer*). A particularly fine example occurs in *The Only Son,* when the mother, sitting in a field with her grown child, asks if he is disappointed in life. He says no. She appears to accept this. They both sit and look at the sky. In the long scene that follows it becomes evident (from their faces, the way they sit, the gradual contentment that pervades the scene) that, looking into the eye of the sky, they have the courage to accept life as it is.

Not, however, that Ozu's characters are passive or indolent. When it comes to things they can do something about, they are quite active, even argumentative. The elder brother is put smartly in his place in *Early Summer* when he says, with the air of uttering an unchallengeable truth, "It is deplorable—women have become so forward." "No, that's not true," says the daughter with spirit. "It is just that we're normal now [after the war]. Men used to be far too self-important." (2, 132.) We have earlier seen other examples of this kind of remark, which puts things into their proper perspective and separates the large immutable problems from small daily annoyances. In *Passing Fancy* there is a scene in which the father cuffs his little boy again and again, though without hurting him. This is the way fathers often discipline their children. The boy, however, responds with sudden rage, and begins hitting his father with every intention, at the time, of killing him. It is a moving, even shocking scene. The father, arms at his side, makes no defense at all, but allows himself to be battered by the boy. He has correctly divined the difference between small things and large; his son is experiencing something enormous.

Such an impasse is rare in Ozu's pictures. Usually his people accept one another's differences with a kind of pragmatic readiness as ordinary in Japanese life as it is rare in contemporary Japanese film. The idea is expressed in a conversation between the eldest son and his wife in *Tokyo Story*. The mother is ill and they have to go to Onomichi. "What about black clothes" [for mourning], she suddenly wonders. "Maybe we'll need them," admits her husband. "Well," she says, voicing typical Ozu wisdom, "Let's take them and hope we don't have to use them." (11, 839.) His characters also accept differences of opinion with complete equanimity, as though they knew that in this passing world two things commonly thought antithetical can and do happily coexist. In *Equinox Flower* husband and wife are talking. She says: "Remember how we had to run into the air-raid shelters when the planes came during the war? Setsuko was in primary school and Hisako had only just begun to walk. And I used to think in the dark that we might all die together." "That's right," says her husband. "I hated that period," he says. "Nothing to eat, awful people all around you." "I liked it," she says. "We four were always together." (4, 454.) Such a confession of values so completely different never results in argument, sulking, or indignation in an Ozu picture. Once the difference is uncovered, that is usually the end of it. Husband and wife in *Equinox Flower* sit there after discovering a gulf they have lived with for years, all but unaware of it, mutually enjoying the summer sun, the light on the river.

It is perhaps easier for people to accept the grand verities of life, such as aging, death, etc., than it is the smaller but no less real immutables—set differences of opinion between husband and wife, for example. In Ozu's characters, however, such difficulties, though observed, are never commented upon. When one accepts one's life, one accepts everything in it. Such a view allows one to be objective about oneself, and to enjoy an ironic view of life. Disparity is everywhere, but disparity, too, is part of the texture of life, and is for that reason acceptable. Nature, one's self, one's place in nature, this is a fit object for art, for philosophy, for contemplation.

The central figure in an Ozu film is often a character with the ability to contemplate, to remain for relatively long periods of time seemingly inactive, utterly given over to contemplation. Some scenes of Ozu characters in silent contemplation have become extremely well-known, most of them ones that occur at the film's end: the mother alone at the end of *The Only Son;* the son alone on the train carrying the ashes of his father in *There Was a Father;* mother alone in *Late Autumn,* fathers alone in *Late Spring, Tokyo Story, Tokyo Twilight, Equinox Flower,* etc. Other such moments occur at the end of scenes, and the long still shot of the character simply existing, no longer acting or reacting, is usually given some small reason; often it is the weather, or some other natural manifestation. In *There Was a Father,* a scene of considerable emotional power, the son apologizing to the father, is suddenly broken when the latter turns suddenly, listens, and remarks on the bird singing outside. (The bird is used again with much less effect in *The Munekata Sisters.*) The effect is one of stillness and expectation, of a quite ordinary event that is somehow special.

In *Tokyo Story* the mother and daughter-in-law, side by side on their *futon,* stop speaking; the scene continues as the mother fans herself, a look of contentment on her face—a scene of the simple savoring of the moment. In *Tokyo Twilight,* the father and son-in-law are talking when the latter looks out the window and says, "It's snowing—I didn't expect snow." (3, 249.) We watch them watching for a time, neither saying anything further. In *Equinox Flower* the mother, who is working, looks out the window and then, having remarked on the fine weather, sits down to watch it for a time. In *Late Autumn,* the daughter's friend is on the roof of her office building. "Beautiful days like this are wasted here," she remarks. (9, 191.) Nonetheless she turns to enjoy the beautiful day and for a time we watch her enjoying it. In *The End of Summer* the two daughters have finished talking. One of them looks up at the sky and says, "Another hot day" (1, 200), and the two women sit looking at it. In *An Autumn Afternoon* the son and his wife have finished their small quarrel over the golf clubs and she turns with, "Oh, what a nice day" (5, 546), and he joins her, and they look out the window for a time.

One function of such unusual appreciation of the weather, unusual even in weather-conscious Japan, is precisely to break a scene of some emotional tension, and Ozu usually prefers to break rather than resolve, at least in the middle of his films. An unavoidable inference is that the weather, nature, the world that exists outside man and his petty concerns, is much wider, much more mysterious, than we usually think. When we allow ourselves to appreciate it, or even to regard it, our thoughts are soothed, our spirits renewed. The idea of anyone sitting and *watching* the weather is one admittedly inimical to the West, but not, as yet, to Japan.

Another function of such scenes, empty as they are of all story content, is to provide a hiatus—a word that Webster's Unabridged nicely defines as "a break or slight pause necessary to keep distinct . . . without contraction or elision." Invariably occurring at the ends of sequences, they stretch the scene in the manner of a fermata in music; they sometimes attenuate it until it vanishes. One reason for Ozu's fondness of the device was his regard for character and consequent unwillingness to exploit it in any apparent story-forwarding manner. But another was that he wished to keep the various parts of his film separate, and to impress, through emptiness and length of scene, the importance that moments of silent contemplation had for his people. These scene endings are caesuras. In music the term usually means a pause marking a rhythmic point of division in a melody; in Ozu's films they indicate and usually precede a change in the direction of the story.

Often the hiatus consists of empty scenes. The various still lifes in his films (the best known of which include the vase in *Late Spring* and the corridor, stairs, and room at the end of *An Autumn Afternoon*), recall both what once happened in these rooms and the characters who lived there. Such scenes often occur at the beginning of films as well, where they are less noticeable because they are taken to be introductory material. *Late Spring* opens with a typical series of three placing scenes, followed by the tea-ceremony scene with the daughter, whom we will later come to know well. There follows immediately three more empty scenes—the stone at the entrance to the tea room, some trees, the temple roof

—and then we return to the tea ceremony. While some empty scenes serve as psychological reminders, ones that occur so early in a picture can serve only as punctuation: in *Late Spring* they separate the introduction of the main character from the beginning of the film's story. By this means Ozu calls greater attention to the daughter. He has set her off in brackets, as it were (he has also really introduced her: she bows at the audience, an action that is natural because she is bowing to the others at the ceremony but that also, because of Ozu's continuous frontal position, ensures that she acknowledges us as well), and has now differentiated her completely from the other girls enjoying the tea ceremony.

Though sometimes the "empty" scene, whether or not it has people in it, seems almost formalistic—the first scene in *Floating Weeds* opens with a shipping clerk, a secondary character, saying, "It's so hot, what a hot day" (1, 21), and closes with a close-up of the same character (1, 47) saying, "It'll be another hot day today," with both lines of dialogue followed by long still shots of the man—usually it is correctly formal in the sense that it is an integral part of Ozu's dramatic construction and serves to convey his interpretations. More will be said about these hiatuses later, but at present it should be noted that while one of their functions is grammatical, another is psychological. They tell us that Ozu characters are people capable of sitting back, of being contemplative.

They can also surprise in a way relatively rare among screen characters. One of the reasons is the often elliptical construction of their story. The golf clubs in *An Autumn Afternoon* and television set in *Good Morning* suddenly appear. So much has been made of them that one half expects plot complications involving these objects. Not at all. In the next scene there they are, their arrival unexplained. In one film the wife, in the other the father, has apparently gone out and gotten them after having argued at length against doing so. The deaths in *Tokyo Story* and *The End of Summer* similarly come as a complete surprise to us. We know something is wrong, someone is ill. But by the time we see anything, the characters are dead. In *Late Autumn* we have been following the efforts of the older men to get the young girl married.

When she and the young man appear in the coffee shop together, we are almost as surprised as the older man who had intended to introduce them. Neither he nor we had known that they had simply gone out and met each other. We and the father in *Equinox Flower* are equally surprised when the young man asks for the hand of the daughter. The father asks his wife, "You knew nothing about it?" "Nothing at all," she says, though it transpires that she did. "This is a shock," he says. (5, 505.) And so it is, because Ozu left out the scene in which the girl told her mother everything.

Ozu made his films this way in part because he wanted to obviate the obvious and to deny any toehold to plot. In addition, however, he wanted us to be surprised—particularly, perhaps, by men and women we thought we understood acting out of character. Their inconsistencies (a film in which characters are static—*A Hen in the Wind,* for example—is rare) force us to discover new depths in them and readjust our opinions, a continuous process for the audience during any Ozu picture, a process that is perhaps more gratifying in film than in life. Ozu's films are made of so little, his characters composed of so apparently few "traits," that one is in retrospect both intrigued and baffled at how surprising they can be. He rarely gives his characters any identifying props (our being shown that the father in *Late Spring* takes *Also Sprach Zarathustra* along in his suitcase, and that he apparently fails to read it, is an exception) and makes little visible differentiation between them (though much differentiation in the dialogue), and yet they surprise. In most cases Ozu creates surprise by showing us an incongruity between what we had been led to assume about a person and something he or she does. In *An Autumn Afternoon,* after the daughter has been told about an approaching marriage, the son says to his father, "I was afraid she'd cry." "Yes," says her father, "or show some disappointment." "She took it quite coolly," says the boy. "Yes, fortunately," says the father, pleased that his daughter has behaved just as she ought, just as he thought she would. After a pause the father goes to look in on the girl. When he returns the son asks, "What's she doing?" "Crying," says his father. (7, 861.) They were wrong. The girl was only human, and being only human she can surprise them and us.

Sometimes the character tells us something completely out of character, which we must thereafter accept and remember. One of the nicest of the many nice people in *Good Morning* is the pleasant and even-tempered young teacher. Nonetheless he at one point tells the girl in whom he is later interested: "After my mother died I kept on feeling bad about the quarrels we had had. Even now it bothers me. Once when we lived in Fushimi we had some really nice dolls. They were all set up in a row . . . but one day I lost my temper and I broke them all. . . . I still remember what she looked like when she found out what I'd done. And it was all over nothing, too. And then she died that same autumn." (8, 989.) We are not, I think, supposed to deduce that this regret is the reason the man became so nice—that would be false as well as sentimental. Rather, we are supposed to be surprised, and to realize that however nice a person may be he also does un-nice things.

In *Early Spring* some of the characters show us they have learned, from Ozu, as it were, that the proper way to assess character is to observe what the character does not do. Some of the office people are talking about Sugimura and one of the girls. "Didn't you notice?" asks Chako, another girl, "Sugimura and that girl—it's very suspicious. They never sit next to each other in the train. And, didn't you notice yesterday?—they avoid each other in public. They act like they don't know the other one is there. It's very suspicious." "What's wrong with that?" her friend wants to know. "Well, it's odd. Why don't they talk?—like you and I do." "But I was never interested in you," he says. "Well, that was rude," she counters, but his response still proves her point. (6, 539.) In fact the guilty girl herself has already, in the fifth reel, proved the point that people's behavior belies their feelings. She has had her little affair with Sugimura, and he has in the morning been, even for a Japanese male, rude and brusque. He walks out on her. And yet we see her alone in the room with a small, secret smile on her lips as she combs her hair and hums a little tune. We had expected her to be hurt by his lack of tenderness—it was their first time together, too. Not at all. She is far too sure of herself. She knows, too, that you must read for motive inversely. Such coldness must, she appears to believe, argue for a great deal of warmth; so much rudeness for a great deal of affection.

Ozu's characters often display opposite extremes of emotion, usually quite dramatically, often very suddenly. Perhaps the finest such switch occurs in *The End of Summer*. The older sister comes down to see her father after his first stroke. When he appears to be recovering, she says with many a smile and nod, "Well, if he's going to live after all, then I want to get back to Nagoya," and, lack of sympathy personified, leaves. (5,799.) Later, however he does die. At his funeral, where she sits smiling, nodding, very chatty, she says: "Well, he ought to have died when we were all here last time. But then he always did as he pleased. Selling all those nice old things that belong to all of us. He was really not a very nice person, but he was awfully lucky. And now he's dead. . . ." She suddenly pauses and, before our eyes, bursts into tears, gasping out between her sobs, "And it's all over." It is a powerful moment in the film. Our realization that she, a selfish person, has had some inkling of the quality of her own death does not suffice to explain why we are so moved. It is, rather, Ozu's simply and dramatically indicating that beneath every one of the emotions we normally show, the emotions from which we have chosen to build our ostensible character, there lies its opposite. When such concealed emotions, powerful and long denied, break out, they show —no matter who we are—how akin we are to everyone else.

Occasionally people in Ozu's films are defined not by what they say or do not say, do or do not do, but by the direct observations of outside commentators. Almost never the main characters, such commentators usually appear briefly in the picture, make their comments, and disappear. In *Floating Weeds* the old actor is going through the streets of the seaside town on his way to meet the woman by whom, years before, he had a son. He passes two of the village women. One turns and says, "That's the actor." The other responds, "He's very old." (1, 186.) We are being told, though we do not fully realize it till later, that the man is perhaps too old to be a good actor, which we suspect, and that he is probably too old to be a good husband and father, which he will later prove. Having made their comment, at the time apparently gratuitous, the two women disappear from the film.

Sometimes comments from outsiders point up a parallel, often a comical one, to a character we are supposed to take seriously. In

Tokyo Twilight the younger daughter is being questioned by the police. Ozu cuts to another person under interrogation, someone we have not seen before. "Speak up, do you do this very often?" the policeman asks him. "No," answers the man. "What do you steal women's underwear for anyway—don't you have a wife?" asks the policeman. "No," answers the man. (7, 479.) The little cartoon-like scene is, first, a joke, and Ozu can rarely resist a joke; at the same time it reflects on all men who do not have wives, including the hero of the film, whose wife has left him. Such an oblique comment on a major character is rare in Ozu, perhaps because it is rarely successful.

More often the outside comment is used to reinforce the theme of the film. At the end of *Early Summer* two ladies are talking: "Look, a bride is passing," says one. "I hope she'll be happy," says the other (13,1184), and indeed a happy marriage is the conclusion of the film. Something similar occurs in *Early Spring* when two servants, making their sole appearance early in the film, start talking about wedding portraits. The beginning of *Equinox Flower* contains a beautiful example. The film opens at Tokyo Station, where two railway men, never to be shown again, are sitting and talking about the brides they have noticed that day. The first says, "Certainly a lot of married couples today." "Not many pretty brides though," responds the other. "See the one who took the 3:15?" asks the first. "The fat one?" asks the second. "Well, that's the best we've had today." After a pause the first man observes, "There's a storm warning out." To which the second adds, "Well, bad things follow good. Look, there's another." (1, 2.) This light, humorous scene sets the theme (happy marriages), suggests the complications that follow (storm), and inverts the conclusion (good things follow bad).

If the above scene works it does so mainly because it occurs at the beginning of a film, the theme of which we do not as yet know. At a film's conclusion, such a scene does not usually work. It seems mere reiteration. The otherwise impressive ending of *The End of Summer* is marred by such a scene. The father has died; his body is being cremated. We watch the smoke rise from the chimney—all that now remains of that very human and lovable man. Into our elegy Ozu suddenly intrudes two peasants at work by the river. "So, someone died after all—there is the smoke," says the woman. "Yes, that's so," observes the man. "It's pitiful if it's someone young instead of someone old," she continues. "Yes," replies the man, "but new lives replace those who've died." To which she replies, "How well nature works." (7, 988.) This is *mono no aware* with a vengeance. The bald statement, coming directly after an unusually rich orchestration, is needless and obtrusive. The fact that the commentators are simple peasants, apparently spouting folk wisdom, does not much assist. Of no help at all, of course, is the fact that these are patently no peasants, but the famous and talented actors Yuko Mochizuki and Chishu Ryu.

(One reason for their appearance was that Mochizuki had been in only one Ozu film, and wanted to be in another.[22] Also Ryu had to be fitted in somehow. On occasion, Ozu, usually so stern about his films, could be astonishingly accommodating. During the filming of *Tokyo Twilight*, Nobuo Nakamura was to pour a glass of whiskey for Isuzu Yamada. As always they used real whiskey, just as they always used real food, even for rehearsals. They rehearsed the scene and then, before they shot it, Ozu whispered to Nakamura so no one else could hear, "Turn the bottle around so the label shows." The reason was that the Suntory Whiskey people regularly gave the director large quantities of whiskey, and in his later years at any rate, Ozu was a great whiskey drinker.[23])

Usually, of course, the comments of outside parties in an Ozu film support rather than undermine the film's impact. There is a very beautiful scene toward the end of *Early Spring,* one that is rich, ironic, apt, and enigmatic. The young man has been transferred, and, on his way without his wife to the new position, stops to meet with an older friend in Kyoto. They sit talking near a bridge. The conversation stops, and just then a racing shell skims across the river in the background, the young crew bending over the oars. The elder man watches them go by and then says, "You young men are happy." (15, 476.) That is all. He suggests that he is not, but then neither is the young man sitting beside him. But we know that for the younger things will change—and we have just glimpsed that vision of youthful vigor, a racing shell, as it flashed across the scene. The comment enlarges on character but it is at the same time properly diffuse. It suggests complications, it enlarges rather than limits.

There is another kind of outside comment used by Ozu that is less common but even more powerful. This is the comment offered by an invisible character, someone who is not there. The dead elder son in *Early Summer,* killed in the war before the picture opens, is present in many scenes before he appears, as it were, in the conversation of his parents at Ueno Park, where they break off their conversation to watch the lost balloon soaring into the sky. Another example is the dying friend in *Early Spring.* We have heard so much about him that he has come to personify the disasters to which the other characters occasionally seem near. Toward the end of the film we actually see him, and in the next scene he is dead. The dead elder son indicates what might have been, and the dying and dead friend seems to indicate what, unfortunately, is possible. Perhaps the best known of these invisible characters who comment through their absence is the mother in *Late Spring.* She is not even mentioned until the end of the film (11, 732), and yet she is in every scene because her absence is so deeply felt by the other characters. And this feeling in turn defines them. Both father and daughter seem to be dwelling on what their lives would have been if she had lived. The dead mother is in a sense a personification of *mu*—a concept to which we will return but which we may at present partially define as an empty space that is also a part of the pattern.

We have in this chapter been discussing how Ozu and his collaborator constructed their scripts: how they relied, initially at least, entirely upon dialogue; how the joke or light comment became a motif; how this in turn often became a parallel; how the main theme was elaborated; and how the characters were formed. In actuality, of course, all this happened at the same time. Here the method has been schematized, to make it easier to apprehend. Ozu and his collaborating scriptwriter obviously did not think in terms of motifs or parallels any more than they pondered *mono no aware* and *mu.* And, as we have seen, the end result of this work was not story but character.

Any artist this interested in character, and this adept at creating it, is inevitably, I think, a moralist. This is certainly true of artists who long ago created characters so strong we still believe in them —Jane Austen, Tolstoy, Dickens, Chekhov. Along with this interest and ability comes a concern for excellence in anything pertaining to practice or conduct, a concern for what is proper and what is ethical. The moralist in Dickens is immediately apparent because he takes up questions of right and wrong; in Ozu's case it is less a question of what is right and what is wrong than a question of what is and what isn't. The message of an Ozu film—to the extent that one can be sorted out from the sum experience of the film itself—is, perhaps, that one is happiest living in accord with one's own imperfections and those of one's friends and loved ones; that these imperfections include aging, dying, and other calamities; that man's simple humanity must, in the end, be recognized and obeyed.

Seen in this light, Ozu was a truly moral man, a profound moralist who wanted the greatest good for the greatest number of people. As a realistic, even pragmatic man, he knew that this was an impossible aim, but considered the hope itself important. He was also an artist, and thus expressed his moral views only indirectly. To assemble moral comments from various films and then present them as a coherent moral statement, as I shall do below, does Ozu disservice as an artist, and obscures the strength and, to the West, the originality of his moral viewpoint. It does, however, offer some approximation of the moral effect of an Ozu picture.

Though Ozu, particularly in Japan, is often thought of as affirming traditional values, particularly in his later films, this is not quite true. He accepts these values, and he occasionally criticizes them—though to be sure, it all depends on what you mean by tradition. I take it to mean a series of assumptions about life that have been handed down from ancestors to posterity, an inheritance largely unremarked, a body of assumptions largely unspoken. When a society becomes self-conscious about its traditions, it means they are losing their viability.

One object of Ozu's criticism throughout his career, beginning with such early pictures as *The Life of an Office Worker* and *Tokyo Chorus,* has been the texture of Japanese urban life, traditional in that it has been unthinkingly passed on from generation to generation for over a century. In *Early Spring* the young office clerk who is the leading character is in a bar with an older customer, Hattori. He and Kawai, a fellow worker, are talking with him. The latter asks, "How many years have you been working there, then?" Hattori answers, "Just thirty-one years." "Well," says Kawai, "then you'll get your retirement pay." "Hardly," answers Hattori, "that's just the point. I had hoped after retiring to open a small stationery shop near a school someplace. I thought I would have a happy life. But the retirement allowance isn't large enough. And that's the way it goes. I've known only loneliness and disillusion. And I've worked thirty-one years to find that life is just an empty dream." (15, 411.) This sentiment is later echoed by another older friend, Onodera: "A company can be a cold thing; . . . at my age I feel it more and more." (15, 474.) In *Good Morning* the father of the two boys is talking to an older next-door neighbor, Tomizawa:

> TOMIZAWA: Reaching retirement age—that's an ugly word. It's like being told you're half dead. The company seems to think that a man no longer has to eat after he reaches retirement age. But he does—and drink, too. My wife says that I have to go out looking for a job, but at my age that's hopeless. Life is an empty dream. FATHER: But surely your retirement allowance— TOMIZAWA: No use. They calculate these things. They don't give you that much. Thirty years of work. Rainy days, windy days, pushed around in crowded trains. A dream—nothing but an empty dream. (3, 86.)

Later in the film the boy's mother says, "We'll have to start thinking, too." "About what?" asks the father. "About when you retire." He nods. "Probably so." (5, 86.)

Life is a dream. This is a familiar Buddhist concept, radically updated. Originally the observation that the world is a mirage was meant to console the sufferer, but in Ozu's universe there is no afterlife. That life is a dream means one has had no life at all. We may feel that Ozu overstates the case, but he does so with compassion and even restraint.

The inequalities of Japanese urban life—and of life in general, to be sure—are soon recognized by Ozu's characters. In *I Was Born, But . . .* the two little boys reproach their father: "Why do you have to bow to Taro's father?" demands one of them. "Because his father is a director of my company." The child then asks, "Why don't you become a director, then?" The father answers that it isn't that easy. "I'm only an employee. He pays me my salary." "Don't let him," says the boy. "No," says his younger brother: "You pay *him.*" The father tries to reason. "If I didn't let him pay me, you couldn't go to school, you couldn't eat." The boys see neither justice nor sense in such an arrangement. In the following scene the father admits to the mother: "I know how they feel. . . . It is a problem they'll have to live with for the rest of their lives. . . . But will they lead the same sorry kind of lives that we have?" (7, 120.) At the conclusion of the film, Ozu leaves no doubt that they will.

Ozu's view of life is not, indeed, a comforting one. In *Early Summer* a character observes that life is like a game of chance: "Happiness is only a hope—hope more like a dream, like hoping you are going to win at the racetrack." (5, 447.) In *The Flavor of Green Tea over Rice* this concept is elaborated. A character is complaining about pachinko, the ever-popular pinball game. "It's bad that a game like this should be so popular—I'm sorry I opened this place. . . . It will invite decay, it will ruin the national morale." (5, 641.) Its attractions are later explained by a friend: "Pachinko develops into a passion. . . . It allows you to feel isolated while in a crowd and to enjoy a kind of solitude. Just you and the ball become one and so you are completely alone. Blissful solitude. And then you realize that this ball is in itself a kind of cycle. And the whole game becomes an epitome of life itself." (6, 745.)

If life is a dream, a hope, a game, then we, the players, cannot do much about it. One reason is that this is the way it is; another is that human beings are simply not the special creatures they think they are. In *Floating Weeds* one of the actors denounces a plan to steal the funds and abandon the troupe: "Never. . . . the only difference between us humans and animals is that we aren't ungrateful" (7, 1046), a distinction he himself erases when he steals from the others and runs away. In *The Flavor of Green Tea over Rice* one of the characters says angrily to another: "Look, Setsuko, we aren't dogs or chickens, it's true . . . ; and you may think that we are higher beings or something, but in the eyes of god we are mere animals." (7,843.) Though Ozu does not linger on such heights (the very next line is, "You like these noodles?"), we know what he thinks.

Another reason we cannot change the world is that the world itself changes all of the time. In *The End of Summer* Manbei is speaking with his mistress: "And we wouldn't have met that day if I'd taken the first streetcar." "That's right," she agrees. "Fated to meet." "And then we didn't meet for nineteen years." "And to meet at a place like that." He remembers: "A bicycle race. Well, life is a running stream, forever changing." "Our world has really changed," she agrees. "It's disturbing," he says, to which she adds: "I do miss the old days. Remember the tea shop?" "And the night we went snow viewing, and the firefly hunt—that moonlit night." "I remember that all right," she says. "That was the night you turned me from a girl into a woman." (2,328.) The theme of the world in change is sounded again and again in the films of Ozu. In *Tokyo Story,* for example, the mother says when she sees her child: "I'm so glad I lived to see this day. The world has changed so." (2, 115.) To which the children reply: "But you haven't changed at all."

This is the way of the world, the old no longer change, the young continue to change, as the parents in this picture discover. Yet the parents never cease to hope that their lives will find some vindication in those of their children. The happiness they seek is a mirage. Most of Ozu's films are about parents and children, all of whom suffer a degree of disappointment. As Shuichi says in *Late Spring:* "Raise them and then off they go. If they don't get married you worry, and if they do you feel disappointed." (10, 689.) In *An Autumn Afternoon,* Hirayama and Kawai are talking. "You know," says the former, "when you come down to it, a son is best. Girls are no use." Kawai answers: "Boy or girl, it's all the same. They all go off sooner or later." (8, 962.) As the father says in *Tokyo Story,* talking about a son lost in the war: "To lose one's children is hard; but living with them isn't easy either." (7, 561.) This disappointment is built into the human condition, as many an Ozu character learns during the course of the picture. They begin by hoping that all will be well, that things will turn out as they wish; they often end by consoling themselves that at least they have suffered less than others they know.

In *Tokyo Story* the mother finally turns to the father and says: "Some grandparents seem to like their grandchildren more than their own children—what about you?" "I like my children better, but I'm surprised at how they change," he answers. A bit later she ventures, "Children don't live up to one's expectations." "Let's think," he says, "that ours have turned out better than most. They're certainly better than average." "We are fortunate," she says. "Yes, I think so," he concludes. (10, 781.) In *Early Summer* a similar conclusion is reached. One of the characters says: "Our family is every which way, but we've done better than the average—why, we've done lots of things together. We shouldn't ask for too much. We've been really happy." (13, 1189.) Of course they have not been happy in the way he implies; he himself had already (13, 1179) seen the breakup of the family as inevitable.

Ozu shows in his films both the natural reluctance of the old to let go of the young and the natural impatience of the young to be rid of the old. He is not, however, interested in comparing the virtues of the one with the shortcomings of the other. What Ozu chronicles, rather, is the impossibility of accord. Those critics— mainly young Japanese critics of a decade or so ago—who found Ozu old-fashioned and reactionary were obviously misreading his films. And those other critics who complain that Ozu lost interest in social problems obviously restrict their definition to political problems, since there are no social problems greater than the unavoidable misunderstandings between the generations, the indubitable unfairnesses of any society, and man's yearning for security in a world susceptible only to change.

And the end is always there, staring us in the face. When asked why he seems so sad, Kawai in *An Autumn Afternoon* says, "Solitary, sad—after all, man is alone." (6, 648.) Man is alone, and as one of the characters toward the end of *The End of Summer* remarks, "Life *is* very short, isn't it?" (7, 914.) The conclusions of many Ozu films—*Late Spring, Tokyo Story, Late Autumn* among them—underline this common fate. It is so common, indeed, that its appearance in films as in literature always surprises. Loneliness and death are in a sense such banal facts of human experience that only a great artist, a Tolstoy, a Dickens, an Ozu, can restore to them something of the urgency and sadness that we all someday experience. Ozu does this through a deliberate description of the facts, a full display of them, and—surprisingly in one so often described as an apologist for the traditional—by confrontation. Ozu is one of the very few artists whose characters are aware of the great immutable laws that govern their lives.

The son in *I Was Born, But . . .* says that if all adult life is like his father's, then he won't grow up. In *Late Autumn* one of the girls is disappointed that their friend did not wave. "And we were such good friends, too," she says. "Yes," answers the other, "but time passes and friends part." The first girl is struck by this remark. "Is that all friends are? Are men that way, too? Well, if that's all friendship means, then I think it's just disgusting." (5, 554.) Later in the film, the daughter is complaining about her problems. "But that's how life is," says her mother, a remark heard again and again in Ozu's pictures, a statement neither condemning nor condoning. The mother adds, "Grown-up life isn't as pretty as you might think. So you can just stop being a child." (7, 960.) In the very beautiful and moving scene at the end of *Tokyo Story*, Noriko, the daughter-in-law, is speaking with Kyoko, the younger sister. The latter is crying. "Even strangers would have been more considerate," she says of her brothers and sisters. "Look, Kyoko," says Noriko: "At your age I thought so, too, but children begin to drift away from their parents . . . ; everyone has to look after his own life." Kyoko looks up: "Really? Well, I won't be like that. That would be too cruel." "And so it is," agrees Noriko. "But children become like that—gradually. And, then, you too . . ." "I may become like that?" asks Kyoko. "In spite of myself?" She stops, then says, "Isn't life disappointing?" Noriko smiles, a beautiful, gracious, accepting smile, and replies, "Yes, it is." (14, 988.)

If Ozu's characters can accept life as a hope, or a game, or a disappointment, it is *because* they are aware they see life that way. Even the foolish men and women in Ozu's films are unusually canny about their own character, and the wise are often profoundly knowing about themselves; they know what kind of person they are, what their limitations are, to what ambitions they may aspire. It is this unusual degree of self-knowledge, which of course does not preclude blind spots and illogic, that enables the

Ozu character to take an ironic view of life. He is concerned but not enmeshed. This self-knowledge leads neither to cynicism (as it does among the characters of Ivy Compton-Burnett, who display a preternatural degree of self-knowledge) nor to sentimentality (as it sometimes does in Chekhov, whose people's self-knowledge usually extends only to limitations). Rather, as in Jane Austen, self-knowledge leads to a balanced sense of life and self, an understanding of the world and one's place in it, and an unexalted but nonetheless accepting opinion of one's own capabilities. In this sense Noriko, and so many of Ozu's young women, are like Emma. Having come to know themselves, they may hope for contentment.

It is here that morality enters into the Ozu film. What Ozu is saying is not that the old way is the best way, or that youth must have its fling, or that you come into the world and leave it all alone—though all these thoughts have their places in the Ozu universe. Ozu is saying, rather, that within the given constraints, one forms one's own character by consciously deciding upon this course or that. One does not delve into oneself, find there a character already formed, then recognize it as one's own. Rather, out of the inchoate material of human nature one forms a single human being, inconsistencies and all.

Morality exists that one may have a guide through the labyrinth. Ozu's morality, like that of most Asians, is simple. You act in a way that is consistent with nature, for you observe your kinship with other beings and perceive that you are a part of the nature around you, neither its slave nor its overlord. You observe the laws of your civilization until the point at which they seriously interfere with your own well-being, and then you make a compromise. You behave like the guest in this world you truly are.

You are a transient in a transitory world. With a feeling that goes far beyond the demands of good breeding, you gently celebrate *(mono no aware)* those very qualities which threaten (and eventually extinguish) your personal entity. You do so because you are part of this world and you know its rules, and you accept them. They are right because they are.

To achieve this relationship with the world, you learn to choose. We watch the people in an Ozu film choosing and deliberating over and over again, usually in the knowledge that in

71

choosing one forms one's character. You are what you do, and nothing more nor less; the sum total of your choices, your actions, is the sum total of yourself. In choosing, you not only create self, you transcend it. You are, in a way, the self you always were, but the awareness of alternatives brings awareness of the most important fact of human life: there is no immutable inner reality, no inner person, no soul. You choose what you will become.

Here, perhaps, is the reason why Ozu's characters have, as has been mentioned, no past. They may refer to times past, but we never see them. Ozu is one of the very few directors who never once in his entire career used a flashback. A person's past has done its work, but it is not interesting. Of his people you may truly say what is important is not what life has done to them, but what they do with what life has done to them.

One understands, then, Ozu's dislike and distrust of plot. Plot is possible only if it is agreed that a character is a certain kind of person with a certain kind of past who will therefore predictably do certain kinds of things and not others—that he is, in short, limited in a way people never are, before death. One understands also why inconsistency of character is so important to Ozu: it is a sign of life because it is a sign of choice. Choice is important to all of Ozu's people, as it is to all of us, which is one of the things that makes them so lifelike. What is involved, one must add, is nothing so sweeping as absolute free will. The freedom of Ozu's characters is, from the first, restricted. They are after all, human, which implies certain constraints; they must live together, another constraint; and they are part of a larger society, yet another constraint. They are offered not the *à la carte* menu, but the *table d'hôte*. Limitless choice exists no more for them than it does for anyone, but the range of choice is wide enough to be meaningful, to let Ozu's people form their own character.

And this, finally, is what the Ozu film shows us—character being formed through choice. We have seen the various ways in which this is done; we may now more fully appreciate the enormous difficulty of the task. Ozu and his collaborator had to work as their finished characters have to work: pondering, deciding, choosing. The Ozu character has only his own concerns, director and writer had the concerns of all their dramatis personae. No wonder Noda said that even after forty years of writing scripts, each new one constituted a tremendous problem. "What should this one be like, and how should we go about it—this was something that made us both sweat." [24]

Yet the picture would stand or fall with the script. Ozu consequently was always much relieved when it was finally finished. Chishu Ryu remembers:

> Ozu always looked most pleased when the scenario was completed . . . ; by the time he had finished writing it—about four months of work—he had already made up every image in every shot so that he never changed the script after we went on the set. And the dialogue was so polished that he would not allow even a single mistake. . . . He told me how happy he was when the script was done, but he also told me, though jokingly, that he was often disappointed to find how his images came apart when he started working with the actors. [Still,] once the film was completed, even if the acting was poor, he never complained. Even when we were certain that he was disappointed in us, he took all of the responsibility as his own and never spoke of it to others. This alone gives you some idea of his character. [25]

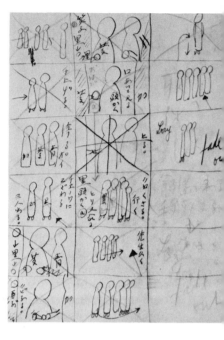

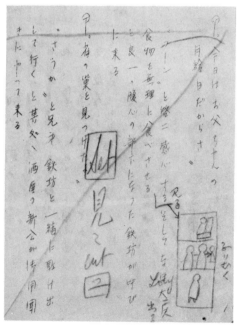

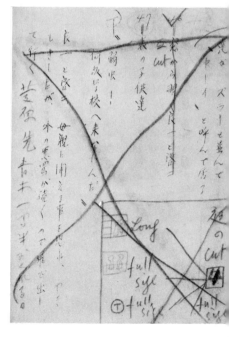

1. *Title page*

2. Boys: Because today is father's pay day. That's why we're not going
to school.
The boys stare at Keiji, then turn to look at the dog being fed against
its will. Long [shot].
Tetsubo, who has become Ryoichi's buddy (*buka*) comes to call them.
SET—see cut 2.
"I found a sparrow's nest." "Is that so?" say the brothers. They run
off with Tetsubo. Then comes Shinko from the sake-shop to call for
orders.
Three drawings. "He turns back."

3. *Fifteen drawings*

	laugh	
[crossed out]	Kuro Suga	
lifting hand	Suga bowing scratching head looking at his open mouth Kato	
stops short Kato Suga Aoki	take out	long fade out
three come out Masa Kuro ring game	Kuro scratching head (A) take and put back Kuro discovered and goes	
Kuro Suga Aoki	the teacher comes	
playing ring game shaking head Kato		

4. Children are lined up. They shout: "Yai!"
46.   Ryoichi and Keiji looking out of the window.
47.   Children in front of the house. A child:
Cowards!   Why don't you come to school?
Ryoichi and Keiji are afraid that their mother will hear, they are
nervous about it. But since the insults from outside continue they rush
out. Sugahara goes ahead, Aoki lags behind about three meters.
Drawings. Garden Cut [Scene].

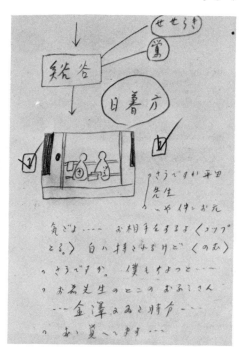

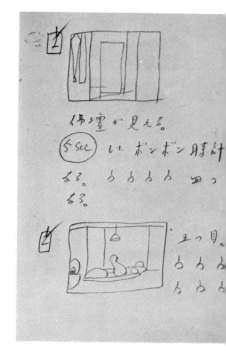

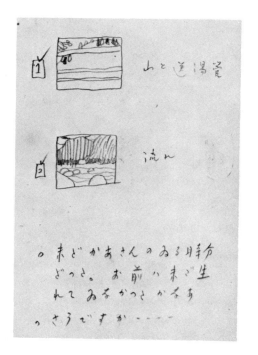

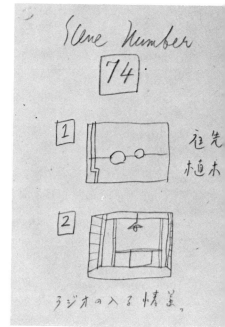

1.   little stream
        valley   nightingale
                toward evening
    Drawing of scene (1)
    (1) How is Professor Hirata?
    (2) He's very well_____.
            . . . I'll join you. (Takes up glass)
            This *shiro* [whiskey] is a bit much for me. (Drinks)
    (1) Is it? Then give me a little. Do you remember Miss Ofumi at
        Professor Hirata's . . . when you were at Kanazawa?
    (2) Yes, I remember her.

2. (1) *Drawing.*   Mountains and hot-spring pipes.
    (2) *Drawing.*   Stream.
    (1) It was when [your] mother was still alive.
        And you weren't born yet then.
    (2) Is that so?

3. (1) *Drawing.*   The buddhist altar.   [After] five seconds the sounds
        of an old-fashioned clock (*bon-bon dokei*). It sounds four times.
    (2) *Drawing.*   [New scene   Then] the fifth sound.
                    Six further sounds.

4. Scene Number 74.
    (1) *Drawing.*   Garden plants.
    (2) *Drawing.*   Scene when radio is heard.

Tokyo Story (*1953*)
The written version, the printed version, and 36 stills from the
finished sequence (Stills read down, not across)

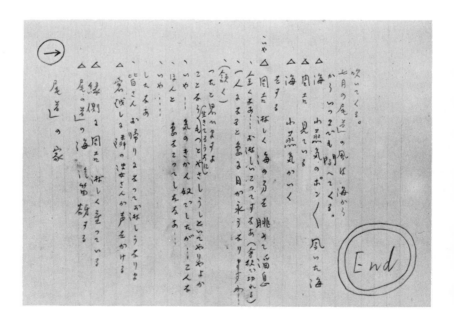

78

33. A song is heard in the distance, children singing a school anthem. A hilltop from which the sea is seen. All the children are sketching. Kyoko is watching them but also keeps looking at her watch. Then she goes over and looks down.

A train, distant shot.

Close-up of Kyoko looking.

The train, shot from the window.

Noriko, in the train. She looks out of the window.

From the window. The mountains of Onomichi.

Noriko looks wanly at the mountains. Looks at the watch left her by her mother-in-law. Loud sound of train whistle.

      The House in Onomichi.

The sea, sound of train whistles.

Shukichi sits alone on the porch.

The woman from next door looks in at the window and speaks.

WOMAN: Everybody has gone off, haven't they, you must be lonely.

HE: *Iya.*

WOMAN: It was all so sudden wasn't it.

HE: She wasn't a sensitive woman, but if I'd known it would turn out this way I'd have been nicer to her. Living alone, I feel now that a day lasts too long.

WOMAN: Yes, probably so. You must be really lonely.

He looks out over the sea and sighs.

The sea, some boats on it.

Shukichi looking.

Again the sea, smoke from the boats, a calm still sea from which one can hear the sounds of their whistles. (The wind in July in Onomichi comes from the sea.) End.

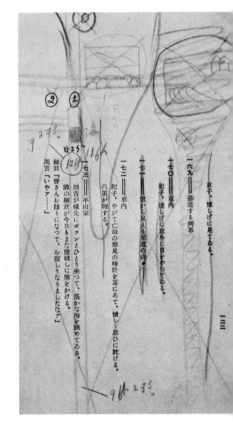

一六九＝＝募遠する列車

京子、懐しげに見てゐる。

一七〇＝＝車内

紀子、懐しげに意外に目をやつてゐる。

一七一＝＝窓から見える尾道の山々

一七二＝＝車内

紀子、やがて亡母の形見の時計を耳にあて、懐しく息ひに耽ける。

汽笛が鳴る。

一七三＝＝平山家

周吉が縁先にポツンとひとり坐つて、遙かな海を眺めてゐる。

細君「皆さんお帰りになつて、お寂しうなりましたねァ」

周吉「いやァ……」

——三——

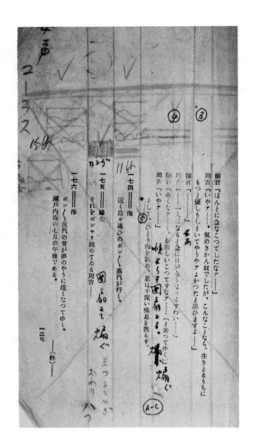

細君「ほんとに急なことでしたなァ……」

周吉「いやァ……。気のきかん奴でしたが、こんなことなら、生きとるうちに、もつと優しうしといてやりやァよかつたと思ひますよ……」

細君「……」

周吉「あ丶」

細君「一人になると急に日が永うなりますわい……」

周吉「丶丶」

細君「お寂しいこつてすなァ……」（と去つてゆく）

そして、ひとり海を眺め、思ひは尽深い嘆息を洩らす。

一七四＝＝海

遠く島々通ひのポンポン蒸汽が行く。

一七五＝＝縁先

それをボンヤリ眺めてゐる周吉。

一七六＝＝海

ポンポン蒸汽の音が夢のやうに遠くなつてゆく。

瀬戸内海の七月の午後である。

——（終）——

——三——

168. Kyoko looks out [of the window].
169. An advancing train.
170. In the train. Noriko looks wanly from the window.
171. The mountains of Onomichi seen from the train window.
172. In the train, Noriko puts the watch to her ear, then sinks into memory. Sound of train whistle.
173. The Hirayama house. Shukichi sits by the veranda and looks over the distant sea. The woman from next door comes to the window and talks to him.

> WOMAN: Everybody has gone off, haven't they. You must be lonely.
>
> HE: *Iya.*
>
> WOMAN: It was all so sudden wasn't it.
>
> HE: She wasn't a sensitive woman, but if I'd known it would turn out this way I'd have been nicer to her. [Written in: *Nya*] Living alone, I feel now that a day lasts too long.
>
> WOMAN: Yes, probably so. You must be really lonely.

He takes a round fan and fans himself. [Written in].
He looks over the sea and sighs.
174. The sea—a boat serving the distant islands goes by.
175. On the veranda, Shukichi vacantly stares into the distance. [Written in: He fans himself].
176. The sea. Sound of the motor boat becomes distant as a dream.
It is a July afternoon in the Inland Sea.
A female chorus. [Written in].
Rasuto (Last). [Written in].

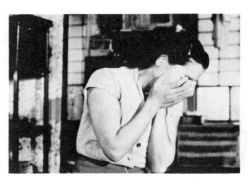

OPPOSITE AND FOLLOWING P,
Early Spring (*1*
The opening sequ

86

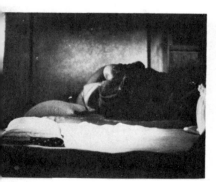

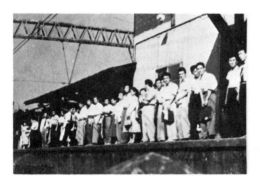 

Good Morning (*1959*)
Family plan and map

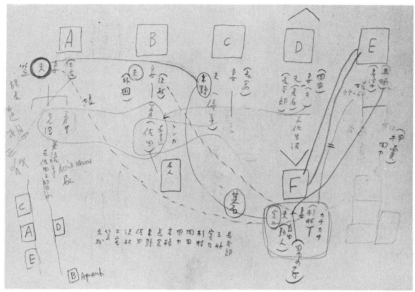

A	B	C	D	E
Husband (Ryu)	Husband (for-	Husband	Husband	Midwife (Miyoshi)
Wife (Miyake)	eign) Wife	(Tono—	(Hasabe,	Mother-in-law
	(Sawamura)	retired)	young man,	
		Wife	foreign	
		(Nagaoka)	style life)	
Head of section			Wife (Oka-	
Elder brother (13)			da) young-	
Younger brother (7)	Younger brother,		er	Unwelcome
	fight			salesman
	Friend (Sada)			(Tanaka)
Learn English from Sada				
'I don't know'				
Fart		Go game		F

F
Kachi-kachi
Wife (Sugimura)
Husband (Miyaguchi)
Salaryman
A boy [son]

C
A
E

D

B Apartment

Kuga	Ryu	Miyake	Sawamura	Sada	Tono	Nagaoka
Takahashi	Tanaka	Okada	Sugimura	Miyaguchi	Miyoshi	Hasebe

Floating Weeds (*1959*)
Two pages from the script,
two pages from the notebook,
and six stills

". . . Leave me alone. I said, leave me alone, leave me alone."
Komajuro forces her out of the house. Outside the snow is falling. (1) The inner room. Father and mother, Kiyoshi turns back [Osumi] and looks after her. (2)

13. An alleyway. Snow is falling. Komajuro comes in and grasps Osumi's hand. The side of the Agricultural Association Warehouse. He pushes her and Osumi staggers against the wall. Some of the snow falls from the roof with the impact.

OSUMI: What are you doing?
KOMAJURO: What—what's that? It's about time you stopped.
OSUMI: What are you saying?

People walk along the nearby street (3). Komajuro goes under the eaves at the other side of the alley. Both glower at each other, breathing hard.

KOMAJURO: What do you think you're doing. This is no place for you to meddle in. Go away.

Osumi, breathing heavily stares back at him.

KOMAJURO: What did you want to say to them? What's wrong with my coming to see my son? What's bad about that? Who are you

94

to object to that?—any objections? If you've got anything to say, say it. Stupid!

Osumi says nothing.

Komajuro says nothing.

(1) *Originally the film was to have been shot in Tohoku in the winter.
In the finished film rain is substituted for snow.*

(2) *There is no such scene in the finished film.*

(3) *There is no such action in the finished film.*

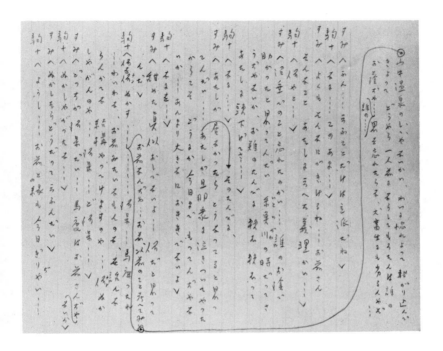

OSUMI:	That's all very well to say.
KOMAJURO:	What's that? You bitch.
OSUMI:	How can you say that . . . . What right have you to talk to me like that?
KOMAJURO:	What's that?
OSUMI:	You've forgotten what happened in Numadare? Who do you think saved you then? You've forgotten what I did at Itogawa too. Every time you were in trouble you begged me—help me, help me. And you bowed and bowed and bowed.
KOMAJURO:	What's that?
OSUMI:	And if I hadn't been there, what do you think would have happened to you? It's only because I begged my patron for

95

help that you're alive today. So just don't talk so big to me.

KOMAJURO: Just pay some attention to who you're talking to. What do you think I am?

KOMAJURO: What are you jabbering about. Who do you think you are? Think what you were before. I can do very well without any help from a bitch like you. Why are you carrying on like this —stupid! Stupid ass!

OSUMI: Who's stupid! You're the stupid one.

KOMAJURO: You've already said that.

OSUMI: So what.

KOMAJURO: Good. This is the last day for you.

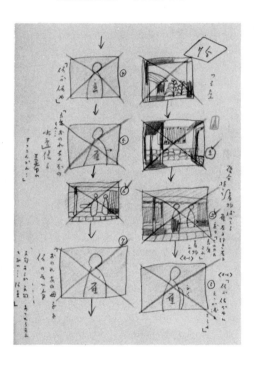
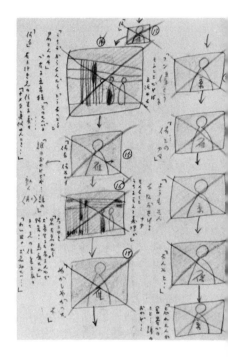

Late Autumn (*1960*)
The opening sequence: two versions, one from the
written, the other from the printed script

OUT.   The first day of writing. April 7, 1960.

(1).   A certain day. A temple yard in Tokyo, the uptown section. Tokyo Tower can be seen in the distance. In the windows of the apartments washing is drying. An old woman is playing with some children. A baby carriage is nearby.

(2).   The priests' quarters. Today is the seventh-year anniversary of Shuzo Miwa. His widow, Akiko, and their daughter, Ayako; Shuzo's old classmates, Taguchi and Hirayama, and his former colleagues at the company, two of them, and other relatives including two middle-aged women. On the table are tea and cakes.

Hirayama comes onto the scene, drying his hands, he has come from the bathroom. He sits down. Taguchi lights his cigarette.

TAGUCHI: Is that right? Sounds good. Where is it?

HIRAYAMA: Where is what?

TAGUCHI: A place where you can get good steak. I hear it's fine.

COLLEAGUE: You know the Homokutei in Ueno? It's in an alley around there. Just an old man and his wife run it.

TAGUCHI: Is that right? I'll go and try it. I often go to that pork-chop place in back of Matsuzakaya [Department Store.] You go there too, don't you?

HIRAYAMA: Yes. I remember when it was still a cart.

[None of this conversation is in the finished film.]

98

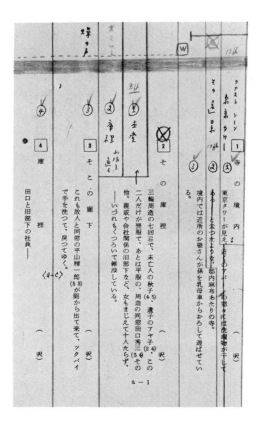

1) Temple yard. Tokyo Tower can be seen. The temple is in Azabu. In the temple yard an old woman is playing with a grandchild she has just taken from the baby carriage.

2) The priests' quarters. This is the seventh anniversary of the death of Shuzo Miwa. His widow, Akiko (45), and her daughter, Ayako (24), are wearing mourning kimono. The rest are in ordinary clothes. First, Hidezo Taguchi (54), former classmate, and other relatives and former colleagues from the company, about ten in all including the women. Everyone is relaxed, talking among themselves.

3) The corridor of the temple. Seichiro Hirayama, (53) another classmate, comes out of the bathroom, washes his hands at the basin and returns to the others.

4) The priests' quarters, Taguchi and the others.

[Ozu's pencillings on this script read: Tokyo Tower, distance scenes; the main hall (*hondo*) of the temple; a boy-priest passes by; noise of cicada.]

99

The End of Summer (*1961*)
*Two pages from the notebooks
and nine stills*

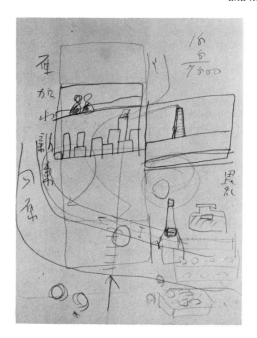

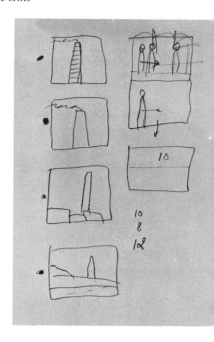

An Autumn Afternoon (*1962*)
*The final sequence: two pages from the
notebook, two pages from the finished script*

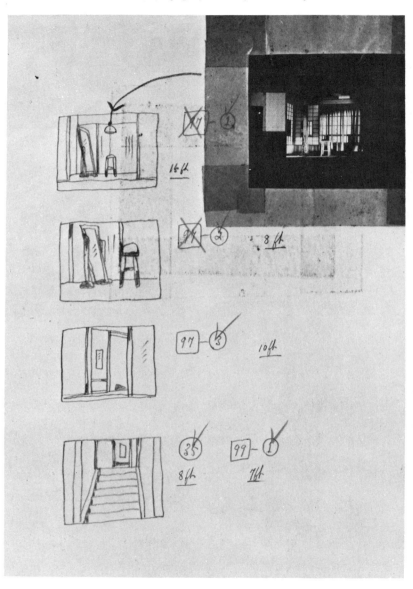

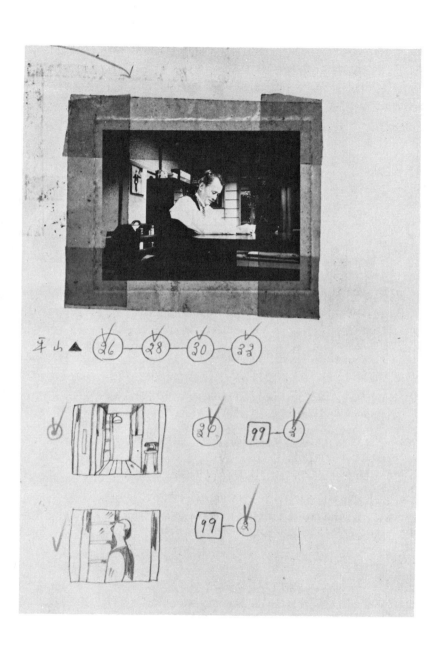

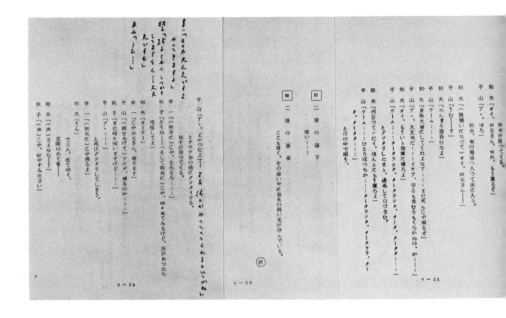

Hirayama takes off his coat as though he is not aware of doing so.
Kazuo comes back.

KAZUO: *Oi*, father—time to sleep.
HIRAYAMA: Yes, let's go to bed.
Kazuo goes into the room in the back and gets into bed.
Kazuo: *Oi*, father!
HIRAYAMA: Hm?
KAZUO: And lay off the sake. Can't have you dying yet.
HIRAYAMA: Oh, I'll be all right. *Ya.* "In defense or attack these plates of steel—"
KAZUO: Go to sleep.
HIRAYAMA: (hums) *
KAZUO: Stop groaning. I'm going to sleep.
HIRAYAMA: (hums) Yes, all alone at the end . . .

Scene 97 The upstairs, dark.
The corridor. The room upstairs.
Here it is also dark and in this darkness there is the dull gleam of the full-length mirror.

* In the finished film, the humming has turned into a war song heard in a previous scene: "Floating fortress . . . pride of the land . . ." etc.

104

SHOOTING

O ZU'S FILMS are shot from an almost invariable angle, that of a person sitting on the tatami matting of the Japanese room.[1] The camera rarely pans, though traveling shots are relatively common in earlier pictures. Fades in and out are seldom found in his later films and dissolves are very rare; usually the sole punctuation Ozu allows himself, particularly in his postwar pictures, is the straight cut.

Ozu thus eschewed cinematic means other directors would think indispensable. As early as 1930 he began to renounce optical devices commonly thought of as essential. He conceded that in *The Life of an Office Worker* he used several dissolves to get a certain effect, but felt that most of the time the dissolve is "a form of cheating." He said that he first gave up fades-in and -out while shooting *I Was Born, But . . .* , having come to feel they were not a part of cinematic grammar, "only attributes of the camera." Later he began to anchor his camera, allowing it very little movement, and adopted the single angle that helps create the distinctive look of the Ozu film.

He thus relinquished most of the major ways through which a film-maker directly expresses himself in film, and severely restricted his means of cinematic comment. Godard once remarked that a tracking shot is a moral comment,[2] and so it is, as is any kind of camera shot because it conveys an attitude toward what is

There Was a
Father. *1942*.
Chishu Ryu,
Haruhiko Tsuda

There Was a
Father. *1942*.
Shuji Sano,
Chishu Ryu

happening on the screen; this use would properly be avoided by a
director wishing to refrain from one kind of direct comment. What
Ozu lost by his renunciation becomes obvious if one examines his
early use of these technical means; what he gained by it will become apparent later.

Just as the dissolve can link different places in a smooth and
economical manner, so the fade can link different times. These
are not the invariable uses of the two, but the most common.[3]

Ozu claimed that the only really good use of the dissolve he ever saw was in Chaplin's *A Woman of Paris,* where different locales are smoothly and efficiently connected. He never said anything about fades, but he early used them in an orthodox fashion, to emphasize a scene and to separate scenes distant in time. In the early *Tokyo Chorus,* one finds Ozu using fades to comment directly on a scene. The wife discovers that the husband has pawned her kimonos; she is shocked and hurt and near tears. Her moment of discovery, however, happens to occur during a riotous hand-clapping game that her husband and children are playing. The excited youngsters insist that she join. Reluctantly, her mind still on her loss, she does so. As she plays with them her face softens, her husband looks at her, understanding what she is feeling, and finally she is smiling through her tears—she, too, has understood, forgiven. It is a lovely scene; we know Ozu thought so, too, because it is the only scene in the film ending with a fade. He is saying, as does any director who uses fade-out in this particular way: there, that was an important scene, that is something to remember.

e Only Son. *1936.*
oko Iida, Masao Hayama

The Only Son. *1936.*
Shinichi Himori, Yoshiko Tsubouchi

Another use of the fade, to separate different times, occurs in *The Only Son.* After a long conversation between the little boy and his mother, the scene fades out on their tears, fades in on a title, fades out and in on the mother alone, now older, talking to another woman about the son, now doing well, she says, in the big city; then fades out, another title, and fades in on the first Tokyo scene, where we are not surprised, after all this preparation, to find the boy now a young adult. This is the classic way a fade is used, once very common.

There Was a Father, a film made just six years later, has a similar scene. After a long conversation between the little boy and his father, the child begins to cry; after a close-up of his face there is a cut to house roofs, then a cut to the interior of a machine shop. The father comes in, older. He talks with another employee and mentions that his son is now twenty-five years old. Though the scenes are similar on paper, on film the difference is enormous. What we feel in watching the later picture is not so much surprise —Ozu has prepared us for something by a long close-up on the child and then the cut to a scene completely unrelated—as a sense of something familiar, something we had known and not remembered, something as familiar as the fact that children grow up and fathers grow old. One reason for our response is Ozu's studied refusal to comment. In the 1936 film we are told; in the 1942 picture we are shown. The later film consequently seems lighter because less ostensible importance is given such scenes as this; in the same way the long fades in the earlier film (there are many, though Ozu said he had stopped using them in 1932) makes it seem more weighty, with each important scene set off in parentheses, as it were. The 1942 film seems not only lighter but less "dramatic," because the conventions we associate with the creation of drama are not present. The 1936 film, by contrast, becomes slightly predictable: certain expectations are raised by the use of fades, and these expectations are invariably fulfilled.

It is more difficult to say which film is the more moving. *The Only Son* is moving in the direct and empathetic way we know films can be; *There Was a Father* is moving in a different way. The assumptions behind the two films, which we, as spectators, naturally infer, differ in important ways. During the earlier picture we soon realize that a story is being told in a way that appeals to our emotions in a fairly predictable manner. We consequently feel the presence of a creator behind the film, one who guides our ideas and emotional responses. In the later picture no specific emotional response is called up at all. As scene follows scene we are given no hint of how we are to react. When the simple cut is the only punctuation, it becomes no punctuation at all in the usual sense of signaling how we are to read, how we are to react. Consequently our ideas and emotions are free, and we have little sensation of a directing intelligence. It is almost as if the camera had made the film and not the director. In the circumstances we must supply the emotional direction ourselves, and doing so, I believe, heightens our emotional involvement, brings us closer than we can be (this applies in real life, too) when our reactions have been foreseen and foreordained. One result is that we find similarities between ourselves and the people we are watching. We think more, but it does not follow that we feel less. The conclusion of *There Was a Father,* though obviously tragic, is not felt to be as hopeless as that of *The Only Son.* The reason is that, in watching the later film, we realize that we are all in a sense alike, that we will all suffer and will all die. We feel not that the mother was a brave, unknowing, and perhaps tragic figure, unique in herself, but that the father was like all fathers, his son like all sons. The fate they suffer we will all suffer; we can only hope to emulate their dignity and honesty.

To return to our original question—which of the two films is the more moving, that is a matter of personal preference. There are many critics, including a number of Westerners (mainly French, for some reason), who maintain that Ozu's later films are cold, artificial, and contrived compared to such earlier films as *The Only Son,* which are, they maintain, warm and human. While this judgment is obviously inapplicable to *Tokyo Story* or *Late Spring,* one can at the same time understand the point these critics are trying to make. They probably miss just the sense of comment and judgment that Ozu so specifically avoids in his later films. For my part, I find the later films the more moving, and I think this is because I am forced to contribute so much to them myself. To be shown everything and told nothing means that I must make up my own mind. Consequently I think harder and feel more during an Ozu film, and hence my experience is the deeper.

Another meaningful restriction is Ozu's stationary camera. Though Ozu rarely used the pan shot (one of the most common shots in cinema), he often mounted his camera on a dolly and cre-

The stationary low-angle shot. *Ozu
shooting The Flavor of Green Tea
over Rice, 1952.*

ated tracking or traveling shots. These can, like any shot, be used
for comment. Specifically they can be used to comment through
contrast, usually side-by-side parallels; to comment by pulling
away; to comment by approaching; and, to a lesser extent, to
comment by showing more of a scene than is possible with a stationary camera. Ozu most often dollies to show his characters
moving and to include more of the background, thus lending the
scene, it is commonly thought, a greater feeling of veracity. There
are many such passages in Ozu's films, notably in *What Did the
Lady Forget?* (where the scene shows the ladies' feet as they walk
along, the sound track carrying their dialogue) and such films as
The Brothers and Sisters of the Toda Family; there are many in
the later films, however, including *Late Spring* and *Tokyo Story,*
the last one probably being the Enoshima hiking scene in *Early
Spring.*[4]

Ozu rarely used the dolly, however, to comment emotionally on
a scene. The dolly-in shot usually means an increase in interest or

feeling; the dolly-back shot usually means disassociation, and can be used for both tragic and comic effects.[5] Such use is rare in Ozu films. (Though it should be mentioned that Ozu's single crane shot, in the penultimate sequence of *Early Summer,* is used for its conventional associations. The sisters are walking among the dunes along the Shonan Beach. The scene begins with a still life of the dunes, then the camera rises to reveal the two girls walking toward the sea. Such a shot almost always means The End: this will not happen again. Here the two are, talking, unmindful of a different future; here we may leave them, at this juncture in their lives.) Rather, one finds Ozu making liberal use of parallel tracking shots to point up contrasts. In *Tokyo Chorus,* for example, they are used to compare and contrast the lives of schoolboys, office workers, and the unemployed. A famous example already mentioned occurs in *I Was Born, But . . . ,* when a traveling shot along the desks of the sleepy and bored schoolboys is cut directly to a traveling shot along the desks of their sleepy and bored office-working fathers.

Such shots in the films of Ozu, however, seem less conventional than they might in the films of other directors because, even in the earliest films, they are relatively rare. They are not part of a style that makes full and continual use of the resources of the camera, but of a style that was, even in the beginning, deliberately restricted. The crane shot in *Early Summer* creates a feeling of finality that is much stronger than it would be in other films because the shot occurs in the midst of static and nonmoving shots: for this reason fades and camera movements have a weight in the Ozu picture that is often dissipated in films that use such techniques continually.

It remains to be said that Ozu's dollies were never particularly skillful. In the hands of some directors (e.g. Murnau, Ophuls, Mizoguchi), dolly shots are miracles of fluidity, extraordinary in their ability to display and to hide. Ozu's dollies, however, are blocks of movement, usually too slow for maximum effect, and in any event shot from so low an angle that more often than not, the effect is one of awkwardness. This awkwardness, however, creates a sense of mystery because we know what a dolly is supposed to mean, we understand a convention that is so taken for granted it

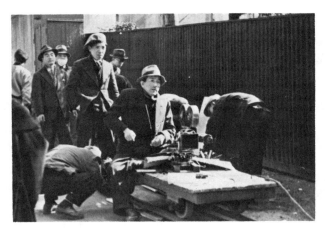

The moving dolly-shot. *Undated snapsh* *Yuharu Atsuta and Ozu.*

is rarely discussed, and Ozu's dollies seem to mean something else. One example occurs in *Early Summer*. With the sisters advancing on tiptoe, the camera moves back to keep them in the center of the frame. They are in a restaurant and are going to surprise the boss of one of the girls. Cut to an empty corridor, the camera dollying forward. The natural assumption is that we are now seeing what the girls are seeing, and that they are moving down this corridor to a soon-to-be astonished employer. Not at all. We are back home, and the girls are already seated around the hibachi discussing their evening out. The effect is jarring and untoward. If the shots had not moved we would have quite accepted the progression. But they were dolly shots, which gave rise to expectations that Ozu has disappointed—possibly out of playfulness (though this is doubtful since Ozu never played with the camera), but probably simple sloppiness.

For a director with a style so severe, an outlook so austere, Ozu could be incredibly untidy. Perhaps we are mistaken in equating austerity with neatness, but even if we are charitable enough to entertain this idea, we are still left with unaccountable lapses in Ozu's films. Actually, Ozu was meticulous about his script, rigid about his editing, severe with his actors, but relaxed when it came to the actual shooting. There is no other way to account for the lapses of continuity in his films. In *A Woman of Tokyo* the teapot is bubbling away in the background, steam rising. Ozu cuts to, of all things, a close-up of the pot itself. No steam, no bubbles, an apparently cold teapot. Then back again to the heroine: no time has passed, it is the same scene. The director simply had not noticed that the pot was bubbling away in one scene and not at all in the next. In the later films continuity is continually broken because Ozu rearranged his props constantly for different camera set-ups. In these cases, however, he knew what he was doing, or at least why he was doing it (for compositional reasons), and if the effect is scrambled on the screen, it is at least the way he wanted it.

Skillful or not, Ozu's often gratuitous dollies generated a feeling of strangeness and mystery that deepened his films. The most notable example of this occurs in *Early Spring,* the last film to use traveling shots. Several times one is in an empty corridor in the office building where the characters work. At times the camera is stationary, at times it creeps forward. The effect is disquieting. In this world of no camera movement which Ozu has established, the slightest movement of the camera calls attention to itself. And in this film we have no idea why the camera is moved. Nothing is to be gained by it; indeed, nothing is in the scene, it is just an empty corridor. Because of the rigid, immobile context, however, the effect is disquieting, mysterious.[6]

When Ozu relinquished, one by one, most of the grammatical elements of cinema, obviously he sacrificed a great deal—most of the means, in fact, through which film directors ordinarily express themselves. The reason is apparent: he did not want to express himself in such a direct way. Just as he refused plot because it exploits characters by interpreting them in conventional ways, so he refused elements of film grammar because they express conventionalized opinion. It should be noted, however, that Ozu himself gave a different reason for his abandonment of the traveling shot. His camera angle was so low, he said, that he couldn't find a dolly large enough to accommodate the outspread legs of his tripod.[7]

If it were truly an either/or situation, then obviously the low camera would win out. It had been a constant element of Ozu's style almost from the beginning, and was clearly essential to his conception of film-making. Usually three feet or so off the floor, the camera simply viewed what was in front of it. Few details are picked out for closer examination (with the exception of the very important still-lifes, which will be discussed later), and the camera's angle and position almost never change. Everything is seen head-on, from the position of a person kneeling on the floor Japanese-fashion. Of the various explanations advanced for Ozu's low camera position, one of the most ingenious is that he happened upon it when making films about children. In *Tokyo Chorus* there is a scene in which we see the parents only from the waist down. This extremely odd scene is explained when the children enter. It was framed for them. Ozu, it is argued, liked the look of this low-angled scene and continued to use it. This explanation may well be true, for it fully accords with Ozu's unique conception of the role of composition in cinema.

Composition in Western cinema is now used—to the extent that it is consciously used at all—to interpret the action, usually by commenting upon character.[8] Earlier, however, another kind of composition was more common—composition that existed for its own sake, for its pictorial beauty. Pictorial composition, originally inspired by traditional painting, presumed that the edge of the image was a frame in which the objects were to be arranged in as pleasing a fashion as possible. Notable examples occur in the films of Stroheim, Murnau, and Sternberg, among others. Perhaps the reason one rarely sees such composition in films today is that its use presumes an agreed-upon standard of beauty. Certainly the efforts at pictorial composition by such contemporary film-makers as Bolognini and Griffi are widely considered precious or artificial.

Ozu's composition, however, is almost invariably pictorial. We do not instantly recognize it as such in his films because we somehow think of pictorial composition as an arrangement of Nature, by which we mean trees, streams, mountains, etc. When we see the lawn scene in Mizoguchi's *Ugetsu,* we are at once aware of pictorial beauty; when we see the same kind of arrangement in any of the hundreds of Ozu's urban exteriors and interiors, our response is less certain. And yet the two film-makers shared many of the same assumptions and proceeded in a roughly similar fashion. Their aesthetic aims were also similar, though one can agree with Yoshikata Yoda, Mizoguchi's scenarist, when he said that Mizoguchi was the more Japanese of the two. He had in mind the

great influence of American cinema on Ozu, but also the Japanese
kind of nature portrait almost always found in the films of Mizoguchi, and never in Ozu's.[9]

Yet, according to Yushun Atsuta, Ozu's cameraman, it was the
need for a pictorially balanced composition that dictated the
director's camera position: low and almost invariably shooting at
right angles to the scene. He remembers Ozu's saying to him:
"You know, Atsuta, it's a real pain trying to make a good composition of a Japanese room—especially the corners. The best way
to deal with this is to use a low camera position. This makes
everything easier." [10] That is, if the camera is positioned low on
the tatami and facing into a room, the black bindings of the tatami do not create in the farther corners the acute angles that
would detract from a composition conceived as frontal and at
right angles to the observer. Rather than seeming to stop at a
point to which the director wishes to draw no attention, they seem
to proceed uninterruptedly to invisibility.

Atsuta also told director Kazuo Inoue he once suggested to Ozu
that paintings were all "taken" from a much more conventional
angle than the low-angle view Ozu favored. Ozu agreed, and
pointed out if you shot a film at normal eye level from a painter's
head-on angle, you would have to include the tatami in the background, and this made it difficult to make the human figures stand
out sharply enough.[11] Tomo Shimokawara has mentioned that a
low angle—which Sadao Yamanaka, who also used it, called "the
dog's-eye view"—makes any composition tighter just by simplify-

e Autumn. *1960.*
o Tsukasa, Mariko
da, Setsuko Hara

The End of Summer. *1961.*
Setsuko Hara, Michiyo
Aratama, Yoko Tsukasa

115

ing it; [12] you can see that much less from a low-angle position.

This low viewing point, however, occurs in some forms of traditional Japanese art, particularly in wood-block prints, especially of genre scenes in which attention is directed to the figure alone. And Gregg Toland placed his camera in the same position in many scenes in *Citizen Kane,* and for the same reason: the low angle made it possible to sharply delineate the various surfaces of the image and to accentuate the one occupied by the actors. (When Ozu adopted this low camera position, probably with the shooting of *Tokyo Chorus* in 1931, Shiro Kido, head of the studio, was reported to grumble that now they had to build ceilings on the sets, a complaint heard from RKO ten years later when Toland's camera placement made ceilings necessary on the *Citizen Kane* sets.)

This low angle has the effect of creating a stage upon which the characters are seen to best advantage. We see them from below, as it were, and the background is distant from the figure. We recognize the theatrical effect at once in a film like *The Little Foxes.* If we often fail to recognize it in the films of Ozu, it is partly because his scenes usually occur in the Japanese house, which is in itself a kind of stage. The traditional house in Japan is elevated off the ground. Many of its walls are really sliding door-windows, which are opened in fine weather to display a truly stage-like interior. In the house is a real little stage, the *tokonoma* alcove, which serves to display, in often theatrical fashion, flowers of the season and, usually, a scroll. Doors to other rooms open onto contrived vistas, and guests are seated with their back to the *tokonoma* so that they can be considered part of the display. Doors are slid open and shut with a degree of ceremony, and corridor-like *roka* lead from one part of the "set" to the next. When Paul Claudel remarked that being inside a Japanese house reminded him of being backstage among the flats of a theater, he was noticing the strikingly obvious.

Ozu was almost alone among Japanese directors in exploiting the theatrical aspect of the Japanese dwelling.[13] He used rooms as a proscenium, as will be later discussed, and since his fixed camera position precluded his following his characters about, their entrances and exits are often as theatrical-looking as they are in real Japanese life. In particular Ozu liked to play with the theatrical aspect of Japanese domestic architecture. Perhaps the best-known instance of such playfulness occurs in *Early Summer*. The daughter is expected to respond to an offer of marriage, and the married brother has told his wife to make certain that the daughter knows this. After the girls have talked for a bit, the daughter goes to the kitchen. At once the wall slides away from in back of the waiting wife. She is surprised and so are we. But it is really a *fusuma*, a sliding door; we had not noticed it before and the brother is on the other side listening. When the daughter returns unexpectedly, he does not have time to close the door and so hastily crawls behind the single panel. She glances in, fails to see him, and closes the door. When she next goes out, the door slides open again to reveal the brother with more advice and admonitions. And so the scene goes. There is nothing more to it, but it is done with an ingenuity, a flair, and a perfect naturalness that is as amusing as it is theatrical.

One of the most charming of these stage-like effects occurs at the end of *What Did the Lady Forget?*—the little dumb show that concludes the film. The husband has been neglecting the wife, but now it is bedtime. Differences are forgotten; the reconciliation will probably take place in the *futon*. The wife has already gone to the kitchen, which is apparently next to the bedroom, but the camera remains where it was, in the living-room-like *osetsuma*, looking down the corridor to a corner of the kitchen. The lights in the various rooms along the way go out one by one as the husband proceeds to the kitchen, and the screen darkens. Finally, all that is left is the small square of the kitchen, a tiny lighted area, occupying only a fraction of the screen, a small stage in the distance where the final pantomime occurs. He appears, yawns somewhat ostentatiously, and goes out; she comes in, smiling, gets the sake things, goes out; he appears again, stops undecided, makes several false starts, stops, turns, then goes off in the same direction as his wife. Fade-out.

Ozu was always fond of putting his camera in one room, pointing it into a corridor-like *roka*, which is the avenue of traffic in a Japanese house, and waiting, as it were, to see what would happen. His films abound in such scenes, with members of the family coming into view and disappearing as they move about the house.

Since the Japanese house is usually crowded, there is always a lot going on. Ozu's films have many charming scenes of these apparently random movements. One remembers delightful examples from *The Brothers and Sisters of the Toda Family, Late Spring,* and *Early Summer,* but the most skillfully choreographed are probably those in *The End of Summer.* In the best of these, the head of the house is playing hide-and-seek with his grandson, with

The End of Summer *1961. Masahiro Shimazu, Ganjiro Nakamura*

both of them wandering on and off the scene. The grandfather, however, wants to go and see his mistress in Kyoto, a desire he knows that his daughter, busy doing the ironing, would most disapprove of. The sequence comes as near a production number as Ozu gets, with the child appearing from time to time, thinking he is playing hide-and-seek with his grandfather, the grandfather appearing from time to time, knowing that he's playing hide-and-seek with his own daughter, and she appearing from time to time, unmindful of the other two, going about her housework. The camera sits and watches, relishing the near misses, waiting for a collision. It is as though one were at the theater, watching a particularly amusing play. Our view is limited, our position stationary; we are not shown what the characters do off-screen, and the delight of these scenes lies in the surprises that await not only the characters but the spectator as well.

That Ozu was very fond of performances is indicated by the number and kinds of actual theatrical shows he includes in his films. There is a Noh performance in *Late Spring,* and country Kabuki in both *A Story of Floating Weeds* and the later *Floating Weeds.* We do not see city Kabuki in Ozu's pictures, but his characters do, and in both *What Did the Lady Forget?* and *Early Summer* we watch them watching it. We do see the *naniwabushi* reciter in the opening of *Passing Fancy,* and we watch the mother in *Equinox Flower* enjoying a *nagauta* performance over the radio. All of these performances are shown in a much fuller and more complete form than is usual in film, with that of the Noh in *Late Spring* going on for some time. Similarly, when Ozu takes us to

The Story of **ating Weeds.** *1934.* *Emiko Yagumo,* *Takeshi Sakamoto*

Woman of Tokyo. *1933. Kinuyo Tanaka, Ureo Egawa*

the movies we see a lot of the picture his characters are viewing. The home-movie sequence in *I Was Born, But . . .* is as long as it is amusing. When the characters in *Woman of Tokyo* go to the cinema, we see the Lubitsch section of *If I Had a Million* almost complete. When the son takes the mother to the movies in *The Only Son*, we watch an entire musical number with Martha Eggerth in Willi Forst's *Leise Flehen meine Lieder*. Not all of us watch, to be sure—the mother falls sound asleep.

It is typical of Ozu in particular and the Japanese in general that we wait until Martha Eggerth drops her scarf and completes her coda before the screen darkens. The Japanese as a whole retain a feeling for fitness, and wait until the end of acts or scenes before making an unavoidable departure. Even at the movies one observes that most Japanese will wait until the end of a sequence before leaving. When the young man goes to the concert alone in *Late Spring* and hears the *Kreutzer Sonata*, Ozu does not let us leave until Beethoven has come to the end of his exposition. It is not simple politeness that restrains the spectator because there are few less polite nations on the whole than the Japanese. Rather, it is the sense of fitness, based perhaps upon an idea of rendering art its due. Ozu extends this regard to forms of entertainment not commonly thought of as artistic: the television *sumo* matches in *Good Morning*, the baseball games actually attended in *The Flavor of Green Tea over Rice* and seen on television in *An Autumn Afternoon*. In Ozu's films one watches such entertainment for a length of time, and departs only at the end of a number or an inning.

When it is the Ozu character who is performing, the same attention is required. The golf scenes in *What Did the Lady Forget?* and *Early Autumn* go on for some time, the one in *An Autumn Afternoon* seems almost too long; is it really necessary to watch this many strokes, one wonders. Ozu would say that it is. The games his people often play demand undivided attention. The delightfully choreographed mah-jongg game in *Early Spring* covers two entire hands; the hide-and-seek in *The End of Summer* consists of several turns; the unconscious games that his characters sometimes play (the corncob manipulation while playing *go* in *A Story of Floating Weeds*, the byplay with the fans between a salaried man and his angry boss in *Tokyo Chorus*, etc.) are extended so that one may see their shapes, observe the rise and fall in intensity.

When the Ozu character performs in any formal manner, then we are obliged to watch the entire selection. Ryu's folksong in *Record of a Tenement Gentleman* goes on for verse after verse; so

The Record of a Tenement Gentleman. *1947.*
Chishu Ryu, Choko Iida (center)

do the more formal songs in *Late Spring, Equinox Flower,* and *An Autumn Afternoon.* In *There Was a Father,* we not only hear the whole song but sit through the entire party that the students give their old teacher. One might argue that such a long party, such singing by the guests, such an observation of *politesse,* is so much a part of traditional Japanese life that its inclusion is not surprising. Perhaps not, yet Ozu is alone among Japanese directors in adhering to the code. All the other directors tend to cut the song short after a few bars, perhaps fearful of boredom, perhaps anxious to get on with the story.

Ozu would have us listen to the whole long song not only out of a sense of fitness, but for its own sake, out of a sense of pleasure. And after all, someone we love is singing, and Ozu communicates to us the respect he feels. It is when the character exerts himself and performs, as it were, that Ozu's respect is perhaps greatest.

In this sense, any task can become a performance. In *The Only Son,* the mother has been given a new pillow, and we watch her as she puts into place the paper wrapper that will prevent its being soiled, a long and intricate business. In *Early Summer* we watch the father feed his mynah bird, an almost equally lengthy occupation. The most celebrated such scene is at the end of *Late Spring,* where the father, now alone, begins to peel a summer pear while we watch. To be sure, a desire for character delineation may play some part in determining the length of such scenes. Yet many of them come at a point when we know the characters so well that a prolonged observation of such activities can offer little new information. Rather, Ozu would have us share his respect for a task, any task, that is done for itself alone.

One is reminded of a Zen aphorism: "When I eat, I eat; when I sleep, I sleep." When one does something one does nothing else; one immerses self entirely in the task at hand, and appreciates it while completing it. A corollary is that in this fashion the present instant, the *now* that all of us are continually and notoriously forgetting, is preserved. The present moment is immortalized in the father's peeling of his fruit. As we watch the skin fall away, it is the concentration on the present we appreciate and, if we are like Ozu, admire. It is when the hands stop moving, the knife remains poised, the peeling remains unfinished, it is when the father looks up with vacant eyes, that we know he is, after all, like us—that the present is now lost in the future with its hopes and its fears, that he is feeling his loneliness.

Film is forever and only (despite flashbacks) in the present historic tense; this is a part of its lasting appeal. As long as it is indubitably now, we will happily sit and watch anything. It is only during a flashback, explanation, or resumé that we feel restive. Our feeling is correct because it is only now, the present instant, that can be felt. All else is surmise. Perhaps this is why Ozu is fond of the performance in any form. His insistence upon performance in both the literal and figurative sense may account for his personal insistence upon the kind of pictorial composition that will emphasize the actors, will set them off, will make them the most visible things within the frame.

**There Was a
Father.** *1942.
Chishu Ryu,
Haruhiko Tsuda*

Early Spring. *1956.
Koji Mitsui, Ryo
Ikebe, Daisuke
Kato, Chikage
Awashima*

Good Morning. *1959.
Masahiro Shimazu,
Chishu Ryu, Koji
Shidara, Kuniko
Miyake*

Ozu often literally frames his people. One remembers scene after scene in which the natural frame of the screen is reinforced with the inner frame created by the sliding doors at either side, the lintel or *ramma* at the top of the frame, the horizontal lines of the tatami at the bottom. These frames within frames set off action in a way that (as many directors have understood) commands attention and by its very artificiality can compel belief. That the composition within these frames is often asymmetrical is another reason why we often fail to recognize it as pictorial. The traditional Western assumption is that the pictorial is centered, or at least balanced in some obvious manner. The balance may be hidden, and often is by the best painters, but it is nonetheless there. Eastern pictorial composition is to the Western eye more erratic. One mass is balanced against another in less obvious ways, and emptiness may be given an equal weight with fullness. The rules governing Eastern composition, however, are actually as rigid (and as handy) as those governing, say, compositional perspective in the West, and they are just as easily learned.

Ozu learned them as most Japanese used to, from childhood on. It is most unlikely that he ever set about consciously planning one composition or another. He simply knew. Chushu Ryu remembered that for interiors he, too, more or less knew where everything would go because Ozu in his postwar films usually used a master plan, and had his sets constructed in accordance with it. Several of these plans have been published.[14] They show a typical small Japanese house: two eight-tatami rooms or one eight- and one six-mat room; a smaller, four-mat room; *roka* enclosing the whole on three sides; stairway to the right; bathroom in the back; kitchen to the left of the stairs. This is the plan of the house in *An Autumn Afternoon* (among other pictures), but sometimes Ozu used simpler structures. Ozu thus knew in advance where most scenes were to be taken, and consequently their composition. That these sets all closely resembled one another reflects Japan itself, where a majority of homes are identical.

Within this set one of the most used places was the *roka,* the corridor that forms the space between outside and living quarters. Over the years Ozu and Tatsuo Hamada, his long-time art designer, designed a shot which pleased them both and which appears again and again. The camera was placed in the *roka* so that it looked toward the kitchen, and this scene occupied a third of the frame; the left third (usually) was the *shoji* of the outside windows; the right was the *shoji* or *fusuma* doors of the inside. Action, if there was any, occurred in the middle third of the picture, and Ozu was sometimes heard to express appreciation of the scene's simplicity.

Decorating the set was not so simple. Ozu, his art director, actors, friends—anyone who wanted to—brought low tables, hibachi, bottles, pots, pans, and other objects in actual use to the set. When a pile had been collected, Ozu set about furnishing the house. As the pile got smaller Ozu would call out and ask what was left. If a bottle was left, for example, he then found a place for it in the kitchen. Though the Shochiku prop department was rarely called upon, Ozu maintained a certain standard for his furnishings. He used only "good" things, though occasionally if someone he liked had given him something "bad," he used that, too. Often he brought objects from his own Kita-Kamakura home (seen in abundance in *Equinox Flower*), placing an expensive *bizen* pot and an empty beer bottle with the same care. The care was always with the same end in mind: satisfactory composition.

Ryu recalled that long before the set was completed, Ozu would be busy with the viewfinder. Even if only a pillar or two were up, the director knew what his compositions would be.[15] Masahiro Shinoda, now a well-known director himself, remembers that when he was assistant director on *Late Autumn*, Ozu used to rearrange all the interiors to suit himself. "He used to say that he particularly disliked all of those straight tatami edges in a row. He'd take a number of *zabuton* pillows and push them along with his feet until they had added what he wanted to the general composition of the scene." He also recalled how surprised he was to discover Ozu changing the arrangement of objects within a single sequence:

> There was this table with beer bottles and some dishes and an ashtray on it, and we had shot the scene from one side and were going to shoot it from the other side when Ozu came up and began shifting the objects around. I was so shocked that I said that if he did that he would create a

bad break in continuity, that everyone would notice that the beer bottles were now on the right and the ashtray on the left. He stopped, looked at me, and said: "Continuity? Oh, that. No, you're wrong. People never notice things like that—and this way it makes a much better composition." And he was right, of course. People don't. When I saw the rushes I didn't notice anything wrong with those scenes.[16]

In the all-important interest of a pleasing composition, Ozu would even move his presumably stationary actors about within a sequence. There is an impossible bit of continuity, or lack of it, in the celebrated scene in *Tokyo Story* in which the old couple are sitting on the sea wall at Atami. In the next shot they have

Tokyo Story. *1953.*
Chishu Ryu, Chieko Higashiyama

changed places, with the father on the left and the mother on the right, though we are to presume that they have not moved. And we do. I, for example, never noticed the switch until it was pointed out to me. Ozu was right, people do not notice things like this.

Do not notice them, that is, when the break in continuity was considered and deliberate; one notices them soon enough otherwise. Often one is too interested and involved in the film to notice. Consequently one tends to notice Ozu's passion for composition at the beginnings of his films, where carefulness can be obtrusive, or where it becomes obsessive. An example of the former is the opening scene of *Floating Weeds,* a very handsome and formal composition—a beer bottle on a pier on the right side, balanced by a distant lighthouse on the left. An example of the

Floating Weeds.
*1959. Opening
shot.*

latter is the red tea kettle in *Equinox Flower.* Ozu's favorite color was red, and he wished to use it to accent certain scenes. The kettle consequently performs a number of surprising acrobatics within various sequences, appearing first on one side of the screen, then on the other, then on a table in the middle of the scene, etc.

If Ozu was somewhat cavalier about continuity, he was extraordinarily careful about the look of the scene itself. Ryu remembers his changing the patterns on the *fusuma* though they were already in place; for his color films he himself chose all the furnishings, including the shade of the tatami bindings and even the material from which the kimonos were made.[17] He was equally precise in the placement of objects within the scene—as we have seen with the beer bottle and the ashtray. Setsuko Hara remembers that in *Late Spring* she was always being told: "No, two more centimeters to the left. No, a bit more. No, no. LEFT, I said." [18] Yoko Tsukasa remembers Ozu's being extremely particular how she knelt down in *The End of Summer:* "It had to be done with Setsuko Hara, and we had to do it at exactly the same time and in precisely the same way." [19]

The end to which all these pains were taken was, of course, composition. Ozu had various ways of creating it, but all were necessarily based on his ideas of balance and geometry. Between scenes, composition usually was not maintained. There are exceptions to this, of course. In *Passing Fancy* several scenes are arranged so that the composition of one echoes the composition of the next: several different large gas storage tanks, each of a slightly different shape, are used one after the other, their place in the frame being invariable. In *The Munekata Sisters* the opening sequence is built on a series of shots identical in composition: (1) a Kyoto pagoda; (2) a tall tree of roughly the same shape; (3) the tower of Kyoto University, again the same shape. What interested the director in the main, however, was the composition of the single shot.

Earlier in his career variable focus afforded Ozu a way of balancing composition. With the far objects in focus, the near out of focus, one composition was created; with the farther objects out of focus and the nearer in we have another composition. Sometimes Ozu would forward dialogue in this common way: the far person, in focus, would speak; the focus would then shift to the near person and he would speak. *The Brothers and Sisters of the Toda Family* has several examples of this method, though it is perhaps the last film in which Ozu used it. This is, to be sure, a standard technique, used by many directors. Ozu differed in using both the dialogue and the change of focus to create an entirely new composition, but one that balanced with the composition of the preceding shot.

More typically, however, Ozu used a single composition that as often as not left the person in the background out of focus, the focus being on a still life in the foreground. In the scene that is the emotional climax of *Woman of Tokyo* (the sister's prostitution has been discovered), a vase and some fruit occupy the foreground while, dim and unfocused in the background, sits the sister.

Often, it is true, such still lifes become repositories for the feelings aroused by the film, but this early in Ozu's career, and in a film that arouses few strong feelings, one can safely assume that the reasons were compositional. Similarly there is a long scene in *What Did the Lady Forget?* in which, while the conversation goes on entirely out of focus, the frame is balanced with a sharply focused still life of a flower arrangement and some golf clubs. A similar shot in *The Only Son,* however, has obviously more than compositional interest. The young couple, out of focus, are talking about the absent mother. In focus in the foreground, making both a composition and its own comment on the scene, is the mother's pillow and pallet. The composition is pleasing, balanced, formal, and pertinent.

Ozu's conception of the uses of composition is apparent in his handling of traveling dolly shots, those scenes invariably so disruptive to planned composition. In *Early Summer* a sequence opens with a dolly to the right along an outside wall. Several objects enter the scene, among them a large outdoor barometer. The motion stops when a balanced composition is obtained, and then Ozu cuts to inside the building, to the married brother's laboratory, where the sequence takes place. In the final scene part of the screen is blocked by a large bookcase. Midway through this scene the camera begins to move, again to the right. The bookcase entirely cuts off the view of the room. When the camera reaches the wall the scene is over and we cut to the next sequence.

A number of things are suggested by the way this short sequence has been shot. First, it is balanced in a formal and temporal manner. We go out as we came in, with the same kind of motion, the same speed. Second, a care for composition has been observed that is irrelevant to character—i.e., does not serve to explain or suggest anything about anyone in the film. Third, there is no matching formal composition at the end of the final bookcase shot, though there was one at the end of the initial shot in the sequence. The calculated absence of such a composition serves to carry us more smoothly into the next part of the film, and is a favorite device with Ozu.

One of its most beautiful uses occurs in the final scene of *Early Summer*. The story is over, the girl is going to be married, the parents are staying with a relative in the country. We see across a field of ripening rice the farmhouse where they are staying. The composition is pleasing, natural. Then the camera begins to move to the right. The farmhouse glides off to the left. We gaze at this moving plain of rice and into this is cut the end title. An almost identical effect is achieved in the final sequence of *Woman of Tokyo*. The callous newsmen leave the scene of the brother's suicide and we see them on the street, watch them go around a corner. Ozu cuts to a closer shot of the corner itself and follows this by a closer shot (of nothing in particular: a lamp post, the sidewalk), which then begins to move slowly to the left. This shot continues for a time along the empty sidewalk, then fades into the end title. By beginning with a formally composed scene and then proceeding into a traveling shot that has no balancing composition at its conclusion, Ozu achieves something like the effect of a parenthetical clause with no final parenthesis. We are left dangling. Since there is no formal conclusion, and since formality is one of the givens of the Ozu film, we feel a pull toward infinity, we feel as though the film, like life, could have gone on forever. Later in his career Ozu achieved this effect by different means. Here we are noting that his conception of composition also included the consequences of its absence. In belying the expectation he has planted of formal composition, as he does in the two film-ending sequences described above, Ozu makes us consider the future. By carefully composing his scenes, by not permitting nature to enter unless carefully arranged, he makes us consider the present. This equation—the unplanned and chaotic indicating sometimes past but more often future, the planned and composed indicating the present—may be observed (or rather, inferred) in all of Ozu's pictures.

Usually the director was not interested, however, in harmonizing the composition of succeeding shots. Each shot is a separate entity, and the cut presents us with another shot that is composed in a fashion that cannot be considered complementary to either of the shots adjacent. Here again Ozu resembles the traditional Japanese architect, who, working in module units, is not really concerned with complementary qualities; he will use tatami in one fashion or style alongside *fusuma* of a different style.

Ozu, then, was interested in composition within the single shot. Inside this frame Ozu worked to create the kind of geometry necessary to satisfy his sense of beauty. Things are usually seen at right angles, balanced against each other, and the people, as the most important things in the scene, are worked into a frame already prepared for them.[20] Thus, in a conversation, though people will sometimes face each other, just as commonly they sit side by side, seen by us from the front or from the side. How they are placed is often determined by where they are.

As earlier noted, when Ozu and his fellow writer were creating the dialogue script for a film, they sometimes gave no indication where a conversation was taking place. It was only in the second or third drafts that they decided where their characters were to be. Paul Schrader has made the interesting observation that

> if an Ozu character is in a certain location, a certain type of conversation will ensue. In the home Ozu characters discuss domestic arrangements (finances, housework, what other family members are doing); at the office they make concrete arrangements (future meeting places and times); in a restaurant they reminisce and discuss social problems (marriage proposals, what other members of the family are doing); in a bar they reminisce and express disillusionment (the *après-guerre* generation, office life).[21]

While this pattern is not invariable, as Schrader himself concedes, it is consistent enough to deserve comment. The process of creation, however, was perhaps the other way around: a certain kind of conversation was written, and then the director and his fellow writer decided which of the four major locations used in Ozu's films was appropriate.

In the same way, the setting has a definite bearing on the placement of actors within the scene. In part this is to be explained by the seating arrangements of various locales. In a bar, for example, or a small restaurant or sushi shop, characters must obviously be side by side since they are sitting against a counter. In a large restaurant (where they have usually asked for a private *zashiki*) they sit facing each other across a table as they do at home. In the office they either sit one at his desk, the other in the chair provided for visitors, and hence face to face, or—if they go to the rooms provided for meetings in large company offices—they face each other across the homelike table. The position of the characters, so often suggested by the seating arrangements, rarely seems unnatural.[22] Nor is it meant to be symbolical; in an Ozu film people are not necessarily on intimate terms if they kneel side by side. Side-by-side conversations, with both actors facing the camera, also do not seem unnatural in the films of Ozu because the characters have known one another for years. Only the young ever need introductions in these pictures; the others, all old friends, need not pay one another the full attention rendered by a face-to-face position. Sato has suggested, in discussing the influence of the novelist Naoya Shiga on Ozu, that the people in these films all seem to live in the same village: they know one another and so, like Shiga's people, they behave themselves; they also have the good manners of those who know they are being watched.[23] At the same time, although the placement of Ozu's characters seems natural, it also suggests a degree of formality (as does, indeed, traditional Japanese life itself). The formality expresses the order Ozu finds in the lives of those who know how to live properly in the present, and also the slightly ironic regard of those who know themselves well enough to regard their surroundings, their friends, and themselves with objective detachment.

Of great assistance to Ozu in showing this order is the fact that his compositions, like most Japanese pictorial compositions, are in the main horizontal. Such compositions, in Western as well as Asian art, suggest the known, the content, even the serene. Vertical and diagonal compositions, by contrast, suggest striving, the

OPPOSITE (READING DOWN):

Lost Luck. *1930.*
Tatsuo Saito, Mitsuko Yoshikawa

Young Miss. *1930.*
Tokihiko Okada, Kinuyo Tanaka' Tatsuo Saito

The Record of a Tenement Gentleman. *1947.* *Choko Iida, Reikichi Kawamura*

Late Spring. *1949.*
Setsuko Hara, Jun Usami

The Flavor of Green Tea over Rice. *1952.*
Koji Tsuruta, Shin Saburi

Tokyo Story. *1953.*
Eijiro Tono, Chushu Ryu

Tokyo Twilight. *1957.*
Setsuko Hara, Isuzu Yamada

Equinox Flower. *1958.*
Kinuyo Tanaka, Shin Saburi

unknown, even the discontent. The invariable low horizon of the
Ozu film (whether the actual horizon is visible or not) helps create
the accepting atmosphere of these pictures—a mood that compet-
ing and active verticals, so often seen in the films of foreign directors, would destroy. Perhaps this is why the diagonal composition
so common in the West remains relatively uncommon in Japanese
films (with such obvious exceptions as Kurosawa, Ichikawa, etc.)
and quite rare in the films of Ozu.

The screen in an Ozu film is often divided compositionally (the
grandmother and children in *Tokyo Story,* boys going off to
school in *Good Morning,* etc.), but the division is usually horizontal. When a diagonal division is used, so far as I can ascertain there
is never a thematic reason for it.

Western cinematographers (e.g. Eisenstein) have long insisted
that a diagonal composition produces a feeling of tension. Indeed,
this has become one of the compositional conventions of film, and
we are presumed to feel tension when we see an obviously diagonal composition. Whether the diagonal composition itself produces
the feeling, however, is open to question. In many Western paintings diagonal compositions inspire the opposite feeling, and in
Asian painting, too, one finds many restful diagonals. It is doubtful, at any rate, that Ozu used his rare diagonal compositions for
any purpose but to break the chain of horizontals that constitutes
the compositional skeleton of his films. A case might be made for
the diagonal bar composition of the opening sequence of *The End
of Summer,* since the girl is undecided about her future and the
man is really there to look her over as a possible wife. But what
can one say of such compositions in *The Only Son* and *There Was
a Father,* or of the diagonally composed scene in *A Hen in the
Wind,* in which mother, friend, and child sit on a hillside discussing
the most mundane and tension-free matters?

Of course Ozu is no stranger to the attractions of symbolism,
compositional or otherwise, but it does not occur to him to use
composition to create symbols that are often direct and thus by
his lights usually unsuccessful. In *A Hen in the Wind* there is a
scene in which the hero, enraged with his wife, stands near an
overhead lamp. A large moth flutters about the light, casting a
shadow over the hero's face, obviously supposed to suggest the

turbulence of the man's thoughts. In *The Munekata Sisters,* the bad husband of the elder sister, a man whose death from alcoholism has been telegraphed for several reels, is reintroduced into the story by one of the introductory shots Ozu liked so well. In this case, however, the director has chosen not his customary genre scene, but a shot of a large, dead tree, followed directly by a shot of the alcoholic husband; the audience is left to draw the only conclusion it can. One scene of *The Only Son* is almost ruined when, after the mother has gone, the son, talking about her with his wife, absently picks up the baby's bottle and distractedly puts the nipple in his mouth—a symbol of filial attachment so blatant that only the context of the picture and the brevity of the action save the scene.

Much more satisfying are those "symbols," if they may so be called, of uncertain meaning. In *Early Summer* the old couple are sitting in front of the museum in Ueno Park, and their talk turns to their dead son. In the midst of this conversation the wife looks up and then draws her husband's attention to what she sees: a bal-

Early Summer. *1951.*
Ichiro Sugai, Chieko Higashiyama

loon, probably lost by a child, soaring up into the sky. They follow it with their eyes and talk no more of their son. Later in the film, when the father is waiting for the train to take him to Tokyo, he looks up and sees a cloudless, empty sky. We are thus reminded of the dead son and the conversation in the park. At the same time we feel that something ineffable, something unspoken, is being suggested, something perhaps to do with loss, with the transience of life, with our place here below under the blank, bright eye of the summer sky. In *A Hen in the Wind* a mysterious object is called repeatedly to our attention. The husband has left his wife. He walks, sits down, and looks at something. We are eventually shown that it is a large circle of rusted pipe, the kind used for sewer conduits. The next morning, we again look at this big piece of pipe. Several times more it serves as a transition between unrelated scenes. Finally, when the husband visits the whorehouse where he thinks his wife once went to earn money for their sick child, we are given another long look. We know what the beginning Freudian would have to say about this large but dirty conduit, but we do not know what Ozu would have to say. This enhances the attraction of the object and its mysteriousness. We cannot, finally, say what it means.

Completely satisfying, so much so that they can no longer be considered symbolic, are those many small scenes in Ozu's films of objects, always perfectly ordinary, everyday objects, which serve not to symbolize but to contain emotions. Ozu refused, as we have seen, to comment directly on his characters by their placement within a scene. Direct comment, symbolic scenes— these are usually alien to Ozu precisely because they constitute an unfair comment on character, unfair because they pretend to sum up something as complicated as a character with something as simple as a symbol. Ozu prefers something more subtle: the still life. The hanging lanterns in *Floating Weeds*, the flower arrangements in *Equinox Flower*, the single vase in the darkened room in *Late Spring*—what do these mean? They are apparently still lifes, objects, photographed for their own beautiful sakes. This is not, however, quite true. Take the vase in *Late Spring*, for example. Father and daughter, soon to part since she is getting married, are on their last trip together. After a day in Kyoto they are going to

Late Spring. *1959.*
Setsuko Hara, Chishu Ryu

bed, and they talk about what a nice time they have had. After
the lights are put out, the daughter lies awake. She asks her father
a question. He does not answer. From this point on the continuity
is:

a shot of the father asleep
a shot of the daughter looking at him
a shot of the vase in the alcove, over which is heard the gentle
    sound of the father's snoring
a shot of the daughter who seems to be half smiling, a long shot
    of the face, almost ten seconds
the vase, another long shot
a shot of the daughter, her mood entirely changed, near tears.

The vase serves as a pivot. Though it *means* nothing in itself
(not even repose, sleep), it is the pretext for an amount of elapsed
time; it is something to watch during the period in which the feelings of the daughter change. It is difficult to say why this is more
satisfying than the ordinary way of doing it, i.e. having us watch

137

the change on the actress's face. Perhaps one reason is that Ozu imposes a kind of impersonality, a sort of coolness, between the daughter and us. Not by seeing her, but by seeing what she sees (a vase alone, solitary, beautiful), we can more completely, more fully, comprehend. In being shown only the vase during the crucial seconds when she comes near tears, we are put into the position of having to imagine her feelings. Although we do not necessarily imagine that she will be near tears when we next see her, the vase has occupied our attention while we were occupied with her feelings (there being nothing else to think about at this point in the film), and we consequently accept her feelings, no matter what they are. We have been led into an emotional situation, and at its climax are given nothing to look at. The surge of our own emotions, and *Late Spring* is a deeply moving film, creates a reciprocal emotion that, because we have put ourselves into it, becomes for us real. This is obviously very far indeed from the simplicities of symbolism. There is more to be said about this sequence, but for the present, I will simply indicate its quality by quoting Schrader on this scene: "The vase is statis, a form which can accept deep, contradictory emotion and transform it into an expression of something unified, permanent, transcendent." [24]

If Ozu usually refuses interpretative composition, he nonetheless refuses to be limited by the formal, balanced, horizontal compositions he almost invariably uses. A better way of putting this is that the rigid geometry of the Ozu scene sets off the fluid and natural actions of his characters.

Just as he divided his scene into fore and background planes so that his actors would be visibly set off, so Ozu arranged his rigid schema so that the characters' gestures and reactions would appear, almost by contrast, natural. The Ozu scene is balanced, asymmetrical, pleasing to the eye; it is at the same time rigid and uncompromising, as all empty compositions are. When the actor enters and behaves in a way contrary to the expectations created by such a formal decor, the result is an often touching spontaneity. This composition, then, exists but to be broken. As the director has repeatedly demonstrated, the flicker of an eyelid or the quiver of a lip can be as moving as oceans of tears. In film as in poetry, the meaning of a single scene, a single word, even, often depends on what went before and what comes after. If the promises implicit in a fairly rigid compositional pattern are not realized, if instead we have an apparently unpremeditated action, the emotional power of the scene is all the greater because of the context.

Ozu's composition is always broken by emotion. The emotional climax of *The Brothers and Sisters of the Toda Family* occurs when the youngest son returns from China and discovers that his elder brothers and sisters have been neglecting his mother and younger sister. This occurs at a formal family get-together. The camera is outside looking in, thus viewing the entire room. The family is sitting in front of separate small tables arranged in an L-shape. The youngest son is at the far right of the back wall, and next to him in a row are his brothers and sisters. At the elbow of the L sits the rather unpleasant elder sister and next to her, consequently along the left wall and at right angles to the others, sit the mother and youngest daughter. The occasion is formal, the composition rigid.

As the scene progresses the youngest son begins discussing what the others have done to the mother. They attempt to maintain the decorum they feel suits the occasion, but his accusations are so intemperate, and yet so just, that one by one, without having eaten, the brothers and sisters and their spouses decide to leave. As they depart holes begin to appear in the composition. What was formal and balanced is now upset. When they have all left, the composition is hopeless: the two women at the extreme left, the son at the extreme right. Then, in a movement that reflects the new living arrangement the three will find together, the son stands up, crosses to the two women, and sits down in front of them. The result is a new composition, one that is again balanced but this time informally. The straight row of the siblings with its answering parallels in lintel and tatami is gone; instead there is on the left the pleasant family huddle balanced by the large amount of empty space that is the remainder of the screen. The new composition is intimate, a genre scene, and it fits perfectly the story, the mood, the persons of this film. All of this, moreover, is done with such naturalness and ease that it does not draw one's thoughts to the composition (unless one is writing a book on Ozu), and yet the director's eye and art have both enriched and revealed the meaning of the scene.

Sometimes, though rarely, the composition is broken and not resolved. In the still and formal world of Ozu, the effect can be devastating. Perhaps the most shocking such scene occurs in *There Was a Father*. The father, preparing to leave, is sitting on the tatami, waiting for his son. It is a formal composition, with the father on one side, balanced on the other by the wide open window of the inn. The son goes to the next room and we go with him. The maid runs in to say that something has happened. We cut back to the same scene as before. The shot is the same, but the father, before so perfectly balanced within the frame, is now sprawled upon the tatami, quivering and jerking. Since we love the father we would be distressed in any case, yet undeniably a part of our sudden horror is that the composition has been shattered; chaos has entered. We are watching a very real-seeming scene of a man we know and understand having a stroke; at the same time we are witnessing a metaphor for the violent end of an ordered and human world.

Usually, however, the composition is broken more gently. People will behave with that quiet dignity and formality for which Ozu's characters are known, but then will come a moment when emotion speaks, and when the composition is rendered imperfect by some completely natural gesture. The formality, pleasing as it usually is, of a person contained and self-assured, is exchanged for the informality of a person unsure, ill-at-ease, or perhaps momentarily given over to some slight emotion, signalled by smiles or laughter. We feel suddenly and poignantly the raw humanity of this person, the reality of his perhaps intemperate but certainly familiar emotion. One of the most beautiful examples of such a scene occurs in *Late Spring,* when the daughter and her aunt bow at the same time.[25] Rather, they are supposed to bow at the same time and we expect them to, but the daughter—who now believes that her father will be remarrying and consequently leaving her— delays her bow for an instant. She wavers, leans slightly to one side, recovers herself, and bows, but the perfect composition that would have been created (as it is in *The End of Summer,* for example) by two perfectly synchronized actions is broken; in its stead we are given a glimpse into the human heart, an organ informal by nature and spontaneous by definition.

None of this should be interpreted as meaning that Ozu considered informal composition superior to formal composition, or that when formal composition is broken, its only use is in the breaking. The question is more complicated than that. Formal composition in an Ozu film represents the way things are not only on formal occasions, but every day: this is how we ordinarily see things, in some kind of balanced pattern. When emotion enters, however, the balance is altered, exchanged, as it were, for an idea of human frailty, of human emotion. In film after film one sees such moments of emotional tension both created and explained by the sudden violation of a compositional convention we have come to accept. It is just this contrast between the rightness of the geometry and the sudden intrusion (playful or tragic or unthinking) of the human, the natural, that prevents the Ozu schema from itself appearing unnatural. Just as we, like the Japanese, accept the Ozu house as a stage, just as we fail to notice the pictorial composition at all, so we accept the ordered demeanor of the traditional Japanese and fail to consciously notice any unnatural constraints. Like the Japanese, however, we feel such constraints, and when they are broken, we feel, as they do, relief.

Composition, scene length, selection—all these help create the revelatory moments in the Ozu film. The main contribution, however, must necessarily be that of the actor, because it is he who must dramatize not only these moments but the entire film. Though the actor need not know what he is doing (Ozu's actors often seemed not to), it is he who has to do it. Dramatization arises not from his interpretation, but from his presence, which may explain Ozu's attitude toward his actors. Ozu compared his actors to the colors a painter uses, and said, as we have seen, that without knowing what they were, neither he nor the painter could begin to work. *What* rather than *who* the actors were was important. They had to be a certain kind of person in order to effectively play a role. Just as Rossellini chooses actors, as he has said, exclusively for their physique, Ozu chose his exclusively for their character. He knew most of his actors and tended to use the same ones over and over: Chushu Ryu, Choko Iida, Takeshi Sakamoto,

Emiko Yakumo, Nobuo Nakamura, Setsuko Hara, Kinuyo Tanaka, among others, are all familiar faces in Ozu's films. If he did not know an actor well, then before the film began he had to find out about him. Shin Saburi, a big star at the time, remembers that before the rehearsals for *The Brothers and Sisters of the Toda Family* began, Ozu called him in. Saburi expected that they would talk about the film but instead, they talked for a long time of many other things. Looking back on this long conversation, Saburi felt that its purpose was to enable Ozu to get the feel of him, to find out what he was.[26]

The Brothers and Sisters of the Toda Family. *1941*
*Shin Saburi,
Fumiko Katsuragi
Mieko Takamine*

Was Ozu also looking for type? To say he was would be to simplify. After all, he avoided using stars, who are often the very personification of a type. At the same time, however, Ozu sometimes had a type of character in mind and would look for an actor of similar character to play him. He said as much in speaking of *The Record of a Tenement Gentleman:* "There used to be, in Fukugawa where I was born, lots of people like the Kihachi character in this film and others such as *The Story of Floating Weeds,* though they're rare now . . . ; they only owned one *fundoshi* [loincloth], dressed any which way, drank *shochu* [lowest-class sake]. . . ."[27] This is the character he taught or encouraged Ryu and Sakamoto to be on the screen, thus creating the *kihachi* genre.

The Ozu set was almost like a school. The director taught the actors how to do everything. Though he had the types of people he wanted for the kinds of characters he desired, he never let his actors express anything. One of his methods was to use himself as example. "Sometimes he acted out the role himself and it was a pleasure just to be able to watch him. If he had appeared in his own films . . . he'd be known as a great actor." [28] His other and more common method was complete, detailed instruction. "He had made up the complete picture in his head before he went on the set so that we actors only had to follow his directions, from the way we moved our arms to the way we blinked our eyes. That is, we didn't have to worry about acting at all." [29]

In the earlier films Ozu often gave the actor an idiosyncratic, suggestive gesture. The father in *Passing Fancy* repeatedly scratches his throat delicately with the nail of his little finger; Tatsuo Saito in *Tokyo Chorus* keeps rubbing his hip during various scenes; in *A Story of Floating Weeds* Takeshi Sakamoto often scratches his behind. Later, however, such gestures (all of which apparently Ozu had observed in life) disappear, or become less stylized and hence less noticeable. In *Late Spring* Ryu has a habit of running his cigarette holder along the side of his nose, but he does not do it all that often, and, in any event, it is a familiar gesture: rubbing fine-grained burr pipes or holders against the nose is the Japanese way of oiling their finish.

In most of his mature films, Ozu demanded not emblematic gestures, but a wide though restricted range of actions that would achieve the desired effect. Ryu remembers a scene in *There Was a Father*: "Ozu told me to stare at the end of my chopsticks and then stare at my hand and then speak to my child. The simple act of doing these things in that order conveyed a certain feeling. Ozu did not explain the feeling; the actions came first. He told me what to do and let me discover the feeling." [30] Again, in *College Is a Nice Place*, Ryu had to bring his new suit to the pawnshop: "When I received the money from the pawnbroker, Ozu told me to first look at one end of the bill and then to look at the other and then to look up. The feeling of the student at this point was quite sad, and the feeling of having lost his new suit was expressed by the movement of his eyes. And I began to identify with the character.[31]

Many of the actors with whom Ozu worked have similar memories. Haruko Sugimura as the elder sister in *Tokyo Story* had a scene on the telephone where she says she will go to the station to pick up the old folks. Ozu had her hold a fan and follow its outline with her eyes, making thus a complete circle that coincided with the length of her dialogue. Sugimura, a serious stage actress, was confounded. She asked what she was supposed to be feeling. "You are not supposed to feel," was the answer, "you are supposed to do." She did as directed and in the finished scene we feel the half-attentive and somewhat selfish abstraction that distinguishes this rather unsympathetic character.[32] Chieko Higashiyama, who plays the old mother in the same film, first appeared in *Early Summer,* where she discovered that she had to choreograph her teacup to synchronize with her dialogue. Each word went with a different position for the cup in her hand. "He was most particular about where the cup should be in relation to each word." It was very difficult work, particularly since just running through the various positions was not enough. "If you did just the form [*kata*] without the spirit, then that was no good either. Everything had to agree with his image of it." [33]

Any discussion among Ozu's actors of the director's methods soon degenerates into a horror-story competition, with each actor vying to recount an ordeal more terrible than the one before. Choko Iida remembers a single shot in *A Mother Should Be Loved* that Ozu made her do "for four or five hours." Admittedly, it was a difficult passage: she needs to go to the toilet but is holding back, when all of sudden she bursts out laughing at something and then has to run off to the bathroom.[34] Ganjiro Nakamura, in speaking of the rain sequence in *Floating Weeds,* recalls that it took all day, that he and Machiko Kyo ended up feverish, and that Ozu (pleased with the sequence) gave them the next two days off.[35] Ryu remembers a scene in *College is a Nice Place* that Ozu filmed over thirty times. He was supposed to be giving a sick friend medicine, and could not do it to Ozu's satisfaction.[36] It was at times like that, Choko Iida has said, they used to sit around after work and think, "If only Ozu would die or something by tomorrow." [37]

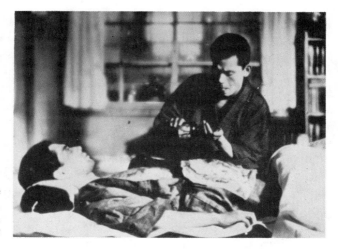

College Is a Nice
Place. *1936.*
Akira Kusakabe,
Chishu Ryu

Mitsuko Yoshikawa remembers a full if nonconsecutive twenty-four hours spent on a single shot in *A Mother Should Be Loved*. She was supposed to turn away from tea-making; the tempo of turning had to be precise, and her glance was not to move ahead of her face. "Why," she finally cried after some hours of this, "do I have to do it this way?" "Because," Ozu explained, "you are not a skillful actress and you must be directed." Later, after the war, when he wanted her for *The Record of a Tenement Gentleman,* she flatly refused. This led to a gentle letter of apology, full of intimations of rectified ways. She went to make the film. "It was just the same. He hadn't changed at all." [38]

If, however, after several days of attempting the same scene or shot he could not achieve the effect he wished, Ozu fell silent, spared the actor further criticism (and made none at all after the film was finished), and chose something from the mass he had already shot. "It was always that way," Ryu has said. "Even if he had to give up he could always find something he could somehow use." [39]

Chieko Higashiyama remembers two nice things Ozu did for her, but they do not substantially alter the impression of an ogre in the studio. First, when the cast of *Tokyo Story* went to Onomichi to study the mood of that southern city, she could not go, and Ozu kindly had someone speak all of her lines in Onomichi-*ben* (dialect) into a wire-recorder so that she would have the proper

145

pronunciation when it came time to film. (An event which led Ryu to remark that it didn't make any difference, "We'll all be speaking Ozu-*ben* anyway.") [40] The second kindness was Ozu's noticing her great fear of heights and constructing, at some trouble and expense, a wooden causeway directly beneath the sea-wall in Atami so that she would not see the ocean and even if she fell would not hurt herself. [41] Both actions would admit interpretations other than kindness—for example, Ozu's determination to get the kind of performance he wanted.

Ozu's method of directing actors reminds one of Robert Bresson, perhaps because both men had a horror of acting as such. Yoshiyaku Hamamura has remembered a very Bresson-like scene. They were looking at the rushes for the scene in *Early Summer* where Haruko Sugimura realizes that Setsuko Hara will marry her son. Hamamura thought the first version should be used because "Miss Sugimura was so good—crying and exulting." Ozu said no, not at all, that she was overacting, and that he did not want anyone's performance to stand out in the finished film. He chose a later take, one made after the actress had lost some of her excitement. [42]

Despite the many similarities between the methods of Ozu and Bresson, however, the end results are quite different. Bresson avowedly seeks to drain his actors of all notions of interpretation, eventually so tiring them that the toneless enactment he desires is achieved. Ozu, by contrast, wanted to imbue his actors with all the characteristics of the people they are impersonating, characteristics that only he knew, so that they could project them whether they understood them or not. [43] This, Ozu's actors are agreed, was very hard work. Ryu recalls:

> Once I followed Ozu's precise instructions more than two dozen times, but each time I failed to convey the proper feeling and finally gave up. . . . Ozu was very strict, [yet] though I was unskillful and often at a loss as to how to play my part, he gave me complete encouragement so long as I followed his directions. Since my clumsiness was well known at the studio, all the staff used to switch off the lights and go off someplace when my turn came. Ozu and I were left alone on the set and he would let me re-

hearse endlessly, giving me all sorts of advice until somehow I at last managed to do what he wanted. . . . Even if I didn't know what I was doing or how these shots would be connected in the end, I was often surprised to find my performance far better than I had expected.[44]

For Ozu this was all part of the business of making films. It ranked, perhaps, only slightly higher (maybe because more difficult) than finding the correct composition, the right *fusuma* paper, the proper vase. The repetitious rehearsals were resented by several of Ozu's assistants, among them the young Shohei Imamura, now a well-known director himself. He told Tadao Sato that during the first rehearsal the actors were just right, but then Ozu required so many repeats that they became stiff, and "when they were at their most doll-like, then the Master would give his approval." [45] Imamura, who had his own ideas about acting, could not tolerate this. He asked to be transferred and he was.

Kogo Noda relates that Ozu made no distinction among the various kinds of directors the popular press insists upon. When asked early in his career if he would become a studio director (*satsuei kantoku*, with emphasis upon camera, editing, etc.), or an actors' director (*haiyu kantoku*), he was unable to answer, apparently seeing no difference between them.[46] This was because he remained in complete charge of his project, making all the decisions himself. Such a director is extremely rare in the history of film, even in Japan, where directors were allowed a creative freedom unheard of in many countries. Some actors feel they never recovered from the experience of making a film for Ozu, others that they owe everything to having worked with him. Ryu has said: "I must confess that I felt I was only the colors with which Ozu painted his pictures, [yet] . . . today I cannot think of my own identity without thinking of him. I once heard Ozu say, 'Ryu is not a skillful actor—that is why I use him.' This is very true." [47]

Some of the techniques Ozu applied to his actors may have been learned from the stage. From 1933 through 1946 he would occasionally write (or help write) and stage skits at such places as the Imperial Theater, the Mitsukoshi Hall, and the Tokyo Theater. Few of these now exist, but they may have been rather like the light sketches that Kafu Nagai, the novelist who in some ways resembles Ozu, wrote for the theaters in Asakusa. Ozu's scene rehearsals for his films have been compared to stage rehearsals, and there is something quite stage-like in Ozu's most common shot. So stage-like do we find it that it has no place in contemporary Western cinema, and its appearance in early foreign films is usually credited to the obvious but unwelcome influence of the theater. This is the single shot of the actor facing the camera, almost directly into the lens. From the earliest extant of the director's works, the 1929 *Days of Youth,* to the 1963 *An Autumn Afternoon,* the shot is ubiquitous. Though the gaze somewhat shifts over the years (it began as an oblique look directed just beside the camera in a manner still fairly common in films; it ended as a face-to-face confrontation with the camera), the shot itself remains much the same: head and shoulders of the actor and the delivery of a single line.

One recognizes the antecedent of this shot. It is American, and is very common in early silent films—those of the Bluebird and Triangle companies, for example, and those of directors such as Rupert Julien. These were, in effect, filmed stage plays. Most were ordinary comedies and melodramas, and all were interested only in telling a story in the fastest, most coherent manner. Close-up and title follow each other at a fairly rapid pace, as the interminable but apparently necessary conversations of these early pictures

Young Miss. *1930.*
Tokihiko Okada,
Sumiko Kurishima,
Tatsuo Saito

**What Did the
Lady Forget?** *1937.
Tatsuo Saito,
Sumiko Kurishima*

Equinox Flower.
*1958.
Chishu Ryu,
Haruo Tanaka*

**An Autumn
Afternoon.** *1962.
Keiji Sada,
Teruo Yoshida*

149

proceeded to an action-filled finale. Such pictures, exported to Japan in great numbers, were avidly studied by all the young directors. It was pictures like these, and not those perhaps more cinematic films made in Europe, that became the model in Japan for continuity. If such a succession of shots now looks strange to us, as it occasionally does, it is because continuity in film has developed beyond this basic stage, and the films we now see make this kind of technique seem primitive.

Basic it may be, but it need not be primitive. It is perhaps the most direct method for registering reaction, and certainly best suggests the subtle interplay that occurs during any conversation. For Ozu, the fact that it was so basic was, naturally, an incentive to continue using it. Also, though the films of Rupert Julien do not suggest it, this kind of continuity was capable of a refinement and subtlety lacking in more advanced forms. The excitement among Japanese directors was considerable in 1925, when Ernst Lubitsch's *The Marriage Circle,* made the year before, opened in Tokyo. For the first time (so far as the Japanese audience was concerned), this ordinary method of telling a story (one close-up, one line of dialogue) was revealed as capable of wit and irony. (So far as Lubitsch was concerned, the lesson may have been learned from Mauritz Stiller's elegant *Erotikon,* a film made four years before and not shown in Japan, and one that *The Marriage Circle* resembles.) The facial expression of the actor could give the lie to the line, or the reaction shot could be logically but wildly at odds with the expected response; a series of such scenes could be formalized into little sequences and then contrasted one with the other; or a series could be followed by another series that paralleled it but suggested different interpretations.

The effect of *The Marriage Circle* on Japanese cinema was enormous: directors as unalike as Gosho, Mizoguchi, and Naruse continued to talk about it far into their careers; the effect on Ozu was decisive. It was a film he often mentioned, and echoes of it are found even in his later pictures. If one compares the 1934 *The Story of Floating Weeds,* made when the American influence was fully assimilated, with the film from which the story was ostensibly taken, George Fitzgerald's *The Barker,* the difference becomes at once apparent. The American film, though employing the one-cut, one-line method, does nothing with it; it is simply used to forward the story. The Ozu film, however, uses the method more or less the way Lubitsch did. The reactions in this picture are particularly subtle, with many of them coming as unexpected and all of them emerging as lifelike. As with so much else in his cinema, Ozu welcomed restriction in his continuity; here as elsewhere, apparent rigidity of the schema made possible the spontaneity of the people within.

For Lubitsch the method resulted in a beautifully stylized, wry, elegant, exquisitely artificial comedy of manners; for Ozu the same method results in a funny, ordered, ironic slice of the human comedy.

That the method often appears artificial is, of course, pa.t of its appeal. In the Triangle and Bluebird films it did not seem artificial because its stage origin was still visible; for Lubitsch it was necessary to maintain the distance without which wit refuses to appear; for Ozu distancing was necessary for irony and for the desired emotional detachment. Even if this were not so, however, Ozu would have been drawn to the method, if only for its super-economy.

Certainly the unnaturalness of anything rarely bothered Ozu. As we have seen, he did not invariably keep to strict continuity and would often move people and props about between the shots of a single scene. Akira Fushimi, one of Ozu's earliest scriptwriters, remembers that in one film the director was taking a shot of a character who was looking at a picture on a wall. He then removed the wall and took a picture of the actor looking at the camera as though he was looking at the picture. Fushimi objected and said it was unnatural, that Ozu should take the character from the back or the side. Ozu said it did not matter whether it was unnatural or not, the main thing was to see the face.[48] Again, during the scene in *A Hen in the Wind* where Kinuyo Tanaka is deciding whether to prostitute herself or not to get money for her sick child's doctor bills, she sits in front of a mirror and looks at herself. There follows a whole series of unnatural shots, with self and reflection alternating four times before she bursts into tears and decides to go to the whorehouse. Kinuyo Tanaka remembers asking if it were likely that a camera would alternately occupy the position of the mirror. Ozu paid no attention and shot the sequence—and very unnatural it is—just as he wanted.[49]

If probability of camera placement did not affect Ozu, neither did other conventional considerations. He sometimes used Sadako Sawamura, an actress famed for her classic profile who possessed, full face, only ordinary appearance. Though she sometimes demurred at nothing but full-face shots, she complained to no avail. She was rarely allowed to show the famous profile. Again, as Setsuko Hara grew older her face changed, and she lost some of her freshness. Although her profile remained unchanged, Ozu withstood all suggestions for profile shots, and Setsuko Hara bravely faced almost invariable full-face lighting and full-face camera.[50]

For Ozu the face was always the most important part of the character. Though he would occasionally show other parts of the body (usually, in earlier films, the hands and feet, shot in the American manner and presumed to be indicative of the character's emotions; *That Night's Wife* is an example), it was for Ozu, as for most other directors, the face, and particularly the eyes, that counted most. Often, in his later films, the actors were directed not to move their faces. All their emotions had to appear in the eyes alone.

In the classical American method of continuity, the gaze is the essence of the scene, and as we alternate between close-ups and lines of dialogue, it is the eyes that capture our attention, in film as in life. In the classical American theory, if A and B are sitting across from each other, then A will act toward the camera with his eyes looking slightly to the right and B will look slightly toward the left. This creates an axis and suggests a straight line. It means that the characters are looking into each other's eyes. "American films no longer hew to this, of course, but for years it was axiomatic," Yoshiaki Hamamura, Ozu's editor, told Sato. Ozu's method, though influenced by the American theory, was different: "In his case, A looks toward the right and B also looks to the right—or to the left, as the case may be, the point being that both look in the same direction." Hamamura told Ozu he was making a mistake. "So he took one scene the way I said and then when we'd seen the rushes, he turned to me and said: 'But, it's all the same, isn't it? It doesn't make any difference, does it?' I insisted, repeatedly, that it made a great deal of difference. He was never able to see it, however, and went right on having them both look to the left, or to the right, and I eventually got tired of complaining about it." [51]

Ozu was, of course, right. As he indicated by the sea-wall scene in *Tokyo Story,* the director can move not only the eyes but the actors themselves and the audience will not notice. Like so much of cinema theory, the classical theory was a paper theorem and meant nothing. Just as we now know that pursued and pursuer need not invariably move in the same direction across the screen, so we now know that the direction of gaze is unimportant. The spectator puts everything together for himself, and will construct a continuity for even the most disparate elements.

Perhaps it was because the face, the eyes, the gaze, were so important to Ozu that, as Sato has noticed, he seemed to have an aversion toward people shown moving sideways. They may enter from the side of the screen, but they at once turn and face front. There is much moving backward and forward within a scene, but little lateral movement. In the same way, Sato noted, Ozu rarely used a partial view of a character. It was nearly always complete, that is, full-face. Such shots as the profile of Ryu peeling fruit at the end of *Late Spring* are extremely rare. They are used only at moments of great emotion, when a full-front shot might imply a lack of respect, a kind of morbid curiosity. From this observation, Sato evolved a theory as ingenious as it is likely.

"Is it impossible to think as follows? In the films of Ozu the characters are all the director's guests. If we are just looking at people on the street, then we see hands, feet, bodies, etc. But if they come into our house we look them directly in the face." We do this for the obvious reasons, but also to show them respect. For the same reason we don't get too close to them. "If the camera has approached a character, it does not move into a close-up, it remains at head-and-shoulders distance—it would be simple etiquette not to get any closer." Further, though a person in repose may be seen in profile, as soon as he speaks the camera moves to a position facing him. "This is only polite."

At the same time, Sato observes, "the characters of Ozu's films, all of them, may be said to behave just as though they were really guests . . . even among those actors who are used to working with Ozu . . . most act stiffly, as though standing on ceremony." [52] And, of course, Ozu's method of working—telling everyone what to do and never why; taking the same tiny scene over and over again—would make an actor even less at ease. We have already seen that Ozu refused to use his character, and now we can see another reason why. For in establishing and showing a kind of guest-host relationship, Ozu is showing the Japanese as they really are.

As a people they do indeed hold back and stand on ceremony. Their language even has a word for this, *enryo,* the English equivalent of which may be found somewhere among "reserve," "constraint," and "diffidence." It is so often observed and so widespread that it might be called a national characteristic. The Japanese, however, only practices *enryo* with someone he knows. With the rest of the world, perhaps to make up for all this diffidence, he has less *enryo* than people of other nationalities, indeed is downright rude. Though this holding back, this standing on ceremony, can be infuriating to the Westerner, it remains one of the most admired traditional qualities of Japan, one widely celebrated on stage and screen.

Ozu's *enryo* however, is neither so strict nor so severe as that commonly exhibited, say, during the well-brought-up young lady's first visit to one's house. It is more akin to common good manners, and the restraint is motivated by fear (of responsibility, of making a mistake, etc., a major reason for the full *enryo*) than by a regard for others. It is a loveable quality, and one equally prized in the West. The difference is but one of degree. The Western host really expects his guests to make themselves at home, hence his urging; the Japanese expects no such thing, hence his urging.

This brings us to the greatest dichotomy in Japanese life, the schism between private and public behavior. Such a gulf exists in all cultures, to be sure, but in Japan is so broad as to be almost ludicrous. People rude to the point of barbarism in bus or subway will bow with the most polite, thoughtful, and fulsome of compliments if, on bus or subway or anywhere else, they meet someone they know. It is not pleasant to think of Setsuko Hara leaving her tea ceremony in *Late Spring,* boarding the train, and then stabbing unknowns with her parasol, or glaring at comfortable offenders until she has secured a seat, but it is not impossible either.

Ozu shows us only one side of this dichotomy, the studied politeness between Japanese who know each other. We are left to infer the other side. He is, as we have seen, similarly one-sided in presenting traditional Japan. For this he has been severely criticized by fellow Japanese, who see in his films only a reflection of genteel bourgeois values. But then Ozu is not trying to present a balanced view of Japanese character as a whole, he is trying to show us the reality of that aspect he is showing us. Just as he remained relatively uninterested in the changing social conditions of his country (one searches as vainly in his films for the great issues of his day as one searches for references to the Napoleonic Wars in the novels of Jane Austen),[53] so he is uninterested in a naturalistic picture of his people. He is interested, precisely, in the known, mundane, and certain society (which Japan also is), that can provide a frame for his observations on life, death, and other imponderables, a frame flexible enough to include the kind of melodrama that is occasionally seen in his pictures, but that firmly rests on an observed nature. For this reason, perhaps, almost all the characters in an Ozu film already know one another before the film begins. On the rare occasion that new people enter one of his pictures, they usually turn out to be the friends of someone we already know. It is a closed, self-sufficient world, governed by formal yet companionable *enryo*. Ozu's films are in this sense rather like parties, with host and guests conversing freely but politely, the main constraint being a mutual regard.

The Ozu set itself resembled a party. Nobuo Nakamura remembers that even during rehearsals, if it was a whiskey- or beer-drinking scene, actual whiskey or beer was served; if it was an eating scene, such delicacies as sea urchins were produced for the munching actors.[54] There were amenities and jokes and sometimes very funny monologues from Ozu himself, providing the entertainment for his party. It was such a pleasant and relaxed atmosphere, so different from the somewhat earnest if not desperate silences observed on the sets of other directors, both Eastern and Western, that the actors were usually agreed—later, at any rate—on what a good time they had had. There seems actually to have been less *enryo* on the set than in the films. Akira Kurosawa, who was very fond of Ozu and whose own early pictures had been rigorously defended by the older director, told Leonard Schrader how much he regretted that this aspect of Ozu did not more often find its way into his films; that he was so funny and so charming and so much himself that the formality of the Ozu *mise-en-scène* did not do justice to the man.[55] (Although this is undoubtedly true, it should also be observed that Kurosawa was a proven foe of *enryo* and all it stands for, i.e. its feudal associations, the seemingly willful abnegation of self involved, etc. Most of the humor of a film such as Kurosawa's *Sanjuro,* for example, results from watching *enryo* being undermined and then exploded.) One may imagine, however, that the party atmosphere on the Ozu set diminished once work had begun. Forcing an actor into exhaustion so he can achieve the properly toneless, expressionless reading does not sound like fun for anyone. When I visited the set for *Late Autumn,* Ozu was charming to everyone until the work began. We sat around and laughed, and he told stories until the lighting had been properly arranged (it was the Chuzenji hotel set). Ozu still kept the jokes coming after that, but as he worked with his actors a different atmosphere appeared. It resembled that of a school with Ozu as teacher, or of an operating room with Ozu as head surgeon. People became slightly more formal with one another, there was an air of self-consciousness (not displeasing to the Japanese), and at the same time a feeling of camaraderie and joint effort. I was not witness to such celebrated examples of the Ozu will as his forcing an actor to repeat the same line dozens of times, but I did observe that for a director he seemed unusually wary. He moved carefully, would scrutinize the scene with the same slightly quizzical expression one notices (in films at any rate) when the scientist is watching to see if the experiment will turn out all right. Once the shot was in the can, however, there were more smiles and jokes, and the somewhat rueful but pleased-with-himself air of the high school champion who has pulled off a difficult athletic feat. And through it all the dominant note was what seemed to me a limitless concern for everyone on that set with him.

For all these reasons—the early example of Lubitsch and other Americans, the observance of *enryo,* the deep feeling of regard—Ozu preferred the full-face shot so common in his pictures, so uncommon in the films of other directors. One may be more precise regarding the effect of this shot. We regard the full-face gaze (in our entertainment, at any rate) as disconcerting, and it is often successfully used to achieve just that effect.[56] Perhaps this was not always so (examples of early American films, including those of Lubitsch, suggest that it was not), but the conventions of film change, and at present such a shot is exceptional. That it is not exceptional in the Ozu film, that it is the norm, is precisely the point. In all his mature work, Ozu directed in particular the actor's face. We hear few stories of how Ozu told so-and-so to hold his hands or place his feet. That was left to the actor himself, and he responded in the natural manner of folding his feet under him and, if they were not otherwise occupied, clasping his hands. As we have seen, however, Ozu was extraordinarily careful about what was done with the inclination of the head, the mouth, and above all the eyes.[57]

The assumptions behind such an extraordinary way of directing actors are interesting for what they suggest about the Ozu film itself. Since we are not shown shuffling feet or nervously twisting hands, or bodies bent into the positions known to indicate various kinds of stress, etc., we are also not shown any involuntary or unconscious actions. When such an action does occur—the blank stare of surprise or disbelief, for example—its appearance is brief because the face always knows what it is doing, even if the hands and feet often do not. The underlying assumption of an Ozu film is that a person is always in control of himself. Although an actor may make a number of "unconscious" gestures such as rubbing his hip or stroking his nose or scratching his shin, in themselves they do not enable us to "read" his character. In this sense Ozu's actors never give themselves away. We are not allowed that vicarious and easy (and hence cheap) pleasure of knowing more about the character than he himself does. If we do indeed know more about him than he seems to, it is because of something he has consciously done, usually said, and not something that we (thanks to the director) have pounced upon. If we see through him it is, in a way, his own fault. But given this kind of character delineation, the whole question of fault never rises. We accept the character as he is; we do not perhaps accept completely his own evaluation of himself. And one of the reasons we accept him is that such a discrepancy is never put to any use—no story line ever turns on it, no plot complication ever evolves from it. Such a disparity exists because it exists in life.

When a character does exhibit emotion, that is, becomes unselfconscious enough to exhibit it, this marks the point of greatest tension in the film. The means are usually the same, tears. But the point is, of course, that the person knows he is crying; he would not know that he was wringing his hands and exhibiting "anguish" or "nervousness" or skin rash, or whatever we chose to read into an involuntary action. It is precisely because the act of crying is not involuntary (and we adults are responsible for our tears; we *choose* to cry) that we do not feel superior to the Ozu character. He does his own interpreting for himself; we are content merely to observe, without reaching for psychological explanations. In one sense, there is nothing to explain.

By looking us directly in the eye, as he does so often in the Ozu film that it comes to seem routine rather than disconcerting, the character appears before us as a fellow human being with his dignity intact; he is not at all the laboratory animal found in some films. Although an enormous amount of careful manipulation obviously has taken place (from the genesis of the character in the script, through the rigors of the actor impersonating him, to the editing of the final version), it is not the kind of manipulation common in other films. In fact, since the ends in view are so grand, and their realization so complete, one calls it not manipulation, but by its proper name: creation. Since the goal is presentation of the imponderables of life itself, one rarely senses the intervention of the director, just as one does not apply the word sentimental to movies that are so often "about" getting married. This is because Ozu makes us share his assumptions, which are, in the main, that people are fairly good, have their own dignity, are honest with themselves and others, and often display a beauty which is that of truth; they know the worst and can live with it.

One result is the extraordinary immediacy of the Ozu scene. The gaze compels belief. This is why we look hard at people when we want them to listen; this is why the practiced liar knows enough to look you straight in the eye. And it is for these reasons that we pay more attention during an Ozu film, that we sit straighter and try harder, that we in fact behave like the guests we are.

EDITING

O F THE THREE stages in the creation of a film, i.e., scriptwriting, shooting, and editing, Ozu considered editing the least important. Ideally, the film was finished when the scenario was done. Like the architect with his blueprint, the carpenter with his working-plans, and indeed the majority of film directors in all countries, Ozu considered the last stage an almost mechanical matter. Even while writing the dialogue script, as we have seen, he would sketch the way the scene would look when filmed. By the time a scene was written, he had already decided approximately how much time it would occupy on the screen.

Ozu thus differed dramatically from the kind of director who feels that editing is an important creative step in the making of a film. So far as one can tell, Ozu took none of the delight in the cutting of a film that Pudovkin and Eisenstein have recounted for us. For them, as well as for a number of other directors— Kurosawa and Ichikawa included—the editing stage is the point at which the film is created, the previously existing bits being only so much lifeless celluloid beneath their animating hand. Whatever the validity of such a claim, Ozu could or would not avail himself of its creative potential.

One reason was that editing, a process of selection, is so fraught with opportunities for editorializing. Editing, as has been pointed out often enough, offers the director his last and best opportunity to interpret his material. But, as we have seen, Ozu did not want to interpret; he wanted to present. Consequently there was for him only one way of editing, and this was by following the script. He followed it carefully and undeviatingly because the impact of his film depended on his realizing previously calculated effects, mainly those concerned with form and tempo. It is to his rigorous adherence to his own rules, among other things, that we owe the feeling of inevitability in the finished picture.

Since the form of the Ozu film is almost as invariable as that of any of the parts, one can begin by looking at the shape of the picture itself. More often than not it is circular: though any number of things may have happened, the film ends near where it began. As early as *Tokyo Chorus* this formal predilection is noticeable. In that film the opening scene is in the schoolyard, where the stu-

Tokyo Chorus. *1931. Kenji Oyama, Tokihiko Okada, Tatsuo Sato*

dents are singing their school song and the last boy makes a tardy appearance; the final scene is the reunion, where again the school song is heard and again the last boy (now an adult) comes in late.

There are many later examples: one might mention that both *Floating Weeds* and *The Story of Floating Weeds* begin and end in travel, *There Was a Father* and *Equinox Flower* begin and end with trains, etc. *The Only Son, The Record of a Tenement Gentleman, Late Spring,* etc., end in the same room where they began. The best-known example, of course, is *Tokyo Story.* At the beginning of the picture the grandparents are packing for their trip and the neighbor lady appears in the window; hers are among the first words in the picture, "Your children will be looking forward to your arrival." (1, 20.) At the end of the film the grandmother is dead and the grandfather is sitting in the same room; the same woman appears, again at the window, and says—the last words in the film—"You will be very lonely." (14, 1070.)

A circular form in film almost invariably results in a full, final, and completed feeling. Life has revolved, and we are back where we started but with a difference. Showing us this difference is the purpose of the film, and the definition of what we have experienced. It must be added, however, that Ozu was often not content merely to close the circle. Rather, he showed that the form was really spiral, often beginning a new if similar film in the final minutes. At the end of *Equinox Flower,* for example, the secondary story (the Kyoto girl's efforts to get married) is picked up and continued for a scene or two; in *Good Morning,* the fight among the housewives is patched up only to break out anew in the penultimate scene, etc. At the same time the new story, the one we see just the beginning of, is obviously going to resemble the one we have just seen. A spiral but otherwise unchanging pattern has been suggested. One begins to feel that there are very few situations in this world, and that one repeats and echoes another; one feels that these are archetypal situations (a description that certainly would never have occurred to Ozu), and that they are, to that extent, rituals. They serve, in part, as metaphors for the human situation. These are of course only feelings, and feelings are of course only unformed ideas. The realism, the naturalness, the spontaneity of the Ozu film prevent one from being very conscious of such feelings during the experience of the film, but they are there, and they help create the still and timeless feeling of Ozu's world.

If the film itself is often circular, the sequence is almost invariably so. It consists of but three kinds of shots, the classical three of primitive cinema: (1) the long shot, which is used to show solitude, precisely because it isolates, or humor, because it isolates and makes apprehendable, or aesthetic beauty, because it gets us far enough away to see it all; (2) the medium shot, which is the standard unit of the Ozu film, the "business" unit during which most of the action (i.e., dialogue) occurs; (3) the close-up, which is used for heightened moments, either with or without dialogue; it is used less frequently than the others and is never allowed to enlarge itself into the "big" close-up.

Each shot has its place within the Ozu sequence, and the order of the sequence is usually 1-2-3-2-1. That is, the camera begins in a far position, moves nearer, and then retreats to its original position. While this happens the business of the sequence is completed, and we move on to the next sequence. Musically, this form is analogous to the a-b-a pattern, simple binary form, one of the most immediate and satisfying formal experiences possible by reason (in films as in music) of its firm apprehensibility and perhaps also, though this is more metaphysical, by reason of its circularity. The circle, after all, is a balanced, continuous, geometrical form congenial to the human mind. This sequence in Ozu is like the paragraph (his films have no chapters), and within these paragraphs the shot then becomes the sentence. One reason for the satisfaction we feel both at the end of the Ozu film as a whole and at the conclusion of each of these paragraph-like sequences is that the circular form presupposes a return. The idea of the return, like the idea of the circle, is something we find emotionally compelling.

Again a musical example seems most apt. Mozart is master of the return because of the freshness, the surprise, the astonishing "newness" of the theme when he completes the return in a sonata-allegro or rondo. For one thing we are back in the home key, always a gratifying feeling; for another we return home (as in the finale of the *Jupiter Symphony*) doubly enriched because we gratefully return to the familiar and because that familiar is suffused with new beauty. A formal parallel between Mozart and Ozu is precise because the effect is rarely formalistic, as it is in some

John Huston films and some music by the sons of Bach. In Ozu's films we are led in circles by the dictates of the story, by our apprehension of its various patterns, and by a severe visual logic. With true art—the art that art conceals—Ozu triumphs in making a formal device *appear* natural. Perhaps the main reason for this is that the structure of the Ozu film is, on the terms the film itself establishes, so logical. There is a definite reason for each shot; remove one of them and you have a different, less satisfying picture. The logic in the Ozu continuity is in this sense extreme. Let us look, for example, first at the way Ozu introduces a sequence, and then at the way he moves us from one sequence to another.

From *Tokyo Chorus* on, the Ozu film invariably begins with a series of placing shots. These correspond roughly to the 1-2-3 pattern noticed within the sequence, and the effect is to lead directly to the place of the first sequence. Some examples are:

The Only Son: A close-up of a hanging oil lamp, the sound of a clock striking; a doorway through which is seen another lamp, people passing, another clock striking; a signboard, name of the factory where the mother works; inside the factory, mother working, the story begins.

The Brothers and Sisters of the Toda Family: A street along the wall of the family estate; a still life of plants and birds, later shown to be the father's; the lawn, cameras standing on tripods, ready to take the family's portrait; inside the house, the family, the story begins.

A Hen in the Wind: A gas tank; another gas tank at another angle; yet another gas tank, with a road and a house; inside the house, the mother, the story begins.

Late Spring: The Kita-Kamakura railway station, the sound of a railway bell; another view, nearer, the steps, daisies; a temple room; inside, the tea ceremony, the story begins.

Early Summer: The sea, a dog on the beach; a hill seen from a window in which a birdcage is hanging; a hallway, the sound of a music box; father feeding his birds, the story begins.

Early Spring: A large advertising sign and a small row of houses; another view, the whistle of a train; another view, showing tracks with a train coming; inside house, the couple asleep, the story begins.

163

Late Spring. *1949.*
Kuniko Miyake, Setsuko Hara (left)

Good Morning: Scene of a housing development, poles for laundry lines, high-tension wire; closer view, houses, alleys; farther view, schoolboys walking, the story begins.

Late Autumn: Tokyo Tower; the tower from farther away; a temple, sounds of cicadas; inside the temple, a character enters, the story begins.

An Autumn Afternoon: A Yokohama factory, white and red chimneys; the same scene seen from a window; an empty corridor; one of the characters at his desk, the story begins.

Such introductory scenes serve a number of functions. Most important, they draw the spectator from the general to the particular, making certain that we understand where we are and what the physical extensions of the characters are. We are also refreshed from time to time by repetitions of scenes like these. It becomes apparent from the examples above, however, that Ozu's method was not formalistic to the extent of his insisting upon an invariable 1-2-3 pattern. We move farther or nearer almost at random among these three shots because Ozu's concern is that we receive an impression of the place, and hence his method is properly impressionistic. We see what his characters see daily, and we are expected to react to and understand the kind of people they are.

An assumption here suggested by Ozu is one that always startles

164

the West: a man is where he is; his environment moulds his character, or induces those choices that taken together become his character. A more important assumption, however, is that unless we are thus shown the perimeters of this character, we cannot begin to understand him. Consequently, Ozu takes care in introducing us to his milieu, and once we are in it makes certain we never are lost.

There are some spectacular examples of Ozu's extraordinary care in this regard. The train ride in *Late Spring,* the taxi ride through Tokyo in *The Flavor of Green Tea over Rice,* the suburban train sequence in *Early Spring,* the bus tour in *Tokyo Story* —all are literal; that is, we recognize the stages along the way, the sequence is shot chronologically. The hiking sequence in *Early Spring* begins on the Shonan beach, with the island of Enoshima in the background. We then see the hikers progressing along the beach, their trip marked by various oddly shaped but not celebrated rocks, which only a person familiar with that stretch of coast would recognize, each precisely where it should be in relation to the progress of the hikers. The train ride in *Late Spring* is even more impressive. The line itself runs through Kita-Kamakura, Ofuna, Totsuka, Yokahoma, and ends in Tokyo. The sequence is as follows:

Kita-Kamakura station, people waiting
The train pulling away, entering the tunnel
Inside train, emerging from tunnel
Inside train, father and daughter are standing
Scene from train window, the stretches between Kita-Kamakura
    and Ofuna
Daughter standing
Father, sitting, offers daughter his seat
She smiles and refuses
Train entering Ofuna
Inside train, view of the Ofuna Kannon monument passing
Father and daughter both sitting, both reading
She looks out window onto outskirts of Totsuka
Several scenes during which they talk
Inside train, Totsuka station passing from view
Train, passing outskirts of Yokohama-Hodogaya

Yokohama, train vanishes from sight
The Hattori building on Ginza in Tokyo, train music stopping
with this stationary image.

This may seem a simple thing, such chronological travel shooting, but it is not. Action and dialogue must be synchronized as if
to a passing background, the stages of which must be noted. All
this must be presented in sequence, to convey the feeling of a
journey. The trip may be shortened (in actuality the trip from
Kita-Kamakura to Tokyo takes one hour, half of which is occupied by the Yokohama-Tokyo run, not shown in this three-minute
sequence), but its essence must be there. Most directors do not
consider such sequential shooting important. They shoot various
scenes at various places and various times and then somehow
make it work in the editing. That it usually does not work is, of
course, a fact well known. We have all seen examples of impossible
journeys made by consequently impossible characters. When this
kind of sequential shooting is brought off in Western cinema, as in
the celebrated walk through midtown Manhattan in *The French
Connection,* the sequence is widely and properly applauded. Ozu,
however, can be counted on to do this, out of a rare regard for
visual truth. His reasons are obvious. If we are to believe his film
we must believe all of it; if we are to believe in his characters then
they must live in believable surroundings.

There are, however, additional reasons for the placing shots and
sequences in Ozu's films. Used between sequences, they form transitions, a use that will be examined later; used as part of a sequence, or as a sequence in themselves, they often carry the double burden of moving us from one place to another and commenting
on the theme of the film.

The opening of *Early Spring* consists of fifty-some shots (see pp.
87–92.) The first, as mentioned earlier, introduces the milieu of
the main character's home, and we enter the house to see him and
his wife waking up. When he finally gets out of bed and goes to the
window, we see what he sees, the road leading to the station.
There follows a series of shots that show the office workers
streaming into the city. We see them waiting for the suburban train,
the main character now among them, and follow them to Tokyo
Station. The final shot in this sequence is an overhead scene of the

station plaza. This is revealed as seen from an office window, the window of the main character's office; he is now at his desk, talking to one of his co-workers. The sequence ends with a scene of the clock; it is a little after nine, time to go to work.

This opening is a sustained experience that moves us from one pole of the character's life (home) to another (office), and does so in a careful and logical manner. Temporally it has moved us about two hours since he got up at seven, and has also shown us the texture of his life by indicating that this is what he does every day. Moreover, and this is of equal importance, Ozu has shown us that this is what all white-collar workers do. We have seen them, hundreds of them, on their way to work. It is but one repetition out of the thousands which make up their lives that we have seen, and yet in a sense we have seen them all. By showing us this single two-hour period of the morning in such a laconic and detached manner, with nothing at all irregular or dramatic occurring along the way, Ozu successfully evokes at the very beginning of his pictures one of his major themes: the boredom and meaninglessness of such a life.

Equally effective but more subtle are the scenes that make up the final minutes of *Tokyo Story* (see pp. 78–86). Here Ozu confronts a different problem. The story itself must be concluded, and at the same time a feeling of sameness, or ordinariness, of this kind of thing happening naturally and often within the context of life must be suggested. The grandfather, left alone after the death of his wife, is telling his daughter-in-law that she should forget his son, her dead husband, and remarry. She weeps. Ozu cuts to a schoolhouse and the sound of children singing. After the establishing shot of an empty corridor we see the youngest daughter teaching school. She looks out the window and we see what she sees: a train pulling away from Onomichi where they live. The next shot is not of the interior of the train, but of the father alone. Then, in the next shot, we see the train as it moves away. Only then is the daughter-in-law seen, sitting in the train and looking straight ahead. This is followed by a scene of the port at Onomichi very similar to the one that began the film.

The order of the shots and their relative length suggest more than the story has suggested. If Ozu were merely photographing the story, the order would be different: we would see the younger daughter looking out the window, then the train, then the daughter-in-law in the train, then back to the daughter, etc. Ozu has inserted views of the father and the port within this sequence. There are four "subjects" to the sequence rather than two, and around these four the rest of the sequence revolves. Only after the port shot do we return to the daughter in the window; then we cut to the father and the neighbor lady, a scene followed by three shots of the father alone, the last from farther away than the others, and two more shots of the port, the second farther away and, again, very much like the shot that opened the picture. We are given, in other words, only two shots of the daughter in the window and one (long) shot of the daughter-in-law in the train, yet this is the ostensible story of the picture, this is where the drama supposedly lies. Twice as many shots are used to illustrate the nondramatic, i.e., the father sitting alone, as he will until he dies, and the port of Onomichi, an extension of the father, but one that has played no part in the film at all. Another director making this film might well have included a shot of the man alone, but it is, I think, only Ozu who would have refused to console himself with a final shot of the daughter-in-law going off into a happier future. His reasons are apparent. Not only does Ozu not believe in this consolation, or in any happier future, he also refuses to compromise his theme, the illustration of which logically leads us to this last survivor of the family as it was.

By ending the drama (the daughter-in-law) before he ends the film, by returning to the father, by showing us the by-now familiar port shots, which reoccur like closing chords in this final coda, by referring, finally, to the larger context of city, sea, mountains, he also suggests that what we are seeing occurs every day, that it is common, that it has happened before and will happen many times over, that it is the way of the world. The dissolution of this family, the transience of this world, the disappointment of this life— this is the theme of *Tokyo Story,* and this is what Ozu has illustrated in these final frames.

Ozu's "empty" or nondramatic shot, which we have so far seen used as introduction, as conclusion, as establishing, as commenting, has a number of other functions. Perhaps most often such shots are used as transitions. The passage from one place to another in the films of Ozu is always direct and economical, but it is not unvarying. Just as the opening milieu of a film is shown in a series of three stationary and empty scenes, so changes of milieu are usually indicated by two shots. The first shows us an outside view of the place we have just been, the second an outside view of the place we are going. There are so many of these transitional pairs in Ozu's films that a listing would require inordinate space and add little to what the reader could readily observe for himself on seeing almost any Ozu picture.

These paired scenes, however, are not the director's only method of transition. Early in his career he several times used the time lapse. In *That Night's Wife* we watch night give way to day in a dawn sequence lasting only three or four seconds, with the light spreading over a still life that includes the window; in *The Only Son* he uses the same effect to the same end, daybreak; and in *Passing Fancy* we see a five-second sunset, the light fading from a still life of the father's clothes hanging on the wall. He also used objects for transitions. In *That Night's Wife* we see the head policeman playing with his gloves behind his back, a close-up; the same gloves, in close-up, are slammed down on a desk at headquarters. In the same film we move into close-up to watch the hero tie his shoes, then cut to a close-up of his wife's shoes as she lies on the bed, worrying. This unexceptional cutting, part of everyone's cinematic vocabulary during the 1920's and 1930's, Ozu "gave up." He retained the logic of such cutting, but instead of using the subjectivity of director or audience (the close-up), he used that of the character, what he did or what he saw.

A very direct transition of this sort occurs in *Early Spring*. The wife of the main character has had an argument with her husband and leaves the house early. She walks down the road, passing the house of one of his friends. The friend, painting a doghouse out in the yard, looks up and greets her. He goes into the house and his wife looks out, noting that her neighbor has gone by. We thereafter stay with this new couple and do not follow the angry wife. This simple, conservative device has moved us neatly from one scene to the next. More often the same effect is achieved by the simple cut. In *The Munekata Sisters* we are told that the father is dying of cancer; the daughter, hearing this, bows her head; the father at

169

home, apparently healthy, is talking to the younger sister. Association has moved us naturally and quickly from one scene to the next. In *Good Morning* the little boys are talking about the natural ability to fart. One of them says his father is wonderful, a real expert. We cut to the father sitting in a chair reading the newspaper; after a while he obligingly farts. In the first reel of *An Autumn Afternoon* there is a scene at the ballpark; we cut to a Ginza restaurant where the same game is being watched on television. In *Early Summer* the family is at the Kabuki, and we watch them enjoying it; we cut to a room in the friend's house where the two girls are listening to the same performance over the radio.

Since we experience only what the characters are experiencing, this kind of transition appears both logical and natural, something that arbitrarily chosen objects (pairs of feet and the like) do not. Often, too, the transitional device is not only something the characters see, but also something they hear. The second reel of *Tokyo Twilight* finds brother and sister in the eel shop with the clock striking the hour; cut to the clock at the railway station, milieu of the new scene, showing that it is just one o'clock. Often, time alone occupies an otherwise empty stretch at the end of the scene, and in this way prepares us for a transition. In *What Did the Lady Forget?* we wait for the clock to strike three before going into the following scene. In *Early Spring* Noriko has left her girlfriend's house but we stay behind to watch and hear the large grandfather clock strike 3:45—a rather lengthy Big Ben sequence. In *The Munekata Sisters* we have to watch the blinking sign of the Bar Accacia coffee shop for five seconds (it lights for one second; we watch it on three times, off twice) before we can continue. In *Early Summer* the family leaves the room and we stay behind to listen to the clock strike ten. In *Late Autumn* we stay behind at the funeral to listen for the second stroke of the drum. One might call these indeterminate transitions. We do not know what is coming next, but we know that something is and we consequently prepare ourselves for it. Such scenes are common in the works of many directors, of course. As transitions they are particularly effective for Ozu's purposes because they do not direct our attention, but merely invite it.

The other function of the indeterminate transition, as of many of the empty scenes in Ozu's films, is logical in that the next scene shows the characters engaged in an activity that it would have taken them some time to get to. While the film time of any of these empty end scenes never duplicates the time it would actually take the characters to move from one place to another, the imposed waiting interval suffices. We are prepared for something new after even a few seconds of empty screen.

This may explain some otherwise inexplicable scenes in Ozu's films. Perhaps the best known is the scene, otherwise empty, of the big soft drink sign during the bicycle ride along the Shonan beach, in *Late Spring*. Noriko and the young man have been having a conversation; we cut to a long scene of the soft drink sign, and then to the two of them wheeling their bicycles along the beach. Ozu needed time to get them from the highway to the beach, and he got it by showing us a large sign in the interval. This method of construction is by no means unknown in the works of other directors, but there it often occurs because they have made some error in continuity and have, fortunately, enough "free" footage that they can cut away and thus save the continuity. In the films of Ozu such scenes are included in the finished script. The sign is essential, not incidental, because it is actually there, where the characters are. It, too, is part of the environment; it, too, exists.

Throughout his career Ozu has also used objects as transitional devices. The scene in *Woman of Tokyo* in which the brother discovers his sister's prostitution ends with a shot of the tea kettle in his room, which is followed by a direct cut to the hand basin in the whorehouse. Water (possibly to be thought of in its lustral capacity) thus serves as a transitional device, though its effectiveness is considerably weakened when Ozu reverses the sequence in returning to the brother. In the same film the girlfriend is called to the phone while entertaining the sister. Left alone, the sister looks around the room and sees a large clock, of which we then see a close-up, followed by a cut to a whole wall of clocks. It transpires that the friend is taking her telephone call in a clock shop. Again the sequence is reversed to get us back to the room. This weakens the device by making it so obviously formalistic, but in this case the transition was very weak to begin with. One feels at once that the call from the clock shop is only a flimsy pretext for the clock transition. A similar transitional device is used more successfully in *The Only Son* to get us from the house to the school and back. In this film the pivot object is a sleeping baby. We see the baby asleep, then a long sequence at the school, then the baby asleep again. The effect is considerably heightened because the baby never once wakes up during the entire film; it is always and simply asleep.

At other times the same technique is used with greater discretion and economy. In *The Brothers and Sisters of the Toda Family* there is a beautiful and logical transition composed entirely of objects. The family is worrying about the ailing father, and they sit on pillows in a kind of grouped still life while we hear a clock ticking. We cut to a number of hats, each perched on a *zabuton* pillow (indicating a formal occasion with a number of people attending), and, replacing the clock, the beating of a drum: the father has died and this is his funeral. In *There Was a Father,* the tragedy with which the film begins is set forth in a series of five shots (four beautifully managed transitions) that occupies only about ten seconds of screen time: the boys rush out of the boarding hotel by the lake; they run along the pier; a grove with funeral markers and grave stones; an overturned boat; the funeral itself. We are never shown the drowned children. Instead, we are shown first a graveyard and then the boat in which they drowned, and then, almost before this can register, a long shot of the funeral during which everything we have experienced in this ten seconds sinks in, all the more deeply felt for the elliptical yet logical manner of presentation.

The object-as-transition device is put to elaborate use in *A Story of Floating Weeds.* We have seen that the young man, son of the itinerant actor, rides a bicycle. This vehicle becomes a pivot for transitions throughout the film. The first occurs when the boy meets the girl he will later probably marry. He is on the bike talking to the girl; the girl moves away, smiles; the bicycle on its stand at home; a scene with the boy and his mother. The second such sequence is composed of a scene in the house; the bicycle as last seen; girl and boy (bikeless) by the railway track. The third occurs after the boy has run off with the girl: the bicycle at home as before and the boy's empty desk; his mother, worried. The bicycle makes its final appearance at the end of the film: the vehicle is in another room, the room is dark, some kind of storeroom; other shots of the empty house; the station, and on to the final sequence.

Like so many objects in Ozu's films, the bicycle serves not just as a transitional device, but for a multiplicity of purposes. Its last appearance in particular serves to suggest that the boy has grown up, that the bicycle will be ridden no more, that adults do not ride bicycles. It also serves as a pivot between outdoor and indoor scenes, as a transition to and from the boy, and as a sign of his presence or absence. The emotional effect of such linkages, however, is ambiguous. If it were another director's film one would conclude that something involving the bicycle will happen; maybe its chain will come off and the boy will crash. This being an Ozu film, we expect nothing of the sort. At the same time the bicycle has become redolent with meaning, and if it does not mean trouble, what does it mean? The question is never answered because it is not one Ozu would ask.

The bicycle in this film, like the objects in so many of Ozu's pictures, is a container of emotion. That is, in addition to its other functions it serves also as a focal point for aroused emotions. For it to serve this purpose, however, the object must be free of all ostensible directorial purpose. Otherwise it would not contain emotion, it would discharge it. This emotion, of course, is neither Ozu's nor that of his characters, but the emotion which has been generated in the spectator himself.

Consequently these shots are empty of both people and apparent intention, and they are therefore in themselves ambiguous. Though their use is not unknown in the West and in the East forms part of the vocabulary of traditional art, their use in Ozu is both particular and personal.[1] These empty scenes form a hiatus not only because they deliberately create a pause, "a break with a part missing," but because they do so within a context—the art of film —that presumes all parts complete, all scenes filled. Empty scenes thus create a major aesthetic paradox. "The blank sheet of paper is perceived only as paper, and remains as paper; . . . only by filling the paper does it become empty," Will Peterson has written.[2] If one fills in a corner of the paper, as did the painters of the early Sung, the unfilled portion is filled as well—filled with space, which comments on the corner, gives it body, and creates its context. Similarly, as in the formal Japanese flower arrangement, not only the sprays themselves but the space between them is considered part of the finished work. This is the concept of *mu*— emptiness and silence are a part of the work, a positive ingredient. It is silence which gives meaning to the dialogue that went before; it is emptiness which gives meaning to the action that went before.

This meaning, however, is one which the spectator himself must supply. His choices are limited in the pictorial arts, but in the temporal arts such as film the choices are as wide as he is deep. In an art the context of which is visual experience, he must continue to experience; though faced with emptiness he must choose to experience the empty scene. The effect is one of statis, a literal "standing still," through which he himself must move.

It is in this sense, then, that Ozu's still lifes and otherwise empty scenes become containers for our emotions. The image of the vase in the darkened room to which Ozu returns at the end of *Late Spring* serves not only to bridge the transition between Setsuko Hara equitable and Setsuko Hara near tears, but also to contain and to an extent create our own emotions. Empathy is not the key here. To be sure we do imaginatively project our own consciousness onto another being, but this is perhaps a secondary effect. Primary to the experience is that in these scenes empty of all but *mu,* we suddenly apprehend what the film has been about, i.e., we suddenly apprehend life. This happens because such scenes occur when at least one important pattern in the picture has become clear. In *Late Spring* the daughter has seen what will happen to her: she will leave her father, she will marry. She comes to understand this precisely during the time that both we and she have been shown the vase. The vase itself means nothing, but its presence is also a space and into it pours our emotion. The shot of the vase is a long one, lasting some ten seconds, and it is one that "can accept deep, contradictory emotion and transform it into an expression of something unified, permanent, transcendent." [3] It can do this precisely because it is empty of everything else and because it is so placed (a pattern recognized because it has concluded) that our own emotion, so carefully dammed by Ozu throughout most of the film, is allowed finally to escape. The emotional surge one feels at the end of such films as *Late Spring, Tokyo Story, An Autumn Afternoon,* and many others is not attributable solely to empathy with the character we are watching. By constructing his works in this oblique fashion, Ozu has ensured that we sense something larger than the emotion we are both seeing and feeling, that at the same time we become aware of the universality of all emotion—in short that we feel something of the texture of life itself and again know that we are a part of this universal fabric. Empathy is thus transformed into an appreciation, and experience into personal expression.

Ozu would probably not have disagreed with the foregoing discussion, but he would certainly have questioned the necessity of putting it all down. For him as for all good film directors, the experience of the film was the most important thing. He himself never spoke of *mu,* or *mono no aware,* though he knew what they meant, and I doubt he would ever have seriously discussed them. Indeed there is a question (a not very important one, to be sure) whether Ozu "knew" what he was doing. One possible answer is that the kind of mentality that framed the concept of *mu* had much in common with the one that created *Late Spring* (just as the kind of mentality that created the Kabuki resembles the one that created the sword-fight film, which allows innocent critics to speak of the Kabuki's influence on the Japanese cinema when, in fact, none exists). The question becomes more interesting, however, when one examines the way Ozu created his pictures, and in particular the way he put his scenes together. Sometimes the "empty" codas are written into the final script (see pp. 102 for the notebooks for *An Autumn Afternoon*), but more often the finished film is different from both the early drafts and the printed script (see p. 78, *Tokyo Story*).

Ozu seems to have "known" when the various empty scenes and still lifes would have their finest effect, would most forward the emotion he was both delineating and creating. The long close-up of the vase in *Late Spring,* for example, is not in the original script for that picture. It was something that was added later. Its proper length and position, while not a matter of improvisation —nothing in Ozu's films was—were something that became apparent only during the course of creating the film. Ozu might be said to have "felt" the proper length and position of this and many other such shots. Certainly, his editing methods were largely a matter of "feeling." Hamamura says that Ozu never looked at the movieola in determining scene length. "He'd look up at the ceiling, absent-minded-like." He would then estimate the necessary length of the scene and Hamamura would compare Ozu's figure with the one written down in the continuity script. In most cases they were roughly the same, but in some they were quite different. "He did this so often and with such relish that I think it was one of the things he liked most about editing." [4]

Ozu's feeling for necessary length of scene was peculiar, uniquely his. Hamamura remembers the director seeing *High Noon*. During the sequence in which close-ups of the actors alternate with close-ups of the clock, Ozu suddenly asked how long that clock scene was. Hamamura replied about six feet (the clock having ticked off four seconds), and Ozu nodded, saying he liked that effect very much and next time he would use it. It was not the content of the shot he had liked, but its length.

In determining scene length Ozu made use of several conventions he had evolved. The three introductory or placing scenes were usually of a common length, between six and eight seconds. The same sort of scenes used as a divider between sections of the script were a bit shorter. The various still lifes, emblematic shots such as signboards, lanterns, details of the environment (called "curtain shots" by critic Keinosuke Nanbu because he thought Ozu used them much as a stage director uses a theatrical curtain),[5] were of various lengths depending on their function. The usual "Ginza" shot of coffee-shop and bar signs is sometimes as short as four seconds; the vase in *Late Spring,* on its first appearance, is on the screen for ten seconds.

Another convention that assisted Ozu in editing was the length of the conversation scenes. In most films such shots are cut directly after the line is finished—one cut, one line. Ozu, however, usually continued such scenes past the point of silence, letting the camera run after conversation stops. In a film such as *The Only Son* the conversations are punctuated with periods of silence, up to two seconds long, after each speech. This gives an air of importance, of weight, to almost any conversation, as though replies were being pondered, and contributes to the serious, occasionally even bleak, atmosphere of this film. Usually, however, certainly in most of the later films, Ozu allowed only a second or half-second to elapse between the end of the speech and the end of the shot. Hamamura attributed the change to television, the medium where everything is run into everything else. Ozu reasoned, he said, that television had taught people to accept more and to think faster, and that it was therefore no longer necessary to give the audience two whole seconds to ponder each line. The result is a normally moving conversation with just a slight lag at the end of each line. It is a tempo that both fits and in part creates the feeling of the finished Ozu picture.

The tempo that is thus created is one often described as "too slow," and not only by the hurried West. In 1936 Yoshitaro Omori, a critic otherwise forgotten, wrote of *The Only Son,* "A tempo this slow is equivalent to no tempo at all." [6] Yet Ozu's tempo, while unusually slow for film, is common enough in music or drama. An Ozu-like tempo is considered the crowning achievement of the Bruckner slow movements, and a very Ozu-like "sequence" is found in the last section of Mahler's *Das Lied von der Erde.* "People say Ozu has no tempo," says Sato, "but he does, only it is his own." It is slow and regular, and eventually, says Sato, one recognizes it: the tempo of the Ozu film is, largely, the tempo of the dialogue. [7] This accurate observation is yet another indication of the primacy of dialogue in the Ozu picture. Ozu apparently thought so too. One of the few times Ozu ever lost his temper on the set was in response to a tactless question about shot length. Hisaya Morishige, a famous comedian and an excellent actor, was hired to play the man looking for an eligible wife in the opening scenes of *The End of Summer.* After a few days' shooting, when he and Ozu were drinking together, he began to complain playfully about the short shots in Ozu's sequences. "They are only ten or twenty seconds each," he remembers saying. Then he asked Ozu, "Isn't this because Shochiku actors are so bad that you have to keep cutting? We at Toho can go on for two or three minutes if you let us." [8] It was an unfortunate remark. Ozu got up and left, and though he soon returned, temper under control, Morishige is certain to this day that Ozu was deeply offended.

Perhaps Ozu was angered by this unwarranted slur on people he had worked with for years, perhaps he was having enough trouble already with an entirely new staff (that of Toho), or perhaps he was simply tired of being told he had no tempo.

In cutting as in everything else, Ozu's technique had but one object—the revelation of character. Consequently his waiting, listening camera records not the heights of emotion (not usually at any rate), but those moments, those signs, that both precede and follow such moments, these little tropisms through which believable emotion is to be apprehended. The "portraits" he thus achieves are almost entirely responsible for the emotional richness of the Ozu world.

One might examine one of them within its own context, noticing the order of the shots. This is the scene at the Noh drama in *Late Spring*. Ozu wanted to show the daughter becoming aware of her father's interest in another member of the audience, a widow. He wished to show the daughter's becoming convinced that the fa-

Late Spring. *1949.*
Setsuko Hara, Chishu Ryu

178

ther intends to remarry. Because some very delicate and indefinite feelings are involved, Ozu eschews dialogue; rightly, he wanted to show rather than state. The only sounds during the entire sequence are those of the Noh itself. Yet the anecdotal point of this three-minute sequence occupies only a fraction of those three minutes. The rest of the time we watch the father, his delight in the Noh. The sequence runs as follows:

Medium shot of Setsuko Hara and Chishu Ryu at the theater watching the Noh
The Noh play itself
Long shot of the audience including Hara and Ryu
Close-up of Ryu's pleased face
Medium shot of the actors in the Noh, the *shite* (main actor), etc.
Medium shot of the *waki* (second actor) and the chorus
Medium shot of Hara and Ryu
The play
Medium shot of the actors
Long shot of the play
Ryu, he bows to someone
Hara, she looks, then nods
Kuniko Miyake, she bows in return
Hara and Ryu, she turns to look at her father
Miyake watching the play
Hara, her eyes downcast
Medium shot of Hara and Ryu
Close-up of Hara, again looking at Ryu
Close-up of Ryu pleased with the play
Close-up of Hara, sad
Close-up of Miyake watching the play
Close-up of Hara, sadder
Long shot of the audience, including Hara and Ryu
Long shot of the play
Close-up of Hara, sad, bowing her head
A tree in the wind, the music of the Noh continuing

Ozu used twenty-six shots to achieve the effect he wanted. There is not one wasted moment; each scene follows the other with a rigorous visual logic. Both before and after the anecdotal point of this sequence is made, the camera stays with the father, whose supreme delight in the Noh (and our delight in his) is the real, the emotional, point of the scene. Thus we have an anecdotal point that is disquieting (the daughter's fears) and an emotional point that is reassuring (the father's delight). One answers the other, and a less worried daughter would have seen that the Noh meant much more to her father than the lady across the way. Something is revealed about both his character and hers, something that could not be said, but had to be observed.

This sequence could have been constructed with about five shots, one for each character, and one or two for the play itself. The central point would have been that the daughter does not want the father to marry. It would have been made rapidly, and we would then be rushed to the next sequence. By the end of the film we would probably have forgotten the entire incident, or remembered it only as a plot complication. As it stands, however, this sequence in *Late Spring* is unforgettable. This is because Ozu has added shot after shot as a painter would apply brush strokes, each one contributing to the final impression. Further, he edited not to contrast scenes but to compare them, to create an incremental structure in which scenes sustain one another. In doing so, he created a feeling of actuality, he forwarded his story, and he took the amount of time we needed both to be convinced of what was happening and to apprehend the event's emotional effects on father and daughter. Finally, but perhaps most important, by creating that final image of the tree in the wind covered by the music of the Noh, he created a rare conjunction of a physical and spiritual state. It is this effect which director Yasuzo Masumura described when he said that "most Japanese directors are realistic. Consequently they always exaggerate. Ozu is different. . . . Each of the shots may be uninteresting, but their rhythm is something like that of ripples or waves, and from their conjunction a mood arises." [9]

In the creation of such a sequence, the crucial factor is the placement of the cut. In this sequence, as in so many of Ozu's films, the point at which the shot ends determines the meaning of the shot. Here, as usual, Ozu places his cut after the emotional point, not the anecdotal point, is made. Just as he often stations his camera and then waits for conversation to begin, using mid-close-ups only when the character is speaking (which has led Sato to observe that the Ozu camera never enters the drama; it enters just like a member of the audience and waits for the drama to begin),[10] so Ozu rarely cuts directly away from either action or dialogue. He waits for his characters to fall into repose, whether it be the one second or so of repose after a single dialogue line or those long scenes of hiatus in which the character sits and observes the weather, or looks at nothing at all.

Though Ozu sometimes connects shots by cutting on movement,[11] a technique that the Japanese call "American" and that is supposed to render the cut "invisible" but never does, more usually his camera remains on its subject until all motion has stopped. Only in moments of great emotion (the weeping in *Late Spring* and *Tokyo Story,* the atypical "romantic" kiss in *Early Spring*) does Ozu cut from a continuing action. And here one feels that if it is discretion that keeps his camera rolling, it is also discretion that, in these scenes, cuts it off. In his cutting, too, Ozu once again refuses to exploit his characters, either by prolonging scenes of intense emotion or by ruthlessly clipping off their film life in the interests of what is called a tight film.

The tempo of the Ozu film, then, is not nonexistent, but it is extremely subtle. "Tempo" usually refers to the rate of speed at which a passage moves, but in film the idea of tempo is complicated by the content of the shot: an empty shot seems to move more slowly than a shot filled with action, even if it is the same length. For this reason cinema tempo is sometimes divided into clock time and psychological time. Ozu's time is not clock time, though many of his sequences would have taken in life the same amount of time they take on the screen. His conversations, for example, are composed of a number of shots all about the same length (the length depending entirely upon the length of the spoken line), but the effect (perhaps because of the "empty" waits before and after dialogue) is not that of clock time at all. In keeping with Ozu's goal of character delineation, the effect becomes that of psychological time. As the characters experience film time, so do we.

We have already examined Ozu's preoccupation with clocks and with sitting and listening to the hours strike in otherwise empty scenes. Time is there, staring at us, but its effect is not that of the raw seconds passing. Since we see it from the viewpoint of the characters themselves, we can only view it as *their* present; since we believe in them we consequently believe in it. And it is quite different from the time ticking away on our wrist. The tempo of the Ozu film is, indeed, somewhat like the regular ticking of a clock. The scenes tick off like seconds, one following the other at a nearly inevitable pace. There is no fast cutting, though there are a number of long scenes that remain uncut. Whatever else it may be used for, tempo is not being used to manipulate our emotions.

If the scenes are all more or less the same length, then our appreciation of the Ozu tempo must come from the content of the shot itself. Indeed, a revolutionary aspect of the Ozu style is precisely that the tempo is almost entirely psychological tempo, and is created by what is in the shot. An analogy with music, another temporally mysterious art, may make the point clear. The pattern shown below is not invariable in the Ozu picture, but it occurs often enough to generalize on the basis of it.

1. the placing shot, often with nothing in it, or the establishing shot, with the characters in repose—a long shot ... *largo*

2. the people, movements, the beginning of the action—often a medium shot ... *moderato assai*

3. dialogue, the anecdotal point—close-ups ... *allegro*

4. the after-talk, moving away from the anecdotal point—sometimes close-ups, sometimes medium shots ... *allegretto*

5. the return to repose but with a difference, the emotional point, gradual silence, gradual emptiness, or both ... *poco a poco larghetto*

It will be apparent that just as the visual form of the Ozu sequence is, as we have observed, the binary a-b-a, so the temporal form of the sequence is slow-fast-slow, even though the actual scene lengths may be all approximately the same. This pattern is reinforced by Ozu's actual use of sound and music in his films.

All the sound except the music is naturalistic in Ozu, but the extremely detailed sound track is carefully patterned. One remembers hearing over and over again in *Late Spring* the sound of the doorbell that rings when the front door is slid open, or the underlying panting of the gas works in *A Hen in the Wind*. It is their realism that keeps us from recognizing these aural patterns as such. Only rarely does Ozu use sound symbolically. An unsuccessful example occurs in *A Hen in the Wind*. When the husband meets the young whore in the house where his wife once went, the children in the school next door ("Isn't it funny—I went to that school when I was little," says the girl) strike up a song rather too hopeful and innocent. A successful example of the same kind is the children's song at the end of *Tokyo Story*, where it creates whatever feeling of hope this film allows to remain and at the same time suits the context of the younger sister's school teaching. A supremely successful example is the sound of the clock at the end of *Late Spring*, which becomes louder and louder throughout the final scene of the father sitting and peeling the fruit, an effect that finally sounds almost threatening and, at the same time, makes us realize that the father now has only time left him.

And just as different locations give rise to different conversations, so different circumstances give rise to different sounds. One of the most common of these commenting sounds is music going on somewhere else. Troubled scenes as different as an argument scene in *Good Morning* and the death-bed scene in *Early Spring* have the same background, someone several apartments away engaging in vocal practice. I once told someone that Ozu's ideal music was someone next door practicing Mozart, and only much later became aware that such a "typical" scene in fact occurs—in *Late Autumn*.

Like incidental sound, music in the Ozu film is used in an ordained and invariable manner. The quality of the music is, to be sure, troubling to the Western ear. It is almost invariably four-square, vapid, sweet to an uncommon degree, and sounds, to us, a dreadful combination of old-fashioned salon music and hymns played on a harmonium. It sounds this way to the Japanese as well, but for them it is pleasant in its expectedness and reassuring in its sentiment. It is also a known genre: one may buy recordings of this kind of music, now known as "home music." This musical gravy is poured over *Tokyo Story* and *The Munekata Sisters* alike. Only three Ozu films have different kinds of scores: *Good Morning* has a light neoclassical score, complete with overture; *Floating Weeds* has a pleasantly atmospheric score with marimba, accordion, and xylophone; *The End of Summer* has a portentous and inflated score by the only "serious" composer Ozu ever used Toshiro Mayuzumi—he also scored *Good Morning*. Otherwise it is all sweetness and hack orchestration. One might make a slight case for its use: there is, after all, a large public that also likes music boxes and grandfather clocks (both of which appear in Ozu's pictures), and it is, or was, the music of the haute-bourgeoisie. Or, one might find that this is, after all, the kind of music used to accompany silent films, and if Ozu was influenced by Rupert Julien, let us say, he would also be influenced by the kind of music that, in Japan as in America, accompanied a Julien film. Or, one might speak of "alienation effect," the irony of the almost hopeless ending of *Tokyo Story,* for example, being slowly covered by this shroud of mindless saccharine sound. Or, one might remember that Ozu had a tin ear, like most Japanese directors, and in any event regarded the sickly *Träumerei* of Schumann as a "favorite" piece of music. One might consider all this, but the explanation that rings truest lies at hand.

Ozu used to tell his composer, usually Kojun Saito, the house man at Shochiku, to "make it like last time." In other words, Ozu didn't really much care what it sounded like, or whether it was any good or not. For Ozu, music was simply another unit in his module-built film. And its use is invariable. There is title music, always sounding the same, just as the burlap-backing of the titles was always the same; it dies away after the first scene and is replaced by naturalistic sounds. Once the picture has started, music invariably is used only for bridging sequences. Almost anything would do: *The Only Son* uses *Old Black Joe.* At the end of the picture, over the final sequence, the music (usually the same themes as the title music) rises up again and achieves a climax over the end title.

All aspects of an Ozu film, then, dialogue, scene, sequence, sound, were patterned; they were module-like units. Each has its own reason, but they have in common the a-b-a binary pattern, the pattern that returns to its original statement. We have seen that this controls not only the sequence, but the larger form of the film itself. It is a pattern that imposes itself upon the material, no matter what the material is; it is a pattern that renders Ozu's films all more or less alike, in intent at any rate.

One reason Ozu can successfully impose such a pattern upon his material, can do so, that is, without falsifying, is that the sequence pattern is *not* the story pattern, as we have seen with respect to the final sequence of *Tokyo Story* and the Noh-watching sequence in *Late Spring*. The higher authority in Ozu's picture is the unvarying structure of the film itself, and not, as in most films, story or plot. For Ozu is not concerned with explanation, not concerned with the past, with what went before—which is always in itself a kind of explanation or apology. He is interested in the *now,* in the present moment, this very instant, and the reality that this implies.[12] Perhaps this apparent paradox—a rigid structural system allowing for a reality that implies the instant now—is the paradox underlying all the art we know as formal or classical. Certainly the immediacy of the Byzantine mosaic portraits is occasioned in part by the rigor and sameness of their patterns; certainly much of the joy of a Bach fugue is caused by the inflexible rules of fugue-writing itself, just as part of the magical realism of a Vermeer interior is attributable to the rigid geometrical composition. Or, better, perhaps all this life and joy and recognizable realism results from the overcoming of various rules and patterns. Perhaps it is restriction that creates amplitude; perhaps less always means more.

CONCLUSION

THE film is finished. We have followed its development from conception through the creation of the script, from the shooting of the picture to final editing. In so doing we have traveled the road Ozu himself took dozens of times. And yet, we are far from the experience of the finished film. Most of the available facts and references, together with my inferences and deductions, are here—a small and lifeless pile when contrasted with the known experience of the Ozu film. This is, of course, the problem with books on film. The writer tears apart what the film-maker has so painstakingly assembled, exposing a structure the director has been careful to hide. The effect of the film, the creator's prime concern, eludes us; the experience of the film cannot be duplicated, only dissected. Several facets of the experience have already been discussed in this book; one salient one remains.

We have seen of how little the Ozu film is made, how few the parts, how often identical the means, how many the repetitions. In the construction of these films we have seen a unity of time and space rare in contemporary cinema. One has felt in the recurrences a kind of ritual. There have been few stories, all more or less similar. A sameness has extended through nearly three decades of work.

Not only do Ozu's methods of construction vary little from film to film, they are all elementary; that is, they all derive from what is now considered the primitive stage of cinema history.[1] Though the finished picture is in fact complicated, subtle, even sophisticated, it is important to Ozu's art that his effects come from this elementary base. The particular emotional experience that is the Ozu film owes much, perhaps everything, to the mundane nature of his materials and the elementary nature of his methods.

The Japanese have an aesthetic category for such a work, namely the concept of *wabi*. In practice it means that the more ordinary, even poorer, the container, the stronger the (properly displayed) effect. The plain, the rough, the common—these are the best conduits for the aesthetic spirit. One should, as one old flower manual has it, place "the chrysanthemum in an earthen jar, the pure white lily in a rustic sake bottle, one floating plum blossom in a rice bowl." [2] What is then felt is indicated in a poem from the 1495 *Hekizan Hichiroku:*

> Breaking a plum branch, I put it in an earthen jar;
> Although the blossoms are not yet open,
> The soul of spring hovers unseen.

From the particular (the young plum branch) has sprung the general (spring), and *wabi* as a spiritual tool serves to suggest that the eternal is contained within the transient. This is what Senno Rikyu, the celebrated aesthete and one of those who formed or refined the concept of *wabi,* demonstrated when he learned that important visitors were coming to view his famous garden of morning glories. He destroyed the garden. The visitors, disappointed, entered the teahouse. There in the *tokonoma,* standing in a simple and common vase, was one perfect morning glory. The particular had become the general, the less had become the more, and the visitors had received a lesson in advanced aesthetics.

Ozu's films abound in similar implications. Since they are entirely about people, however, and since Ozu is interested only in character, the implications are not just aesthetic, but spiritual. *Wabi* corresponds to the spiritual means that Jacques Maritain has called the *moyens temporels pauvres:* "The less burdened they are by matter, the more destitute, the less visible—the more efficacious they are. This is because they are pure means for the virtue of the spirit." [3] Ozu's mundane materials and elementary methods make the experience of the Ozu film an anagogic one, and the nature of Ozu's art is correspondingly close to all religious art.

That his films are in this sense religious becomes apparent if they are measured against the dictionary definition of the word. They are concerned with devotion and fidelity, often to an assumed if unnamed ideal; they express reverence, love, gratitude, the will to obey or to serve; they imply a ritual. That they are, at the same time, about no recognizable superior being, not expressly about the service and adoration of a god as expressed in some forms of worship, keeps us from realizing their nature and from recognizing our own religious impulse when it is suddenly revealed to us as we watch the end of *Late Spring* or *Tokyo Story*.

Ozu's films share with a majority of religious art a predisposition to elementary or primitive techniques: "two-dimensionality, frontality, the abstract line, the archetypal character." [4] They also share the assumption that it is through the everyday, the mundane, the common—and through them only—that the transcendent can be expressed. For, as we have seen, it is the combination of the mundane (the ordinary earthen jar) and the living, the promising, the evanescent (the plum branch) that creates the feeling of the transcendent. In the same way primitive religious art, that of Byzantium, for example, encloses in hieratic and mundane design the living and human saint. And in the same way, as we have seen, the invariable and "everyday" geometry of the Ozu scene encloses and contrasts with the reality and humanity of his characters.

Ozu did not think of his films in this way. For him the givens of his pictures were indeed so everyday that, once decided upon, he neither considered nor questioned their effect. This was shown by his surprise that anyone would want to ask questions about his material and his methods,[5] and by his indifference, even obliviousness, to the many similarities among his pictures. Not in the slightest doctrinaire, he early found a way to show what he wanted and saw no reason to change.

"I don't think the film has a grammar," he once wrote. "I don't think film has but one form. If a good film results, then that film has created its own grammar." [6] He was, to be sure, writing of directors with widely differing vocabularies and saying that there is no such thing as one general film grammar (something like a cinematic *style galante*) that all might draw upon. More narrowly, however, he may have been speaking of his own pictures, which by and large *do* have one form. He certainly implies that a film that creates its own grammar is also a good one. One of his reasons for thinking so is that in his films it is the givens (i.e., the grammar) that create the living, the human, the abiding. If his compositional geometry was a given, what interested him in it was the human nature it surrounded and to an extent created. These were the means through which the spiritual was revealed and attained. If the dialogue, for example, is about nothing in particular, one then watches *how* a character speaks, how another reacts. The visuals again assume first importance. We are being shown something, and it is only this that can reveal a spiritual state. Ozu would certainly have failed to understand criticism [7] that seemed to deny that the ordinary can have any spiritual nature at all, since it is only through the ordinary that the spiritual can be revealed.

Ozu regarded his films as extensions of himself. "In principle," he once said, "I follow the general fashion in ordinary manners and moral laws in serious matters, but in art I follow myself. Therefore I won't do anything I don't want to do. Even if something is unnatural and I like it, I'll do it. I don't particularly approve of myself for this, and I know it isn't reasonable; nonetheless, there it is. From this comes my individuality—and this is most important to me." [8] So, we are back where we began, with Ozu himself. For this reason the following and final section, the most important in the book, is devoted not to Ozu's methods but to Ozu himself, the kind of man he was and the kind of work he did.

A man who recognized spiritual attributes, a dedicated craftsman, an artist who devoted himself entirely to a dissolving status quo—there is a word for such a man. He is a traditionalist. He works with what he has and what he finds, staying far behind the vanguard of expanding knowledge and techniques. In this way Ozu is, as the Japanese are always telling us, the most traditional of Japanese directors. At the same time he does not entirely fit the definition of the traditional artist. As the architect Kenzo Tange has written:

> Tradition itself cannot constitute a force. It always has a decadent tendency to promote formalization and repetition. What is needed to direct it into creative channels is a fresh energy which repudiates dead forms and prevents living ones from being static. In one sense, for a tradition to live it must constantly be destroyed. At the same time, destruction by itself clearly cannot create new cultural forms. There must be some other force which restrains destructive energy and prevents it from reducing all about it to havoc. The dialectical synthesis of tradition and anti-tradition is the structure of true creativeness.[9]

Ozu has been both praised and condemned for being a traditionalist. As we have seen, the Japanese public found him to be a kind of spokesman, an artist who had "the real Japanese flavor," and made him their most honored director. And, as we have also seen, he has been criticized as reactionary, formalistic, tradition-bound. That Ozu is a traditional artist is certain; the only question is what kind of traditional artist he is.

I would suggest that Tange's definition of creative traditionalism best fits religious art. The architecture of the Ise shrines has had an enormous influence upon contemporary architecture, including Tange's own. It is traditional, elementary, even primitive, in that its system of beam supports, for example, is no longer needed in our cantilevered days. At the same time this architectural form is by no means dead. Its purpose is to enclose and in part create the spiritual flavor of Shinto, a still viable religion. When contemporary architecture is influenced by Shinto architecture, it carries with it, whether by association or more mysterious means, something of the original's sense of space and spiritual well-being. It is in this spiritual sense that I consider Ozu a creative traditionalist. The attributes of which his films are made, particularly that state of spiritual grace which is the "goodness" of the Ozu character, remain viable; cynicism has not yet eroded a general belief in human dignity; and to an extent nature remains the standard by which man is to be evaluated. Consequently the elementary and, in Japanese eyes, old-fashioned and traditional construction of the Ozu film remains alive.

While working with completely traditional material and using traditional means, Ozu has had the energy and insight to prevent the formal from becoming formalistic, the form from becoming empty, and the spirit from becoming the mere letter. His method is always the same. His anti-traditionalism, to use Tange's term, lies in his completely contemporary viewpoint and his extraordinary honesty. Because of his combination of traits, repetition comes to indicate a self-sustaining vitality; the motionless does not necessarily imply the static. It is for this reason that Ozu's characters have a validity beyond their role in the film. It is possible for us to imagine them continuing their lives. Indeed, it is impossible for us not to. Having spent a few hours with them, we find that we do not want to leave them. We have come to understand and consequently to love them. And with this understanding we come to know more about ourselves, and, with that, more about life.

Yasujiro Ozu. *Ca. 1956.*

BIOGRAPHICAL
FILMOGRAPHY

Y ASUJIRO OZU was born on December 12, 1903, in
Tokyo. During his early years he lived with his parents
in Fukugawa, an older section of the city, but in 1913
he was sent with his mother to live in Matsuzaka, a
large town near his father's birthplace of Nagoya. The reason was
that Matsuzaka merchants (Ozu's father sold fertilizer) maintained the tradition of a main house in the country and a branch
in the city. Ozu and his two brothers were to be educated in the
country while their father stayed and worked in the distant capital. The result was that Ozu was virtually fatherless between the
ages of ten and twenty.

His mother seems to have felt this deprivation and attempted to
make up for it. Tadao Sato has written, "Yasujiro, brought up in
a house where his father seldom appeared, where he could always
have his own way with his mother, was a very spoiled child. As
for his mother, everyone agreed that there was no more affectionate and kindhearted mother than she. She took such very good
care of him one might have thought she would have gotten in his
way. But he loved his mother more than he loved anyone else,
and all through his life he was her little boy." [1] Kogo Noda wrote
that Ozu, who never married, always called her "an ideal
mother," and added that "since Ozu was in a sense a very shy
man, in front of me he would deliberately treat her in a gruff

manner . . . but he was really very good to her. Whenever we went to Ginza together he would almost always buy something to take home to her. When I visited them, she would make jokes such as, 'Now Mr. Noda that you have taken the trouble of coming, and that Yasujiro's wife is unfortunately again absent, please content yourself with an old woman like myself.' " [2]

Several critics have commented on Ozu's early life as a source for several of his films. In early works such as *I Was Born, But . . .* and *Passing Fancy*, the father is despised by his sons, "but as Ozu grew as an artist he began to idealize the role of father, particularly in *There Was a Father*, and later in such pictures as *Late Spring*, *Tokyo Story*, and others." [3] It has also been pointed out that the economic milieu of such films as *The Brothers and Sisters of the Toda Family*, *The Munekata Sisters*, and *Early Summer* recalls that of the Ozu family during this period in Matsuzaka, and that in pictures such as *Late Autumn* and, again, *The Brothers and Sisters of the Toda Family*, Ozu was portraying family relationships as he remembered them. Certainly, he sometimes used scenes from his own life. In *There Was a Father*, for example, the father takes his son to a restaurant and gives him curried rice. Kogo Noda says that the elder Ozu did just that during one of his rare trips to Matsuzaka: treated little Yasujiro at one of the small restaurants near the inner shrine at Ise. [4]

As a boy Ozu was an indifferent student. In 1916 he entered the Uji-Yamada (now Ise) Middle School, while his elder brother, Shinichi, a very good student, attended a much better school and finally went to the Kobe Higher Commercial School, one of the best in the area. Yasujiro's younger brother, Shinzo, was also a good student. Later, perhaps regretting his own lack of higher education, Ozu paid for Shinzo's college tuition. Ozu's many films about college life, from *The Dreams of Youth* through *I Flunked, But . . .* and the opening section of *Tokyo Chorus*, reveal a preoccupation with university life Ozu might not have felt had he ever been a college student. As it was he got no further than middle school. He could not enter the prestigious Kobe Higher Commercial School because he did not bother to take the entrance examination. He was, he is reported to have said later with a degree of pride, in a movie house watching *The Prisoner of Zenda*.

Ozu had early become interested in film. Kogo Noda remembered that "it was in front of a dilapidated old theater called the Atagoza in Matsuzaka that Ozu said, 'If it had not been for this theater, I might not have become a film director. . . .' And he often told me that the movie bug bit him when he saw his first Matsunosuke historical spectacular there. Then he used to go to the Minoza, too, where he saw Italian spectacles like *Quo Vadis* and *The Last Days of Pompeii."* He was also, recalls Noda, fond of the films of Lillian Gish, Pearl White, and William S. Hart, as well as, later, Rex Ingram and King Vidor.[5] About this time, too, he began writing letters to the local *benshi*, lecture-commentators who accompanied silent films in Japan, and they sent him programs from their theaters. In this way he amassed a rather large collection and used to pore over his favorite items, memorizing the plot, and the cast and credits as well. More and more often he would go to nearby cities such as Tsu and Nagoya simply to see movies. On at least one occasion when he told his mother he was going to the mountains with friends, he actually went to the movies in Nagoya. When he returned home he found she knew where he had been. There had been a storm in the mountains, it turned out, but he had returned home perfectly dry.[6]

The reason the young Ozu enjoyed such liberty was that he had been expelled from the dormitory in 1920, when he was seventeen. He still took courses at the Matsuzaka School but had to live at home with his mother and commute, the idea being that she would keep him in the house and make him study. He was even given a passbook. His mother was to sign him out of the house and his teachers were to sign him in and out of class. He got around this by counterfeiting his mother's seal and going wherever he wanted. There were various reasons for his expulsion from the dormitory. He was a spoiled boy, and an unruly one. He loved mischief and he liked to fight. He drank, too—a habit he contracted very early and continued throughout his life. He was known to collect bromide photographs of a Miss Otome Amatsu, a "prima donna" in the Takarazuka All-Girl Opera. Though he had been in the middle of his class during his earlier years in school, he soon found himself near the bottom. The reason was a zero for conduct. Though his teachers could be expected to frown upon his various enjoyments, a zero for conduct was not given lightly. The true reason for the zero and the consequent expulsion, old friends later told Tadao Sato, was a letter Ozu had written one of the junior students, a letter apparently as indiscreet as it was sentimental.

Such letters and such attachments among boys were common in an educational system that so rigorously separated the sexes, and such sentiments are normal at a certain age. In Ozu's school, however, a new principal had thrown the school into confusion by enforcing literally all the regulations previously ignored. When his letter was intercepted, Ozu was expelled. He was not alone, the attractive junior having apparently received a number of such letters from senior students.[7]

Sato, in explaining this incident, mentions the tradition, then still strong, of the *chigo-san*—a sometimes physical relationship between an older and a younger student. But he goes on to find its real roots in Ozu's romantic ideas (derived largely from the novels of Junichiro Tanizaki and others that he and his friends were devouring at the time) and his extreme shyness, which Ozu masked with mischief and insubordination, but never entirely overcame. Sato goes on to speak of his later relationships with women, which were also characterized by shyness and sentimentality. Torajiro Saito, an early friend and mentor, said Ozu would ask for introductions to this actress and that when they were both working for Shochiku, and then would never find anything to say, often turning the longed-for meeting into a joke, or departing with a flippant line or two. He apparently became more seriously involved with women several times, though to what extent neither the women nor Ozu ever said. For years there was talk of Ozu and a Shimbashi geisha (Ozu became very angry with novelist Rintaro Takeda when he wrote a story about this affair), and at least one actress, Kunie Miyako, apparently turned down a marriage proposal.[8]

In any event, Ozu remained a bachelor. Presumably some of the women toward whom Ozu was romantically inclined felt only friendship toward him, and sometimes even less romantic feelings. "He was like a real father to me," Keiko Kishi told Max Tessier.[9] Just as Ozu's lack of a proper father and want of a college education found their way into picture after picture, so too, in such films as *Beauty's Sorrow* and *Until the Day We Meet Again* and, to an extent, *Early Spring,* one finds in a sweet and sentimental pathos the kind of romance Ozu himself seems never to have enjoyed. Sato attributes Ozu's lack of success in this line almost entirely to his shyness: "Shyness means that the ideal is inflated and the real, one's real self, is humbled; in other words, Ozu was a romantic." [10]

Whatever Ozu's reasons for the first of his attachments, the action of the new principal hurt him. Much later, after the war, his old middle-school classmates asked Ozu to attend a reunion they were planning. He was willing enough until he learned that a certain teacher, formerly superintendent of the dormitory and apparently of some importance in the *chigo-san* case, was coming. Ozu, who rarely became angry, turned furious, and said that if that person would be coming, he most certainly would not.

Ozu put up with the expulsion and occasionally made the most of it. When the final ceremonies came, he showed what he thought of his prospects for graduating by appearing in a brand-new uniform, which he had apparently bought himself, while his friends all wore the uniforms they had used for the past six years and expected shortly to discard. When Ozu learned, to his surprise, that he too was going to graduate after all, he told his friends that the only reason was that there was another student who was even worse than he, and the school was afraid of looking bad if it flunked more than one student.

Ozu stayed in his new uniform while he took several examinations for high schools, all of which he failed. Why he did so poorly in all his school examinations has never been satisfactorily explained. The main reason was probably that he took no interest in anything the Japanese prewar curriculum had to offer. He was interested in modern literature, in cinema, and in having a good time, all of which educators of the period frowned upon. Too, his shyness made him avoid competition, then as now the salient quality of the Japanese educational system, and a system in which everything was organized around examinations must have been distasteful to him. Finally he became an assistant teacher, for which a college diploma was not necessary. He was sent to teach in a small mountain hamlet some distance from Matsuzaka, and there he stayed for a year.

How he fared under this system as an assistant teacher in the deep mountains remains unknown. It is known, however, that he drank almost continually, and that when friends came to see him he insisted they stay on and on and on. A year later, when Ozu was twenty, his father called him, his brothers, and his mother back to Tokyo, and had to wire money to pay the drinking debts run up by Ozu and his friends.

After an absence of nearly a decade, Ozu went back to Tokyo to live with his family. Shortly, however, his uncle— apparently an understanding man who knew of his nephew's interest in film—introduced him to Teihiro Tsutsumi, then manager of the Shochiku Motion Picture Company. In due course the young Ozu began work at that company's Tokyo studios in Kamata as assistant cameraman. Why was an unknown graduate from the country able so easily to obtain a rather good post in one of Japan's largest motion-picture studios? Perhaps because the movies in 1923 were not considered quite proper employment, and there was a consequent shortage of bright and enthusiastic young men. Ozu's father at first refused outright to let his son work in the movies, and was only brought around after prolonged persuasion by the uncle. That Ozu knew something about movies and nothing at all about the camera was no deterrent. (Ozu knew mainly American movies: "There were only three Japanese films I could remember seeing, so the executive who interviewed me was rather shocked.") [11] In those days all the assistant did was move the camera from place to place. It was purely physical labor.

It was also highly educational. Hiroshi Sakai, who was among the cameramen for whom he worked, remembers Ozu in 1924 as an earnest, strong young man, who during summer shooting used to wear only a pair of shorts, carrying the heavy Berhauer camera on his naked shoulder. He also remembers him sitting at the feet of Kiyoko Ushihara, one of the leading directors of the period, asking questions about movie-making. One question Sakai remembered was, "What should the cinema of the coming generation be like?"—though he did not remember Ushihara's answer to this earnest query.[12]

Ozu apparently fit at once into studio life at Kamata. There was no repetition of his schoolboy rebellion because he felt contented and free. Kogo Noda, who joined Shochiku five months after Ozu, remembers him happily sunning himself on the lot during the lunch-hour break, or playing catch with Hiroshi Shimizu and Heinosuke Gosho, two other assistants later famous as directors. Ozu himself often recalled what a good time he had had in the early days at the Kamata studios. He once said that he was happy because he was strong, and lugging the camera took all his strength. He also said he knew that in this new company he had an opportunity to get ahead, but "the real truth is that I didn't want to. As an assistant I could drink all I wanted and spend my time talking. As a director I'd have to stay up all night working on continuity. Still, my friends told me to go ahead and give it a try." [13]

He did not at once have the opportunity. He had registered in the army reserves, which was one way to avoid the draft, but was called up at the end of 1924 for what was called a one-year volunteer system. The reserves trained for a year. A good trainee became a lieutenant, the others, corporals. Ozu spent most of his year in the army hospital, supposedly suffering from mild consumption. He told visiting friends, however, that it was just a matter of dipping the thermometer in warm water when no one was looking, coughing a lot, and seeming sad.[14] This was very much Ozu the schoolboy, but his friends were perturbed about his health. Needlessly, it would seem, because Ozu was in later life never consumptive. After a year of idleness he was discharged (not, however, as a sublieutenant), and happily lugged the heavy camera about the lot as though he had not just spent twelve months in a sickbed.

He might have continued as assistant cameraman, said Ushihara, now a professor in the cinema department at Nihon University, had it not been for one incident:

It was all very relaxed, back then and we used to sit around and talk about movies all the time, particularly, for some reason, about cinema theory. All I knew on that subject at that time came from a book written by Frederick Palmer, who talked about correct continuity and things like that. Ozu always argued with me about what

Palmer, and consequently I, thought. Finally, one day I told him that he just wasn't in the proper job. He was talking like a director and not a cameraman, and if that was how he felt, then he ought to try to be one.[15]

This apparently decided Ozu. He went to one of the Kamata directors and asked to be assigned to him as assistant, which he was, at the end of 1926.

Ozu's choice of directors seems surprising in the light of his later work. He did not ask to work under Ushihara, or any of the other more progressive directors. Instead he chose Tadamoto Okubo, a man now quite forgotten and even in his own day not highly regarded. Okubo specialized in the kind of comedy known in Japan as "nonsense-*mono*," a running series of gags held together by a slight story line, a succession of chuckles intended to make the time pass.

One reason for Ozu's choice may have been that such films allowed his sense of the mischievous, as strong in later life as in his student days, full expression. Certainly he fed Okubo a number of gags. Another reason was perhaps Okubo himself, a man with some interesting pretensions. According to Ushihara, he called himself "a truly vulgar director," and loudly refused to have anything to do with art. He wanted to create pleaure out of the most disparate materials: dirty jokes, noisy farce, and what passed for eroticism in 1925. Sato has compared the Ozu of that period with the late Yuzo Kawashima, also of the same studio, who used to call himself and his followers "the Frivolous Group," and whose earlier pictures were never intended to be taken seriously. "Ozu," says Sato, "also obviously belonged among this group of people. And even though Ozu had the most delicate taste, and Kawashima could never refrain from putting a toilet scene in his films, they have something in common." [16]

Ozu remained a bit like Okubo in his distrust of the art of the film in its most pretentious manifestations. In all his tastes—liquor, bronzes, pottery, literature—he admired either the highest or the lowest, both of which he must have found refreshingly free from cant. And it is true that the low has a claim to reality that anything more elevated must strive to sustain. Ozu, too, has his share of toilet scenes, many of them occurring just at the point when one might expect pretensions to enter.[17]

The most important reason for Ozu's choice of Okubo as mentor, however, may have been the older man's notorious laxness. He would sometimes not even appear at the studio, and his assistants would then go on and shoot the film on their own. Okubo was apparently very generous toward his assistants. If during the screening a scene got a big laugh, Okubo would name the assistant responsible. If the scene failed, he would say, "That, I'm afraid, is one of my mistakes." [18] Also, as Ozu soon discovered, one could argue most profitably with Okubo. He would always listen, and if the new idea had merit, it would be adopted. Akira Fushimi, who wrote a number of the early Ozu scripts, said that Ozu could have learned nothing from Okubo except inversely— that is, by profiting from the older director's mistakes. Torajiro Saito, however, who was equally close to Ozu during this period, said that Ozu liked working with Okubo and that the two men helped each other a great deal. In the end, perhaps Okubo's strongest influence was his announced intention of creating pleasure from vulgar materials. Ozu went on to create, with the most mundane materials, art.

During this period Ozu moved from his parents' house to a house he and four others rented near the Kamata studios. They were all assistant directors or cameramen: Torajiro Saito, Keisuke Sasaki, Yoshiyaku Hamamura, who later became Ozu's editor, and Hiroshi Shimizu, later one of Japan's best prewar directors. Another friend came over from time to time—Mikio Naruse, later one of the finest Japanese directors and a lifelong friend of Ozu's. The young men sat around discussing films almost every night. Ozu, says Saito, rarely said much about Japanese films. He always talked about Griffith and especially the recently released *Marriage Circle*. In their ménage Saito took charge of accounts, Ozu did the cleaning up, and Shimizu did the cooking. Something of a gourmand, Shimizu disdained the others' cooking, and, despite such eccentricities as putting sugar in the bean soup, cooked well enough that no one complained.[19]

Ozu was assistant director for less than a year (a period during which he wrote his first script, the historical drama *Kawaraban Kachikachiyama,* later adapted by Masao Arata and filmed by his good friend Kintaro Inoue). He probably would have remained an assistant director for several more years if another unplanned incident had not occurred. One day, feeling particularly hungry, Ozu went to lunch at the studio cafeteria. The place was crowded and the curried rice he had ordered did not come. Ushihara came in, ordered the same thing, and was served at once. When Ozu complained to the waiter, he was told Ushihara, after all, was the director, and not he. At this Ozu, who rarely lost his temper but when he did lost it completely, slapped the waiter in the face.[20] Word of the lunchtime violence soon spread. Ozu was called up before Shiro Kido, then as now head of Shochiku. After Kido had accepted Ozu's explanation, the two men talked about various things and Kido asked Ozu if he could write a scenario, an indication that the studio was thinking of making Ozu a director. Ozu had one, *Kawaraban Kachikachiyama,* but Kido asked for another. So the young assistant director went away and came back with the idea for *The Sword of Penitence,* which he had taken from an American film, George Fitzmaurice's *Kick-In,* a picture he had not seen but had read about in a film magazine. This was accepted. Ozu was a full director.[21]

He began in the *jidai-geki* (period-film) section, the lowest on the Shochiku lot. This was partly his own fault. He had, after all, turned in a period-film script. At the same time, it was the prevailing practice to start the new men low and let them work their way up. His lowly assignment proved most fortunate for Ozu. It was there that he first met Kogo Noda, though the two remembered seeing each other around the lot before that, and Noda agreed to write the script for his first picture.

Yasujiro Ozu,
ca. 1928

BIOGRAPHICAL FILMOGRAPHY

The Sword of Penitence (*Zange no Yaiba*). Shochiku/Kamata. Idea by Ozu, based on the George Fitzmaurice film *Kick-In*. Script by Kogo Noda. Photographed by Isamu Aoki. With Saburo Azuma, Kunimatsu Ogawa, Eiko Atsumi, Iida Choko, et al. Ca. 70 Min. Released October 14, 1927. No negative, prints, or script in existence.

Yasujiro Ozu at the Kamata Studios, ca. 1928

Before the film was finished the Army again occupied Corporal Ozu's attention, though only for a short time. *Zange no Yaiba* was finished by Torajiro Saito, though he says it had all been done already except for one or two scenes. When Ozu returned he made up for lost time, turning out five films in 1928, six in 1929, and seven in 1930.

They would probably have been period films but for the fact that Shochiku's period film unit was transferred to Kyoto and Ozu persuaded his company to leave him behind. Consequently he was allowed to make *gendai-geki* (films about contemporary life), which he did for the rest of his career. Shochiku acceded to his request in part because a number of magazines, among them *Kinema Jumpo,* had praised *The Sword of Penitence.* Ozu himself didn't like the film. "I didn't feel very good about it, it didn't even seem like my own film." [22] Perhaps the reason was the short but exhausting period back in the Army. "Elinor Glynn's *Three Weeks* is all about women and love affairs, and my three weeks in the Army were all about tiredness and frustration." [23]

The Dreams of Youth (*Wakoudo no Yume*). Shochiku/Kamata. Script by Ozu. Photographed by Hideo Shigehara. With Tatsuo Saito, Nobuko Wabaka, Hisao Yoshitani, Junko Matsui, Takeshi Sakamoto, Kenji Oyama, Chichu Ryu, et al. Ca. 50 min. Released April 29, 1928. No negative, prints, or script in existence. A comedy about college dormitory life, based on several American pictures.

Wife Lost (*Nyobo Funshitsu*). Shochiku/Kamata. Script by Momosuke Yoshida, after an idea by Ononosuke Takano. Photographed by Hideo Shigehara. With Tatsuo Saito, Ayako Okamura, Takeshi Sakamoto, Junko Matsui, Ogura Shigeru, Kano Shichiro, et al. Ca. 50 min. Released June 16, 1928. No negative, prints, or script in existence. A light comedy about marital mix-ups, based on a prizewinning magazine story. Ozu didn't think much of the original,[24] but the company insisted he make it into a film.

Pumpkin (*Kabocha*). Shochiku / Kamata. Script by Komatsu Kitamura, after an idea by Ozu. Photographed by Hideo Shigehara. With Tatsuo Saito, Yurie Hinatsu, Takeshi Sakamoto, Yoko Kozakura, et al. Ca. 60 min. Released August 31, 1928. No negative, prints, or script in existence. A comedy about a young man and his misadventures with girls. Ozu believed he learned something about continuity in making this picture.[25]

Pumpkin. *1928. Left to right, Hinemaru Honda, Tatsuo Saito, Yoko Kozakura, Yuri Hinatsu*

A Couple on the Move (*Hikkoshi Fufu*). Shochiku / Kamata. Written by Akira Fushimi, after an idea by Ippei Kikuchi. Photographed by Hideo Shigehara. With Atsushi Watanabe, Mitsuko Yoshikawa, Kenji Oyama, Tomoko Naniwa, Ichiro Ogushi, et al. Ca. 60 min. Released September 28, 1928. No negative, prints, or script in existence. A comedy about a couple who cannot stand staying in the same house and are continually moving. Ozu was pleased with his work, but it was cut by other hands and the resulting product disappointed him.[26]

With this film Ozu began, he later said, to enjoy being a director. He finally felt as if he knew what he was doing; and with his next film, he added, he began to find his own style.[27] The style was, in its beginnings, an adaptation of the Okubo comedy style. Ozu eliminated some of the nonsense, relied less heavily on gags, and tried to make his characters more consistent both in themselves and with life as it is. He also moved nearer the Shochiku house style, one we would now identify as home drama. A little smile, a few tears, a full, warm feeling—this was what Shochiku rightly thought its public wanted. Ozu's contribution was to make both smiles and tears natural, to make the full, warm feeling a genuine one.

Body Beautiful (*Nikutaibi*). Shochiku / Kamata. Script by Ozu and Akira Fushimi. Photographed by Hideo Shigehara. With Tatsuo Saito, Choko Iida, Mitsuko Yoshikawa, et al. Ca. 60 min. Released December 1, 1928. No negative, prints, or script in existence. A home comedy about an unemployed husband who becomes his artist wife's model. When her paintings fail to win

Body Beautiful. *1928. Tatsuo Saito*

204

prizes, she becomes his model, and his paintings (because they are of a nude female) win all the first prizes. Ozu was pleased with the film, as was his company, and *Kinema Jumpo* again praised him.

Treasure Mountain (*Takara no Yama*). Shochiku/Kamata. Script by Akira Fushimi, after an Ozu idea. Photographed by Hideo Shigehara. With Tokuji Kobayashi, Ayako Okamura, Choko Iida, Yurie Hinatsu, Tomoko Naniwa, et al. Ca. 100 min. Released February 22, 1929. No negative, prints, or script in existence. A melodramatic comedy about the jealousy between a traditional young geisha and a modern girl. Shochiku needed this film in a hurry. It was completed in five days.

Days of Youth (*Wakaki Hi*). Shochiku /Kamata. Script by Ozu and Akira Fushimi. Photographed by Hideo Shigehara. With Ichiro Yuki, Tatsuo Saito, Junko Matsui, Shinichi Himori, et al. Ca. 60 min. Released April 13, 1929. No script in existence, 16mm fine grain master with Shochiku. Another student comedy, this one about skiing.

Days of Youth. *1929. Shinichi Himori (far left) and (right) Tatsuo Saito, Ichiro Yuki*

On location for
Days of Youth

Fighting Friends—Japanese Style (*Wasei Kenka Tomodachi*). Shochiku/ Kamata. Script by Kogo Noda. Photographed by Hideo Shigehara. With Atsushi Watanabe, Ichiro Yuki, Tomoko Naniwa, Hisao Yoshitani, Ichiro Takamotsu, et al. Ca. 100 min. No negative,

Fighting Friends—Japanese Style. *1929. Tomoko Naniwa, Ichiro Yuki, Hisao Yoshitani, Atsushi Watanabe*

prints, or script in existence. Released July 5, 1929. A comedy about two truck drivers in love with the same girl. Modeled after the Wallace Beery—Raymond Hatton series of comedies.

I Graduated, But . . . (*Daigaku wa Deta Keredo*). Shochiku / Kamata. Script by Yoshiro Aramaki, after an idea by Hiroshi Shimizu. Photographed by Hideo Shigehara. With Minoru Takada, Kinuyo Tanaka, Utako Suzuki, Kenji Oyama, Shinichi Himori, Takeshi Sakamoto, et al. Ca. 100 min. Released September 6, 1929. Script in existence, but no negative; ten minutes from original print in the archives of the Tokyo Film Center, an affiliate of the National Museum of Modern Art, Tokyo. A college graduate comes to Tokyo to look for a job. He is joined first by his mother and later by his fiancee, all three of them having to live in one small room.

I Graduated, But . . . *1929. Minoru Takada and Kinuyo Tanaka*

It is with this film that several critics have seen the emergence of the Ozu style. Here, they say, he moved from simple light comedy to mature social comedy. The first genre, it is said, is emotional in its origins; the second is by its nature analytical. As social comedy, they also find the film influenced by the politically critical "tendency films" of the period. Finally, they say, Ozu achieved social consciousness, and in this picture turned from the mindless acceptance of the "nonsense-*mono*" to "the stern criticism of the responsible tendency film."

Actually, Ozu's criticism, always oblique, was never stern. His way was to film things as they were and refrain from comment. Condemnation was never total, and his criticism was always general. It showed a society that was genuinely unconcerned about, let us say, the plight of the poor because in actuality there is scarcely a society that is anything else. Just as Ozu did not care for the ostentatiously artistic, so he did not like the politically ideal; both were at variance with any view of life as it is. He, like Okubo, was always ready to accept human nature as he found it. Unlike Okubo, he went on to celebrate it. In this Ozu differed from other directors of the period. Mizoguchi, for example, was making genuine "tendency films," in which a preoccupation with such abstractions as Truth and Justice led to flat characters and unreal situations. Later, Heinosuke Gosho generously sought a remedy for society's ills and thought he found one in polemic. Ozu, uninterested in politics from his school days on, became, as he was more and more able to say what he wanted, even less interested in any easy solution, whether of the Left or of the Right. Nor did he want merely to show "the coldness of society," a favorite theme of serious films of the period. Rather, he wanted to show things as they were, and this he accomplished not with the customary passionate melodrama, but with a dispassionate satire that came very naturally to him.

The Life of an Office Worker. *1929.*
Tatsuo Saito and Mitsuko Yoshikawa

The Life of an Office Worker (*Kaishain Seikatsu*). Shochiku / Kamata. Script by Kogo Noda. Photographed by Hideo Shigehara. With Tatsuo Saito, Mitsuko Yoshikawa, Takeshi Sakamoto, Tomio Aoki, et al. Ca. 85 min. Released October 25, 1929. No negative, prints, or script in existence. A comedy about a husband and wife who look forward to a year-end bonus, only to discover that, because of the general depression, the husband has been fired. He looks for a job, fails to find one, and is finally hired by several friends.

In this picture Japanese critics see Ozu creating his first *shomin-geki.* This genre, originally a kind of home drama, later to have a long and honorable history, was devoted to the lives of the lower-middle-class majority that was, until recently, the economic backbone of the country.[28] The *shomin* were "people like you and me," but in the films of Ozu, Gosho, Yasujiro Shimazu (and later, of Toyoda, Naruse, Imai, Kinoshita, and Chiba), they became something more, something like spokesmen for all of Japan. As a film genre it was highly regarded for its honesty. It may have somewhat overplayed hardship, but at least it did not gloss over life's real difficulties. Ozu's refusal to give either himself or his audience an easy way out found a natural form in *shomin-geki,* but, unlike some of the other directors, he refused to be circumscribed. His pictures, even the early ones, are (irrespective of genre) also about something else. They are, briefly, about character, about people as they are.

OZU

A Straightforward Boy (*Tokkan Kozo*). Shochiku / Kamata. Script by Tadao Ikeda, after an idea by Chuji Nozu, the joint pen name for Kogo Noda, Tadamoto Okubo, Tadao Ikeda, and Ozu. Photographed by Ko Nomura. With Tatsuo Saito, Tomio Aoki (Tokkankozo), Takeshi Sakamoto, et al. Ca. 57 min. Released November 24, 1929. No negative, prints or script in existence. Ozu was much taken with a child actor he had used in the previous film, and made this comedy about him. It had to be slipped into the Shochiku schedule, and was completed in about three days.

A Straightforward Boy. *1929.*
Tatsuo Saito, Tokkankozo, Takeshi Sakamoto

With this film the critic is in possession of most of the ingredients of the mature Ozu films. First, the director of nonsense comedies had already achieved subtlety of style because he was becoming more interested in character than in comedy. Second, through the ordinary home drama of the period he had found his major theme: the Japanese family, either directly or in its extensions, the school and the office. Third, his interest in the family led him to an interest in society at large, though he always preferred to see this larger entity reflected in the smaller. Fourth, his interest in society had led him to the *shomin,* the class that was most typically Japanese and at the same time formed the larger part of his audience. Fifth, interested in character, in the family, in society, he began to find in children a vehicle for his ideas, in particular, for the kind of social satire he was now developing. Sixth, as he grew more skillful in delineating character he grew more discriminating in the means he used to create character; from 1930 on, he began gradually limiting his technical means, giving up fades, dissolves, etc., and eventually creating a plain style that was superbly suited to his mundane subject matter. The simplicity of form and content (which became identical in later Ozu films) was, in turn, responsible for the power and the depth of the mature Ozu picture.

At the same time, Ozu was a commercial director. His films were intended to make money while showing life as he saw it. For this reason he made many films we now consider atypical of his work. It was later that he gained control and was able to make only the films he wanted to make.

208

An Introduction to Marriage (*Kekkon Gaku Nyumon*). Shochiku/Kamata. Script by Kogo Noda, after an idea by Toshio Okuma. Photographed by Hideo Shigehara. With Tatsuo Saito, Sumiko Kurishima, Minoru Takada, Mitsuko Yoshikawa, et al. Ca. 107 min. Released January 5, 1930. Script in existence, but no negative or prints. A picture about that point in a marriage when both husband and wife tire of their mutual life.

An Introduction to Marriage. *1930. Tatsuo Saito, Ozu, and two unidentified friends at the Kamata Studios, ca. 1930*

Walk Cheerfully (*Hogaraka ni Ayume*). Shochiku/Kamata. Script by Tadao Ikeda, after an idea by Hiroshi Shimizu. Photographed by Hideo Shigehara. With Minoru Takada, Hiroko Kawasaki, Satoko Date, Takeshi Sakamoto, et al. Ca. 100 min. Released March 1, 1930. Script in existence, 16mm finegrain master with Shochiku. A film about a young delinquent who eventually reforms.

I Flunked, But . . . (*Rakudai wa Shita Keredo*). Shochiku/Kamata. Script by Akira Fushimi, after an idea by Ozu. Photographed by Hideo Shigehara. With Tatsuo Saito, Ichiro Sukida, Kinuyo Tanaka, Tomiyo Yoko, Chishu Ryu, et al. Ca. 95 min. Released April 11, 1930. Script in existence, 16mm finegrain master with Shochiku. A satire on college life, based in part on the earlier *I Graduated, But* . . .

I Flunked, But . . . *1930. Kinuyo Tanaka and Tatsuo Saito*

This film remained important to Ozu because it was the first one in which he entrusted a major role to Chishu Ryu, the actor who was later central to his work. Ryu, then twenty-four, had appeared in most of the earlier pictures (he was later to say that he had been in all of Ozu's films except for *Beauty's Sorrow* and *What Did the Lady Forget?*).[29] Several critics have maintained that the Ozu atmosphere

209

could not exist without this actor, and Ryu himself soon became aware that he was playing the Ozu persona.

That Night's Wife (*Sono Yo no Tsuma*). Shochiku / Kamata. Script by Kogo Noda, after a story by Osuka Shisugoru (phonetic), probably a pen name for Ozu. Photographed by Hideo Shigehara. With Tokihiko Okada, Togo Yamamoto, Emiko Yakumo, Tatsuo Saito, et al. 100 min. Released July 6, 1930. Script and 16mm finegrain master with Shochiku; print in the archive of the Tokyo Film Center. A romantic melodrama: a father with a sick child turns robber and is caught. Ozu wanted to photograph entirely within one small set (except for the opening), and then had trouble plotting the action. Nonetheless the film was praised, and Shochiku's Shiro Kido was particularly taken with it.

The Revengeful Spirit of Eros (*Erogami no Onryo*). Shochiku / Kamata. Script by Kogo Noda, after an idea by Seizaburo Ishihara. Photographed by Hideo Shigehara. With Tatsuo Saito, Satoko Date, Ichiro Tsukita, Hikaru Hoshi, et al. Ca. 41 min. Released July 27, 1930. No script, negative, or prints in existence. Typical Shochiku, atypical Ozu: a nonsense-comedy ghost-story picture. Made at the spa to which the director had been sent to recuperate by the grateful Kido, who typically said that Ozu had better come back with a finished film. During this time gossip linked the director romantically with his actress, Satoko Date.

Lost Luck (*Ashi ni Sawatta Koun*). Shochiku / Kamata. Script by Kogo Noda. Photographed by Hideo Shigehara. With Tatsuo Saito, Mitsuko Yoshikawa, Takeshi Sakamoto, Tomio Aoki, Ichiro Tsukita, et al. Ca. 60 min. Released October 3, 1930. No script, negative, or prints in existence. A film about office workers and their insufficient salaries. Asked in 1960 what it was about, Ozu admitted he could not remember a thing.[30]

Lost Luck. *1930. Tatsuo Saito and Mitsuko Yoshikawa*

Young Miss (*Ojosan*). Shochiku / Kamata. Script by Komatsu Kitamura. Photographed by Hideo Shigehara. With Sumiko Kurishima, Tokihiko Okada, Kinuyo Tanaka, Tatsuo Saito, Togo Yamamoto, Tomoko Naniwa, et al. Ca. 130 min. Released December 12, 1930. Script in existence, but no negative or prints. A typical light comedy about a girl journalist, distinguished by Ozu's sense of humor and his respect for character. A big, star-filled spectacular, it surprised the studio and possibly the director by winning Third Prize in the prestigious *Kinema Jumpo* polls for that year.

Young Miss. *1930. Kinuyo Tanaka and Sumiko Kurishima*

The Lady and the Beard. *1931. Satoko Date and Tokihiko Okada*

The Lady and the Beard (*Shukujo to Hige*). Shochiku/Kamata. Script by Komatsu Kitamura. Photographed by Hideo Shigehara. With Tokihito Okada, Ichiro Tsukita, Toshiko Iizuka, Hiroko Kawasaki, Choko Iida, Tatsuo Saito, Satoko Date, et al. 97 min. Released February 7, 1931. Script and original negative in existence. Another college comedy, this one about a bearded cheerleader and a young lady of good family. Eventually she tames him and he shaves. Finished in eight days.

Beauty's Sorrows. *1931. Yukiko Inoue and Tokihiko Okada*

Beauty's Sorrows (*Bijin Aishu*). Shochiku/Kamata. Script by Tadao Ikeda, after a story by Henri de Regnier. Photographed by Hideo Shigehara. With Tatsuo Saito, Tokihiko Okada, Yukiko Inoue, Sotaro Okada, Mitsuko Yoshikawa, et al. Ca. 158 min. Released May 29, 1931. Script in existence, but no negative or prints. Two young men, one serious, the other a playboy, meet the daughter of an eminent sculptor. The playboy marries the girl, whom they both love; the serious one gets the statue. Later, she dies and the husband wants the statue. The two men fight; they both die. Some who remember seeing this film say it was not as bad as it sounds.[31] Ozu, however, said that he wanted to make a nice, light picture, got too earnest about it, and it turned out slovenly.[32]

On the set for **Beauty's Sorrows:** *Yukiko Inoue, Ozu, Tokihiko Okada*

Ozu had a weakness for such films, which he never learned to handle. He later remembered that he had tried particularly hard with this film, and it still had not worked. Then he recalled that he had not tried at all with *Young Miss,* and had made a successful picture. Concerning *Tokyo Chorus* he later wrote, "having learned my lesson from *Beauty's Sorrows,* I made this film in my best easy-going manner and it worked." [33]

During his five years of film-making, Ozu had, in part through trial and error, come to realize what he could do best. Though he would still sometimes stray almost wistfully into romance, the kind of picture he did best came to be those he did most. At the same time he began to act more like a director both off and on the set. Now that he knew what he was going to do, he was determined to do it. Little by little this likable man built his reputation as the director who said no. He originally said no to his actors, making them rehearse more, making more and more takes of the same scene. Later he would, for a time, refuse to make talkies. He refused color for a long time, only to succumb in the end. He refused, eventually, to make more than one film a year, and to the end said no to the wide screen.

At the same time, Ozu is also remembered as an extraordinarily affable man—off the set, at any rate—who liked to talk as much as the next man, and to drink a bit more. Always easy-going, he nevertheless refused to be pushed. He knew he was a good craftsman, but now he may have begun to realize he was also something more. This his company did not as yet know. Shochiku had hired him as a simple comedy man, and though they liked his *Kinema Jumpo* award, the studio was, after all, a film factory. Ozu would occasionally go along with their routine assignments, but more and more often he would not.

Tokyo Chorus. *1931. Kenji Oyama, Tokihiko Okada, Tatsuo Saito*

Tokyo Chorus (*Tokyo no Gassho*). Sho-chiku/Kamata. Script by Kogo Noda, after a novel by Komatsu Kitamura. Photographed by Hideo Shigehara. With Tokihiko Okada, Hideo Sugawara, Emiko Yagumo, Mitsuo Ichimura, Takeshi Sakamoto, Tatsuo Saito, Choko Iida, Hideko Takamine, et al. 91 min. Released August 15, 1931. *Kinema Jumpo* Third Prize. Script and 16mm fine-grain master with Shochiku; prints in the archives of the Tokyo Film Center and the Cinémathèque Française, as well as the Shochiku vaults and the personal collection of Shinsui Matsuda. A serious comedy about a married salaried man who (as in *The Life of an Office Worker*) loses his job and must walk the streets in search of one. He has many misadventures, some of them painfully comic, before being saved by his old school comrades.

With this film, what Ozu called his "darker side" and what we would call his mature style began to emerge. Because he did not blame Japan's ills directly on the feudal family system or capitalism, both prime targets of social critics, he was often criticized for a degree of passivity he did not, in fact, possess. Confusing the passivity of Ozu's characters with passivity on the part of the director, Japanese critics sometimes failed to understand what Ozu was doing. Only rarely did he directly criticize social conditions.

In these "dark" prewar films, he was showing conditions in so faithful a manner that they indicted themselves. At the same time he was also quietly celebrating a character—a personal rather than national ideal—that could remain brave in the face of family pressure, could continue to hope in the face of an increasingly restrictive social order, could remain simple, naive, strong enough to continue to have faith in itself. From this stuff of tragedy, Ozu fashioned some of his best comedies.

Spring Comes from the Ladies (*Haru wa Gofujin Kara*). Shochiku/Kamata. Script by Tadao Ikeda and Takao Yanai, after an idea by Ozu under the name James Maki. Photographed by Hideo Shigehara. With Jiro Shirota, Tatsuo Saito, Yukiko Inoue, Takeshi Sakamoto, et al. Ca. 94 min. Released January 29, 1932. Script in existence, but no negative or prints. Another of Ozu's college comedies. Now, however, the university years have become a precarious golden age during which the real problems of the world are seldom understood and all security is false. In this film Ozu was discovering in the educational system, and in the world of childhood, the acute angle from which he could both view and evaluate the adult world.

Spring Comes from the Ladies. *1932.*
Jiro Shirota and Yukiko Inoue

I Was Born, But . . . (*Umarete wa Mita Keredo*). Shochiku / Kamata. Script by Akira Fushimi and Geibei Ibushiya, after an idea by Ozu under the name James Maki. Photographed by Hideo Shigehara. With Tatsuo Saito, Hideo Sugahara, Tokkankozo, Mitsuko Yoshikawa, Takeshi Sakamoto, Seiji Nishimura, Shoichi Kofujita, Chishu Ryu, et al. Original version, 100 min. Released June 3, 1932. Script and original negative in existence, duplicate negative in New York. Prints in the collections of the Tokyo Film Center, the Museum of Modern Art, New York, the Cinémathèque Française, the Anthology Archives, New York, and Shinsui Matsuda. Prints in general circulation in North America, through New Yorker Films.

I Was Born, But . . . *1932. Tatsu Saito, Tokkankozo, Hideo Sugahara*

On the set of **I Was Born, But . . .**
A publicity photograph. Hideo Sugawara, Ozu, Tokkankozo

A typical suburban wage earner lives in his typical house with his typical wife and two small sons, aged ten and eight, who are not typical at all. They see their father, whom they love, bowing to his boss, and later, playing the fool in order to ingratiate himself with his employer. They want to know why, since they themselves can easily beat up the boss's son, he has to act this way. This he cannot answer, and in protest they go on a hunger strike. Though the father punishes them, he also sees that "this is a problem they will have to live with for the rest of their lives," and wonders if they will have to live the same kind of life he has. They probably will. In the end, ethics undermined by hunger, they begin to see that, somehow, the boss is the greater man.

Of this, the first of his great films, Ozu has said, "I started to make a film about children and ended up with a film about grown-ups; while I had originally planned to make a fairly bright little story, it changed while I was working on it, and came out very dark. The company hadn't thought it would turn out this way. They were so unsure of it that they delayed its release for two months." [34] It went on to win the *Kinema Jumpo* First Prize for that year, and is the single early Ozu picture still in circulation.

In this film Ozu brought together in almost perfect form the various elements which made up his style, his personal way of looking at the world. The picture is a *shomin-geki,* and the rigidity of Japanese society is well implied. It is about a family unit, whose members interest Ozu more than the unit. It is about children, who innocently reflect the falseness of an adult society. Ozu goes further, suggesting that such innocence cannot continue. Though the film is a comedy, it is a serious one; the two little boys will never again be the same. Later, Ozu would realize that innocence returns, and he would celebrate the somewhat battered simplicity of his older men who in this cold world have kept, though at great cost, a kind of purity. In this 1932 film, so bright, so funny, he had not yet found it necessary to realize that innocence can, in a way, be retained.

Where Now Are the Dreams of Youth? (*Seishun no Yume Ima Izuko*). Shochiku/ Kamata. Script by Kogo Noda. Photographed by Hideo Shigehara. With Ureo Egawa, Haruo Takeda, Kinuyo Tanaka, Tatsuo Saito, Choko Iida, Kenji Oyama, Chishu Ryu, Satoko Date, et al. Ca. 90 min. Released October 13, 1932. Script and original negative in existence. A kind of sequel to *I Was Born, But . . .* , and an unsuccessful one. It was made when the shooting of *I Was Born, But . . .* was interrupted because one of the children in that film got hurt. Four boys are graduated from college. Three of them eventually have to ask the fourth, the son of a company president, for jobs. He, in turn, gets one of their girls. In both this film and *Spring Comes from the Ladies,* Ozu used very few stars. The reason was that, as head of Shochiku, Shiro Kido had recently adopted the "director system" of making films, and many of the stars walked out. Their walkout gave many minor actors their first chance, and allowed such directors as Shimizu, Gosho, and Ozu to have much more say in what films they made and how they made them.

Where Now Are the Dreams of Youth?
1932. Ureo Egawa and Kinuyo Tanaka

Until the Day We Meet Again (*Mata Au Hi Made*). Shochiku / Kamata. Script by Kogo Noda. Photographed by Hideo Shigehara. With Joji Oka, Yoshiko Okada, Hiroko Kawasaki, Satoko Date, Shinyo Nara, et al. Ca. 110 min. Sound (i.e., music and effects, but no dialogue). Released November 24, 1932. Scenario in existence, but no negative or prints. An atypical story, a romantic melodrama about a prostitute in love with a boy whose father dislikes her; it takes place during the night before the young man must leave for the army.

Until the Day We Meet Again. *1932. Joji Oka and Yoshiko Okada*

Ozu sometimes maintained that romantic love did not really interest him, implying that he was interested only in love between members of a family. And to be sure, his romantic melodramas usually are failures. Critics were agreed, however, that in this film he captured with delicacy and tact the feelings of two genuine people in a real situation. The picture was seventh in that year's *Kinema Jumpo* polls. Ozu claimed he was inspired by his leading actress, Yoshiko Okada. "She was very good, and there is something definitely sensual about her eyes." [35]

Woman of Tokyo (*Tokyo no Onna*). Shochiku / Kamata. Script by Kogo Noda and Tadao Ikeda, after a story by Ernst Schwartz, a pen name for Ozu. Photographed by Hideo Shigehara. With Yoshiko Okada, Ureo Egawa, Kinuyo Tanaka, Shinyo Nara, et al. Ca. 70 min. Sound (music and effects). Released February 9, 1933. Script and negative in existence; print in the Tokyo Film Center.

Woman of Tokyo. *1933. Yoshiko Okada and Ureo Egawa*

Another romantic melodrama, this one a quickie. A girl works hard to put her younger brother through school only to have him kill himself when he learns that she has financed his education by becoming a prostitute. "We started this one before we'd even finished the script," said Ozu. "And it was all in the can eight days later." [36]

Dragnet Girl (*Hijosen no Onna*). Shochiku / Kamata. Script by Tadao Ikeda, after an idea by Ozu under the name James Maki. Photographed by Hideo Shigehara. With Joji Oka, Kinuyo Tanaka, Hideo Mitsui, Sumiko Mizukubo, et al. Ca. 60 min. Silent. Released April 27, 1933. Script and original negative in existence. "Another film," said Ozu, "about a delinquent, something in the style of *Walk Cheerfully.*" [37] It didn't go well, during or after shooting, and Ozu was heard to say that after he had finished it, he just wanted to go on a long trip.

Dragnet Girl. *1933. Kinuyo Tanaka and Joji Oka*

Passing Fancy (*Dekigokoro*). Shochiku / Kamata. Script by Tadao Ikeda, after an idea by Ozu under the name James Maki. Photographed by Shojiro Sugimoto. With Takeshi Sakamoto, Tokkankozo, Den Ohinata, Nobuko Fushimi, Choko Iida, et al. 101 min. Silent. Released September 17, 1933. Script and duplicate negative in existence; prints in the collections of the Tokyo Film Center, the Cinémathèque Française, and Shinsui Matsuda. A subtle and beautiful film about a boy and his father who live together in a tenement, the father working, the boy going to school. The father is attracted to a younger woman, and though nothing comes of it, the boy is worried and disappointed. Offered a new job in a distant town, the father goes off only to leave when halfway there to return to his son. *Kinema Jumpo* First Prize.

Passing Fancy. *1933. Den Ohinata and Takeshi Sakamoto*

One pattern that emerges in a chronological account of Ozu's early work is that after he has said what he wants to say superbly well (as in *I Was Born, But . . .*), there will follow several films in which he appears to be marking time before setting out in a new direction. In the excellent *Passing Fancy* we see a new interest, one that sustained him throughout his career. It was an interest in what we might call (though Ozu never would) archetypal situations. Parent and child live together; one or the other is attracted toward someone outside; there is a marriage; the one left behind must learn to live alone. In *Passing Fancy* the story is the reverse of the one seen in fuller form in *Late Spring, Late Autumn,* and *An Autumn Afternoon,* but it is, in other respects, the same. Between this film and the next, Ozu was again called up by the Army Reserves, this time for only a fortnight. During this stint he was trained in, of all things, poison-gas warfare. Shortly after celebrating his release he made a friend of Sadao Yamanaka, the great period-film director.

A Mother Should be Loved (*Haha o Kawazuya*). Shochiku/Kamata. Script by Tadao Ikeda and Masao Arata, after an idea of Kogo Noda. Photographed by Isamu Aoki. With Den Ohinata, Hideo Mitsui, Mitsuko Yoshikawa, Yukichi Iwata, Shinyo Nara, Junko Matsui, et al. 93 min. Released May 11,

A Mother Should be Loved. *1934. Yoshikawa Mitsuko and Mitsuo (Hideo) Koji*

1934. Script in existence but no negative; one print (with first and last reels missing) in the Shochiku vaults. A family film about the relations between two half-brothers who have different mothers; good character delineation, somewhat spoiled by melodrama. Ozu originally wanted to call the film *Tokyo Twilight,* a title the company turned down in favor of one that deferred to the continuing popular interest in the tribulations of the Japanese mother. Twenty-three years later Ozu used the title for a completely different script—one also slightly marred by melodrama.

Ozu was later to say that he remembered the film very well, "not because it was any good, but because my father died while I was making it." [38] Long before his death, Ozu's father had apparently forgiven him for disregarding paternal preferences and going into film-making. In Ozu's first picture, *The Sword of Penitence,* there appeared an insert shot of a letter. The calligraphy was that of Toranosuke Ozu, who had written it at the request of his son.[39]

The elder Ozu died of angina pectoris. His son was again living at home at the time, and Kogo Noda remembers Ozu's account of his father's death, a scene that apparently resembled the final sequences of *There Was a Father.* At the end "his father turned to Yasujiro and touched him 'though he knew that I was the last person to be relied upon,' and the younger Ozu burst into tears." [40] After that Ozu continued always to live with his mother, but his home life was quite different now, for he was head of what family was left.

Matsuo Kishi has left us a charming picture of Ozu's home live several years before, in 1932, when the father was alive and the family together.

"I opened the old-fashioned door to find a little bird singing in its cage. It was a kind of bush warbler, I remember. Before long Ozu himself appeared in a very quaint costume. He was wearing a long *dotera* [padded gown] over a *satsumakasuri* kimono [a kimono with a typical *kasuri* pattern], and the *dotera* had a *taigyo* [fishing-motif scene] pattern in red with a pale green background. We went through a long corridor and then upstairs to his study, which was small, just six tatami, with a *kotatsu* [foot warmer] in the middle. There were books and paintings and brushes everywhere, all scattered about in the greatest confusion. Though we knew that Ozu always sketched in his continuity, he had never studied painting professionally, but was very fond of watercolors, particularly those of Katsumi Miyake. There was a smart-looking lamp on the table, and bottles of whiskey were lined up on the shelf. In the *tokonoma* [alcove] there was a splendid gold lion head and a gramophone. I asked him to let me hear some music and he responded with his favorite piece, Schumann's 'Träumerei.' " [41]

A Story of Floating Weeds (*Ukigusa Monogatari*). Shochiku / Kamata. Script by Tadao Ikeda, after the American film *The Barker*. Photographed by Hideo Shigehara. With Takeshi Sakamoto, Choko Iida, Koji (Hideo) Mitsui, Emiko Yagumo, Yoshiko Tsubouchi, Reiko Tani, Tokkankozo, et al. 89 min. Silent. Eighteen feet cut from print by Japanese censors before release. Released November 23, 1934. Script and duplicate negative in existence; prints in the Tokyo Film Center, the Cinémathèque Française, and the Museum of Modern Art, New York. Though based on a popular American picture, the story is much different. The head of a small troupe of traveling players

A Story of Floating Weeds. *1934. Takeshi Sakamoto and Mitsuo (Hideo) Koji*

returns to a small mountain town and meets his son, fruit of a casual affair some years before. Ozu referred to the picture as the second of the "Kihachi" films (*Passing Fancy* being the first)—the main character is called Kihachi and is based upon a known "type" of man. *Kinema Jumpo* First Prize.

Ozu turned this slightly melodramatic story into a picture of great atmosphere and intensity of character, one in which story, actors, and setting, all combined to create a whole world, the first of those eight-reel universes in which everything takes on a consistency somewhat greater than life: in short, a work of art. Ozu himself remained fond of this film and successfully remade it in color in 1959, under the title *Floating Weeds*.

An Innocent Maid (*Hakoiri Musume*). Shochiku / Kamata. Script by Kogo Noda and Tadao Ikeda, after a story by Sanu Shikitei. Photographed by Hideo Shigehara. With Kinuyo Tanaka, Choko Iida, Takeshi Sakamoto, Tokkankozo, Kenji Oyama, et al. 87 minutes, silent. Ninety feet cut from print before release by Japanese censors. Released January 12, 1935. Script in existence, but no negative or prints. For the New Year season, traditionally a money-making time for the Japanese film industry, Shochiku wanted to begin a series about girls in various situations. This was the first and Ozu and his staff worked day and night to finish it. Diary entry: Jan. 4 1935. "This is a very ordinary, routine script. Not a good omen for beginning a new year." [42] It was not indeed particularly good (thoughtful friend ruins marriage to save innocent young bride, etc.) and, in any event, Shochiko decided not to continue the series.

An Inn in Tokyo. *Yoshiko Okada and Kazuko Kojima*

Ozu filming **Kagami Shishi,** with Kikugoro VI

An Inn in Tokyo (*Tokyo no Yado*). Shochiku / Kamata. Script by Tadao Ikeda and Masao Arata. Photographed by Hideo Shigehara. With Takeshi Sakamoto, Yoshiko Okada, Choko Iida, Tokkankozo, et al. 82 min. Silent. Released November 21, 1935. Script and negative in existence; prints at Shochiku and the Tokyo Film Center. A proletariat father (Kihachi) and his two young sons look for a job and eventually find transient companionship with a widow and her little girl. *Kinema Jumpo* Ninth Prize.

This beautifully observed film is among Ozu's most realistic. Indeed the term *neo-realismo* has been used to describe Ozu's establishing scenes of the effects of the great depression in Tokyo. Ozu only remembered that "naturally, it was a silent film." [43] He was still holding out against talkies, though every other director in the studio was making them, and he did not much like music and effects being added to silent films he considered finished. This time, however, the company "made me make it just as though it were sound," apparently so that the film would look modern.

Actually, during 1935, Ozu had already made a sound film, his only short subject, the twenty-minute *Kagami Shishi,* a documentary of Kikugoro VI performing the famous Kabuki dance of the same name, which Shochiku asked him to make in response to a request from the Ministry of Education.

One reason Ozu held out so long against sound was that he had promised his cameraman, Hideo Shigehara, that he would wait until Shigehara had perfected the sound system on which he had been working for some time. It was very like Ozu, Kogo Noda observed, "to go on making silents when the company was howling for talkies just because of a promise to his cameraman." [44] An entry in Ozu's diary (June 15, 1935), says: "If I can't keep promises like this, then the best thing would be to give up being a director—which would be all right, too." [45]

College Is a Nice Place (*Daigaku Yoi Toko*). Shochiku / Kamata. Written by Masao Arata, after an idea by Ozu under the name James Maki. Photographed by Hideo Shigehara. With Toshiaki Konoe, Chishu Ryu, Sanae Takasugi, Tatsuo Saito, Kenji Oyama, Choko Iida, et al. Silent. Released March 19, 1936. Script in existence, but no negative or prints. Another film about college students, remembered as one of the best of them. It was about friends in a college dormitory who are graduated, return home, and begin a hopeless search for jobs. Again the director was enamored of his star. The diary entries covering the creation of the picture are filled with references to the charm, beauty, and great attraction of Sanae Takasugi. Ozu called the finished film "dark." We would call it meaningful, and certainly find the title ironic.

College Is a Nice Place. *1936*
Toshiaki Konoe and Chishu Ryu

Ozu and Sanae Takasugi
on the set of
College Is a Nice Place

The Only Son (*Hitori Musuko*). Shochiku / Kamata. Written by Tadao Ikeda and Masao Arata, after an earlier script by Ozu under the name James Maki. Photographed by Shojiro Sugimoto. With Chishu Ryu, Choko Iida, Shinichi Himori, Masao Hayama, Yoshiko Tsubouchi, Mitsuko Yoshikawa, Tokkankozo, et al. Sound (talkie). 87 min. Released September 15, 1936. Scenario and duplicate negative in ex-

The Only Son. *1936. Shinichi Himori and Yoshiko Tsubouchi*

222

istence; prints at the Tokyo Film Center, the Museum of Modern Art, New York, the Anthology Archives, New York, and the Cinémathèque Française. A woman whose husband is no help to her at all raises her only son by herself, working hard so that he can be graduated from a university in Tokyo. Later, she spends most of her savings to visit him. She finds him married and with a child, and he, in turn, spends most of his money entertaining her in the capital.

Ozu at Komoro, in Nagano, during the shooting of **The Only Son,** *1936*

Despite the somewhat novelettish sound of this précis, this film, fourth in the annual *Kinema Jumpo* lists and Ozu's first talkie, is filled with originality, integrity, and the sharpest kind of observation. Ozu said it "was based on an earlier script, *Tokyo Is a Nice Place*—in fact I had begun to shoot that film the year before, then stopped for some reason or other." [46] The film is one of Ozu's darkest. The eventual impossibility of human understanding, the inevitable failure of trust, the indubitable fact that we are alone in this world, all these are shown with tact, wisdom, and a wry charm. The questioning of basic human values—love, friendship, the worth of life itself—which occurs in the later films in passing, as it were, is here unmuted. It is a dark, poignant, and sage film.

One of Ozu's many Japanese qualities was his ability to make unlikely combinations into something original and personal. Here he was working (originally at any rate) with his college genre, but in combination with that favorite Shochiku genre, the film about mother, or *haha-mono*. One reason behind this somewhat unlikely combination was that *haha-mono* always made money, and Ozu's pictures, though by now critical successes, rarely broke even. Another reason undoubtedly was that the only love Ozu ever knew, or at least ever returned, was for his parents. He had in his art shown his rebellion. Now, in this film, in *There Was a Father,* and in others, he was showing his reconciliation. Yet another reason, and probably the most important, was that Ozu perceived the reality behind the genre, just as he always saw the truth in a truism. Films about mothers might be legion, but an individual mother is an individual person with individual problems, and this is what Ozu showed in this fine film.

"It was my first talkie," Ozu remembered. Gosho had made Japan's first successful talkie nearly five years before, and "I even got to thinking that I'd been left behind by the other directors."[47] The reason for the lag, beside Ozu's promise to Shigehara, was that Ozu, who had mastered the silent film, did not know how a talkie should be made.

The film was shot at Kamata, the last picture to be made there, Shochiku having relocated its new sound studio at Ofuna, near Kamakura. "We worked in the empty studios, but the trains were so noisy that we couldn't shoot during the day. So we worked every night, and from midnight to five in the morning I made about five shots." Ozu found that the sound equipment was not a great impediment. Typically, he wanted to use sound to further restrict rather than amplify his style. He particularly liked the idea of the stationary microphone; it forced his actors to move about less, and he could, he felt, get at them better. At the same time, "because I couldn't shuck off the style of silent movies, I got upset. Although I had understood that everything in a talkie should be different, this movie was just like a silent film. . . . But now I realize that clinging to the ways of the old silent film really helped me with what I'm doing now."[48]

What Did the Lady Forget? (*Shukujo wa Nani o Wasuretaka*). Shochiku / Ofuna. Written by Akira Fushimi and Ozu under the name James Maki. Photographed by Hideo Shigehara. With Sumiko Kurishima, Tatsuo Saito, Michiko Kuwano, Shuji Sano, Takeshi Sakamoto, Choko Iida, Mitsuko Yoshikawa, Masao Hayama, Tokkankozo, et

What Did the Lady Forget? *1937. Sumiko Kurishima, Mitsuko Yoshikawa and Choko Iida*

al. 73 min. Released March 3, 1937. Script and duplicate negative in existence; prints at Shochiku and the Tokyo Film Center. A bright and mordant comedy about the upper classes. Into the household of a hard-working, golf-playing husband, and a spoiled, indolent wife comes a modern young niece from Kyoto. Eventually husband and wife are reconciled.

On the set of **What Did the Lady Forget?** *Michiko Kuwano, Ozu, Mitsuko Yoshikawa*

n China, 1939

Shuji Sano and Ozu in Hankow, 1939

Having said what he wanted to say as perfectly as he could in *The Only Son,* Ozu, as usual, went off in search of something else—in this case, a new milieu. Most of Ozu's pictures (with some exceptions, including *I Was Born, But . . .*) had been laid in the old section of Tokyo, the *shitamachi* or downtown, the traditional home of the poor *shomin.* Just before this period Ozu himself had moved from old-fashioned and downtown Fukugawa to the smart and uptown Takanawa; in this film he went to modern Tokyo, to the well-to-do *yamanote* residential district. The Japanese have always made much of this distinction, and still do, even now, when it can be said barely to exist. In any case, it was certainly a novelty in an Ozu film for everyone on the screen to have enough money. He was not out, however, to deride the idle rich. The people in this film are subjected to the same loving scrutiny that Ozu lavished on all his characters

225

(their progeny appear in such late pictures as *Equinox Flower* and *Late Autumn*). The result was a wry, affectionate, and ironic domestic comedy.

In July, 1937, following the outbreak of the Sino-Japanese War, Ozu was called up with all the other reserves and sent to China as an infantry corporal. There he traveled widely, spending most of his time on the shifting front. Knowing how Ozu felt about discipline, and about war, particularly a war as unwarranted and barbarous as this, one may imagine how he felt. Indeed, one is forced to, since he rarely wrote about his wartime experiences in the diaries and almost never spoke of them afterward. It was during this time that he met Sadao Yamanaka, perhaps Japan's finest director of period films, for the last time. Though Yamanaka worked for a different studio, Nikkatsu, he and Ozu had become friends and admirers of each other's work. In the last films of Yamanaka, one can see evidence of Ozu's influence. Shortly after their meeting in China, Yamanaka died of dysentery. Also in China Ozu met Shuji Sano, who had been in *What Did the Lady Forget?* and was later to play a larger role in *There Was a Father*. In the summer of 1939, having served two years, Ozu returned to Japan and to his work.

Ozu's war years, though unpleasant for him, were fortunate in their timing. Shochiku had begun to complain about Ozu's failure at the box office, though they liked his critical notices and *What Did the Lady Forget?* had ranked eighth in the *Kinema Jumpo* lists. If Ozu had remained with his company it might have meant more light comedies and fewer dark overtones. As it was, the times and the Japanese audience had changed sufficiently to allow him to go on doing as he wanted.

His absence, however, had deprived him of Hideo Shigehara, the photographer with whom he had most often worked, who had joined another company. Though Ozu always made his own camera set-ups, and always checked each shot himself before it was taken, his photographer was always much more than the man who pushed the button. He was included in story conferences and had a say in the look of the finished film. When Ozu lost Shigehara, he lost one of the men who had helped him form his early style. When Ozu returned he had to find a new cameraman, a new staff, and for a time, himself.

After his return, he wrote a very good script, *The Flavor of Green Tea over Rice* (*Ochazuke no Aji*). It was never produced, though he used the title later for a different picture. It was about a man and wife who take the customary final meal together before he leaves for the front. Rather than customary rich ceremonial food, they decide on a dish that is among the most simple, the most Japanese. It was to have been a gentle, intimate, reflective film, filled with observations of Japanese character in times of stress. It was rejected by the Censorship Office of the Home Ministry, which passed on all film scripts before production and refused many. The censors declared the script *fumajime* ("unserious"), and perhaps it was by the standards of the day. "Dramatic art must forget the old individualistic and class attitudes," said an editorial in a leading magazine, "and must begin to realize that it has a cultural role to perform in the total program of our new national consciousness."[49] So Ozu continued with another script he had been working on.

The Brothers and Sisters of the Toda Family. *1941. Kuniko Miyake and Mieko Takamine*

Ozu (center) on the set

The Brothers and Sisters of the Toda Family (*Toda-ke no Kyodai*). Shochiku /Ofuna. Written by Ozu and Tadao Ikeda. Photographed by Yushun Atsuta. With Mieko Takamine, Shin Saburi, Hideo Fujino, Fumiko Katsuragi, Mitsuko Yoshikawa, Masao Hayama, Tatsuo Saito, Kuniko Miyake, Yoshiko Tsubouchi, Michiko Kuwano, Chishu Ryu, Toshiaki Konoe, et al. 105 min. Released March 1, 1941. Script and original negative in existence; prints at Shochiku and the Tokyo Film Center. After her husband dies, a mother and her youngest daughter move in with the eldest son. His wife finds this disagreeable and several family quarrels ensue. Eventually, the two women decide to go live with the second son, who has settled in China.

227

"Before the war," Ozu wrote, "no matter how many best-ten awards one received, the salary of the director was always the same—not enough. I went to Kido and asked for a raise. He told me to make a picture and he would decide after he had seen it. So I made this one and lived much better after that." [50] The picture was a box-office hit, Ozu's first, and also won the *Kinema Jumpo* First Prize. Shochiku was delighted to arrange for a long-term contract. One reason for the sudden success was that after three difficult years, the public was better prepared to understand what Ozu was showing. Another was that the public was getting accustomed to family films because the government was pushing them. Ozu, though utterly indifferent to the government's propaganda purposes, had always made family films. The difference between his and the ordinary "national effort" wartime product was that his continued to be honest.

While he was making *The Brothers and Sisters of the Toda Family*, Ozu recalled,

"The company kept after me. They said the film would never be ready in time. You have to finish shooting today, they said. I had only two hours of shooting time left and lots of long scenes to do. I felt bad about not working this out, but most people, I guess, didn't notice the difference. I liked the film; any film I enjoyed making I tend to like, whether it is any good or not. I'm still fond of this picture. Both Shin Saburi and Mieko Takamine were new to me when I used them in this film, and they were just right for it. And they were already very popular—which is why so many people came to see it, despite the fact that Ozu's films were never hits. And after that a lot of people always came to see my pictures. But before long [he was then working on *Tokyo Twilight*] I'm going to start making films that they won't." [51]

There Was a Father (*Chichi Ariki*). Shochiku/Ofuna. Written by Tadao Ikeda, Takao Yanai, and Ozu. Photographed by Yushun Atsuta. With Chishu Ryu, Shuji Sano, Mitsuko Mito, Takeshi Sakamoto, Shin Saburi, Haruhiko Tsuda, Shinichi Himori, et al. 94 min. Released April 1, 1942. Script and duplicate negative in existence;

There Was a Father. *1942.*
Haruhiko Tsuda and Chishu Ryu

228

prints at Shochiku, the Tokyo Film Center, the Anthology Archives, New York, the Museum of Modern Art, New York, and the Cinémathèque Française. A schoolteacher is very close to his young son. When the boy grows up he is drafted, but the father has the pleasure of seeing him married to the daughter of his best friend. After the father dies, the son returns to carry on the family name.

Haruhiko Tsuda, Ozu, and Chishu Ryu on location for **There Was a Father**

Ozu filming
There Was a Father

Ozu had written the first draft of this script before he went to China. (In the same year, 1937, he also wrote the story for *Unending Advance* [*Kagirinaki Zenshin*] for Tomu Uchida, who later filmed it.) After he returned to Japan he rewrote it: "I wrote and rewrote it over and over again, and it could still be improved." [52] One is at a loss to imagine how. This is one of Ozu's most perfect films. There is a naturalness and a consequent feeling of inevitability that is rare in cinema. At the same time there is, with no warping of character or situation, the unfolding of a pattern—the links between the generations —which is seen every day by every one of us, but which has almost never been so perfectly shown. Critics have called the performance of Chishu Ryu in this film one of the best in the history of Japanese cinema, and they are right. *There Was a Father* won the *Kinema Jumpo* Second Prize, made money at the box office, and has become one of the country's most esteemed classics.

It is easy now to forget that this picture and the one before it were made during the Pacific War, yet Ozu must have had difficulties making them. The industry was all but openly government-controlled,

229

and "national policy subjects" were insisted upon. Both these films were nominally about such subjects, i.e., the war, soldiers, home morale, etc., but Ozu made no compromise with his own kind of reality. Refusing to sacrifice his characters to the needs of plot, he was even more adament about exploiting them for propaganda purposes. The subject was on the approved list, but the treatment was so human that the official attitude was inherently criticized.

Ozu stood up for the work of other directors as well. Akira Kurosawa in particular remembers him during the wrangle over *Sanshiro Sugata*. Kurosawa's film was shown to a military board (as were all films), which then criticized it, saying this would have to be cut, that would have to go, etc. One officer even asked (a question incomprehensible to us today) if the young Kurosawa was not interested in aiding and abetting the enemy. To this Ozu replied that either the film was a good one or it was not, that he thought it good, and that they ought to pass it and get on with their work.[53] This kind of remark was enough to send a man to prison in 1943, yet Ozu always escaped. Masahiro Shinoda, later one of Ozu's assistant directors and now a well-known director himself, explains, in recalling this incident and wondering how Ozu got away with it, "he always made such funny jokes, always got everyone in such a good mood, and was so expert in saying a serious thing in a light way, that nothing ever happened to him." [54]

Nonetheless even an Ozu could not entirely escape the *Zeitgeist*. An article in the New Year's edition of a film magazine finds him listing various plans for future films, all having to do with war. The list includes a proposed continuation of *The Brothers and Sisters of the Toda Family*, laid in both Japan and China; a film commemorating the thirtieth anniversary of the South Manchurian Railroad, seen through the eyes of a successful employee of that company who had labored on its behalf for three decades; something called *One Plane Has Not Yet Returned (Imada Kikan Sezaru Mono Ikki)*, and a "revenge period film" (*adauchi-mono*) about the two Soga Brothers and the love between them.[55] How seriously Ozu considered such projects is not known, but he had begun work on one wartime project, the script for *Far Motherland (Harukanari Fubo no Kuni)*. It was based on material in the "War Diaries," and was never finished because the government did not like what it had seen of it (no heroics, no high-flown language, no sacrifice for the fatherland, etc.). Its qualities are best expressed in an alternative title given it by one of Ozu's friends: *Kihachi Goes to War*. In any event, it no longer exists.[56]

Another reason for canceling the project was that Ozu was once more called up by the military. Though he had already served his time in the Imperial Army, the government decided that directors should join the troops to make propaganda films. Originally it was planned that Ozu make a film in Burma, but by 1943 the Japanese were faring so poorly there that he was sent to Singapore instead. Though several films were discussed, none were ever made, though one apparently was begun. It was about the Indian independence movement, which for its own reasons Japan was encouraging. When Singapore returned to British rule, Ozu busied himself burning negatives and prints. Having done his best to make no films at all, he did not want to be judged a war criminal by the Allied Tribunal. Before that time, however, Ozu was casually sabotaging various suggestions for good "national policy" films, and looking at the American films that the Japanese in Singapore had confiscated. Later he said he saw over one hundred.

The director Kimisaburo Yoshimura, in Singapore at the time, remembers Ozu looking at John Ford's *The Grapes of Wrath, Stagecoach, How Green Was My Valley,* and *Tobacco Road;* King Vidor's *Northwest Passage;* Hitchcock's *Rebecca;* Wyler's *The Westerner* and *The Little Foxes; Fantasia,* and *Gone With the Wind.* The film that impressed Ozu most was Welles's *Citizen Kane.* "If you give Chaplin 62 points, this film gets about 85." [57] He looked at it again and again. It was apparently the technique of the film that most interested him, and according to Yoshimura he kept shaking his head in wonder over this effect or that.[58] Thereafter, whenever asked his favorite foreign film, he always said *Citizen Kane,* though it is impossible to imagine a picture more antithetical to his own.

His other favorites, some of which predated his Singapore days, were almost equally surprising. The influence of Vidor and Lubitsch is visible, and his liking for Chaplin's *A Woman of Paris* is reasonable. But he also said that if he had not seen Ince's *Civilization,* he would never have become a director, and that "if there hadn't been a director called Rex Ingram, I would not now be a director myself." He liked John Ford, admired his spontaneity. "When you get to *Roman Holiday,"* he later said, "that man Wyler just isn't spontaneous." [59] One may only wonder at Ozu, the epitome of a doctrinaire nose-in-the-script director, deploring Wyler's alleged lack of spontaneity. One can also question Ozu's further assertion that all this film-viewing changed his style.

Several people have noted, usually with regret, a supposed major difference between Ozu's prewar and postwar films. It has been suggested, as we have seen, that the change derived from his abandoning the proletariat and embracing the bourgeoisie; but we have also seen that this is nonsense. It has been suggested, further, by Ozu himself and others, that repeated doses of Welles and Hitchcock somehow strengthened or diluted the director's style; yet no one has been able to find a trace of any such change. Finally, it has been suggested that Ozu was "brainwashed" by the American way after the war.[60] This is a more serious charge because there are many examples of directors changing styles in midstream to accommodate the ideals of the new conquerors.

In fact, no such thing happened in the case of Ozu. When his first postwar film appeared (another *kihachi-mono,* the last one), everyone was surprised, bewildered, reassured, or disappointed to discover that Ozu had not changed at all. The director himself was rather hard on the directors who were changing their themes and consequently their way of making films to fit the newly imported *demokuratiku* ideas.[61] The changes in Ozu's films, all of them minor, are accounted for by the fact that although he made few pictures during the war years, as a man and artist he kept evolving. We lack the evidence for minor changes and hence wrongly deduce a major one. The natural growth of the Ozu style is apparent when one considers the director's work as a whole. So far as influences on his style went, the foreign films had no more impact than his army experience, the war itself, and the war's democratic aftermath.

In 1945, however, Ozu's military experiences were not yet over. Though no war criminal, he was a POW, and was sent to a British camp near Singapore for half a year. During this time, besides doing the dishes and cleaning the toilet, Ozu reportedly became interested in poetry. When not working, he and his fellow prisoners sat around composing elaborate *renga* (chain verses). Ozu had always written poetry—an unexceptional pursuit in prewar Japan—but he apparently became more actively interested in it in the prison camp.

Then, in February, 1946, Ozu returned to a new Japan. A large part of Tokyo had been destroyed and part of its population killed. Fukugawa, where he had spent his earliest years, had been almost completely destroyed. Ozu set to work amid the ruins.

The Record of a Tenement Gentleman (*Nagaya Shinshi Roku*). Shochiku/Ofuna. Script by Ozu and Tadao Ikeda. Photographed by Yuharu Atsuta. With Chishu Ryu, Choko Iida, Takeshi Sakamoto, Reikichi Kawamura, Tomihiro Aoki, Eitaro Ozawa, Mitsuko Yoshikawa, et al. 72 min. Released May 20, 1947. Original negative and script in existence: prints at Shochiku and the Tokyo Film Center. A

war orphan is found on the streets of Tokyo and sent to live with a middle-aged woman. At first she finds him a bother, but eventually she comes to love him. The boy's father is found and she must give up the child.

The Record of a Tenement Gentleman.
1947. Reikichi Kawamura,
Tomihiro Aoki, Chishu Ryu

Of this film Ozu recalled, "I was still very tired. But the company kept telling me to get a picture out in a hurry. I finished the script in twelve days. No one thought I could work so quickly, and I told them that this was going to be the last time." [62] It was. It was also the first and last time Ozu can be caught making a nod in the direction of civic endeavor, an idea imported from abroad that enjoyed a brief popularity during the Occupation. At the end of the picture the middle-aged woman decides to open a center for war orphans like the one she had come to love. This unlikely, one may almost say un-Japanese, resolve almost ruins the film.

It was during this period that Ozu formed another romantic attachment. This time it was the daughter of a man who ran a restaurant outside the gates of the Ofuna Studio where the director worked. He took her places with him, including a month-long visit to Kyoto, where he again met Mizoguchi and others, and gossip said he was, finally, about to take a bride. Instead, she became his secretary and later married the actor Keiji Sada. During this same period Ozu wrote a script for himself called *The Moon Does Not Rise* (*Tsuki wa Noborinu*). He never filmed it, however, and gave it to the actress Kinuyo Tanaka to direct in 1955.

A Hen in the Wind (*Kaze no Naka no Mendori*). Shochiku / Ofuna. Script by Ozu and Ryosuke Saito. Photographed by Yuharu Atsuta. With Kinuyo Tanaka, Shuji Sano, Kuniko Miyake, Chishu

A Hen in the Wind. *1948. Hideo Nakagawa, Kinuyo Tanaka, Shuji Sano*

Ryu, Chieko Murata, Eijiro Tono, Koji Mitsuo, et al. 90 min. Released September 20, 1948. Original negative and script in existence; prints at Shochiku.

A destitute woman is awaiting the demobilization of her husband when her child falls ill. She prostitutes herself to pay the hospital. When her husband returns, she tells all. He knocks her downstairs but later apologizes, suddenly realizing all she has been through.

Writing ten years later Ozu said: "Well, everyone has his failures. There are all kinds of failures, however, and some of my failures I like. This film is a bad failure." [63] Nonetheless the picture ranked seventh in the *Kinema Jumpo* polls. Even the critics who liked the film, however, complained about some of the more unlikely scenes. Fresh, clean covers on a prostitute's bed in postwar Japan? The heroine falling all the way downstairs in a crowded Japanese apartment and no one coming to see what had happened? Given the film in question, they were right to complain. In the general context of Ozu's style, however, sacrifices of realism to beauty were already visible, and it was through such sacrifices that a new and perhaps higher reality was shortly to emerge.

Though most critics now agree that nothing new was learned during the days of film-viewing in Singapore, and that the unchanging Ozu was, as he himself said, "a tough old buzzard," one possible result of seeing such films as *Citizen Kane* may have been the new aesthetic, beauty for its own sake, in Ozu's later films. In a picture as melodramatic as *A Hen in the Wind,* of course, Ozu's heightened interest in beauty (clean, pretty bedspreads in a whorehouse) is obtrusive. In a film like *Late Spring,* however, the same distortions for beauty's sake in an almost eventless story only enrich the experience as a whole.

Late Spring (*Banshun*). Shochiku/ Ofuna. Script by Ozu and Kogo Noda, after a story by Kazuo Hirotsu. Photographed by Yuharu Atsuta. With Chishu Ryu, Setsuko Hara, Haruko Sugimura, Jun Usami, Yumeji Tsukioka, Tomihiro Aoki, Takeshi Sakamoto, Kuniko Miyake, Yoko Katsurahi, et al. 108 min. Released September 19, 1949. Script and original negative in exis-

Late Spring. *1949. Chishu Ryu, Setsuko Hara, Yumeji Tsukioka*

tence, as well as several duplicate negatives. Prints in various archives and at Shochiku, and in general circulation in North America through New Yorker Films. A young woman, somewhat past the usual marriage age, lives with her father in Kamakura. She is happy with him, and when she hears of one of his friends remarrying, she disapproves. The father, however, feels that he is keeping her from marriage. She refuses several offers. Then her aunt tells her that her father is thinking of remarrying. She is disturbed, but believing that this is what he wants, she agrees to get married. Father and daughter go on a final trip together to Kyoto. When they return, she is married. The father, who had no intention of marrying, is left alone.

Called "one of the most perfect, most complete, and most successful studies of character ever achieved in Japanese cinema," this picture was also one of Ozu's own favorites, along with *There Was a Father* and *Tokyo Story*. The various components of the Ozu style—the *Ofuna-cho*-flavored home drama, the interest in character, the *haha-mono*-like idea of a parent as central figure—are here combined in a perfectly balanced film, the whole of which far transcends any of its elements. One reason for this perfection was the depth of Ozu's feeling and the security of his style. Another was his return to collaboration with Kogo Noda, for the first time since 1935. And another was the new aesthetic that dominated all of Ozu's films from this one on, though glimpses of it had occasionally been visible in earlier pictures. This was a new simplicity in story, structure, and tempo, matched by a firm control over sets, properties, lighting, and actors. The results were, to be sure, not radically different from earlier pictures, but the later films were more laconic and more incisive. *Kinema Jumpo* First Prize.

The Munekata Sisters (*Munekata Shi-mai*). Shintoho. Script by Ozu and Kogo Noda, after the novel by Jiro Osaragi. Photographed by Jyoji Ohara. With Kinuyo Tanaka, Hideko Takamine, Ken Uehara, So Yamamura, Chishu Ryu, Sanae Takasugi, Tatsu Saito, et al. 112 min. Released August 25, 1950. Script and original negative in the Toho archives, print at the Tokyo Film Center. The story of two sisters and their life together, a life complicated by the demands of their family and their interests in the outside world.

The Munekata Sisters. *1950. Hideko Takamine and Kinuyo Tanaka*

235

Of this film Ozu once wrote, "To be frank, I find it difficult to make a film out of a novel. You're forced into reworking the imagination of the author, and then have to select someone to play a role already created. When I write, I always write with an actor in mind from the beginning, and this helps create the role in the film. Actually," he characteristically added, "I found that making this film was easy." [64] All too easy, one is tempted to add. Ozu was further hampered by working for a new company, Shintoho (for the first time in his career), and by Shintoho's insistence on some romantic interest for its big-name stars, something that Ozu never handled very well. Moreover, Kinuyo Tanaka had just returned from America and was full of herself and new ideas on acting, none of which Ozu agreed with; for once, he was heard to grumble about an actor.[65] The film nevertheless won seventh place in the *Kinema Jumpo* polls.

The Munekata Sisters. *1950. Kinuyo Tanaka, Hideko Takamine, Ozu on location*

Early Summer (*Bakushu*). Shochiku/ Ofuna. Script by Ozu and Kogo Noda. Photographed by Yuharu Atsuta. With Setsuko Hara, Ichiro Sugai, Chieko Higashiyama, Chishu Ryu, Haruko Sugimura, Kuniko Miyake, Ken Nihon-yanagi, Chikage Awashima, Shuji Sano, et al. 135 min. Released October 3, 1951. Script, original negative, and prints at Shochiku and in general circulation in North America through New Yorker Films. Various small stories, almost anecdotes, make up this picture of a family. Six family members live together in Kamakura. At the end the daughter agrees to marry and the family is dissolved. *Kinema Jumpo* First Prize.

Early Summer. *1950. Setsuko Hara and Haruko Sugimura*

236

Ozu has told us that plot bored him, and we have seen him gradually releasing himself from its toils. With this picture it becomes apparent how little a role story itself has come to play in his films. Of *Early Summer* Ozu wrote: "I wanted in this picture to show a life cycle. I wanted to depict mutability (*rinne*). I was not interested in action for its own sake. And I've never worked so hard in my life. . . . I didn't push the action at all, and the ending, in consequence, should leave the audience with a poignant aftertaste." [66]

In other words, Ozu had discovered that story did not necessarily mean dramatization, at least not in any gross form. One can see him learning this. The early diaries are filled with complaints about "no story," that is, no visible way of dramatizing what story he has. They are so frequent (the only entry more often encountered is, "Drunk again last night") that one realizes what a problem dramatization was for him. Then suddenly, with one last call for help in April, 1937 ("At the end of my tether—no story," concerning *What Did the Lady Forget?*),[67] they cease. They cease because, from *The Brothers and Sisters of the Toda Family* on, Ozu solved his problem. He did not untie the knot; he cut it. Ozu discovered that neither he nor his films were concerned with story in the conventional way he had been thinking about it. In pictures such as *Late Spring, Early Summer,* and *Tokyo Story,* we see the results. The "story" is simply the recounting (balanced, artful, incisive) of what happened. It became increasingly possible to compress this "story" into a one-line description, though to do so gives no indications of the film's enormous emotional power.

The Flavor of Green Tea over Rice (*Ochazuke no Aji*). Shochiku / Ofuna. Script by Ozu and Kogo Noda. Photographed by Yuharu Atsuta. With Shin Saburi, Michiyo Kogure, Koji Tsuruta, Keiko Tsushima, Kuniko Miyake, Chikage Awashima, Chishu Ryu, Yuko Mochizuki, et al. 115 min. Released October 1, 1952. Script and original

The Flavor of Green Tea over Rice. *1952. Keiko Tsushima, Shin Saburi, Koji Tsuruta*

negative in existence; prints at Shochiku and in general circulation in North America through New Yorker Films. A middle-aged, middle-class couple experience a crisis in their marriage. With no children to create a bond, married life has lost its meaning in routine. They both attempt to improve and hence create a stronger marriage.

The Flavor of Green Tea over Rice.
Keiko Tsushima during the filming of the pachinko parlor scene

About this film Ozu has said: "I took this film out of the drawer where it had been since I'd written it, after the Army wouldn't let me make it. I took it out because there was no longer any reason for it to stay there. Because the times had changed, I rewrote it." He rewrote it to such an extent that it is unrecognizable, and the sharing of the *ochazuke* (green tea over rice) at the end loses its original point. It merely means that the somewhat snobbish wife is coming around to her husband's simple and popular tastes. "I wanted to show something about a man from the viewpoint of a woman, but this film wasn't very well made." [68] Ozu rarely attempted to graft new material onto old in this way, which was wise since his grafting efforts were rarely successful. This film has many admirable things in it, so many that some people prefer it to his finer pictures. But it does not have the perfection of *Late Spring* or *Tokyo Story*.

Tokyo Story (*Tokyo Monogatari*). Shochiku / Ofuna. Script by Ozu and Kogo Noda. Photographed by Yuharu Atsuta. With Chishu Ryu, Chieko Higashiyama, So Yamamura, Haruko Sugimura, Setsuko Hara, Kyoko Kagawa, Shiro Osaka, Eijiro Tono, Kuniko Miyake, Nobuo Nakamura, Teruko Nagaoka, et al. 136 min. Released November 3, 1953. Script and original negative in existence; prints at Shochiku and in general circulation in North America through New Yorker Films. An elderly couple, living in Onomichi in the south of Japan, go to Tokyo to visit their two married children. Their re-

Tokyo Story. *1953. Chieko Higashiyama and Chishu Ryu*

Tokyo Story. *Chieko Higashiyama, Ozu, Chishu Ryu*

ception is disappointing: both the son and the daughter are busy with their own lives and send their parents off to the hot springs resort of Atami, ostensibly as a treat, actually to get rid of them. The only one who is truly nice to them is the widow of their other son, who had died in the war. After the old couple returns home, the children receive a telegram saying the mother is ill. When they all arrive in Onomichi, the mother is dead. After the funeral the children rush back to Tokyo, but the daughter-in-law stays on. She confesses that living as a widow is difficult for her, and the father advises her to remarry. Then, alone, he sits in the empty house.

From this simple anecdote unfolds one of the greatest of all Japanese motion pictures. Ozu's style, now completely refined, utterly economical, creates a film that is unforgettable because it is so right, so true, and also because it demands so much from its audience. Evasions of any sort are rare in an Ozu picture, but here there are none at all. Two generations, a simple story that allows all the characters to change places, a pervading delineation of high summer, and the deceptive simplicity of the film's style—all these combine to create a picture so Japanese and at the same time so personal, and hence so universal in its appeal, that it becomes a masterpiece. Ozu, who was himself very fond of this picture, had little to say about it. After it won Second Prize in the *Kinema Jumpo* polls he said that, "through the growth of both parents and children, I described how the Japanese family system has begun to come apart." Then he added, surprisingly but characteristically, "This is one of my most melodramatic pictures." [69]

Early Spring (*Soshun*). Shochiku/Ofuna. Script by Ozu and Kogo Noda. Photographed by Yushun Atsuta. With Ryo Ikebe, Chikage Awashima, Keiko Kishi, Chishu Ryu, Daisuke Kato, Teiji Takahashi, Kumeko Urabe, Haruko Sugimura, So Yamamura, Kuniko Miyake, Eijiro Tono, Chieko Nakagita, Nobuo Nakamura, et al. 144 min. Released January 29, 1956. Script and original negative in existence; prints at Shochiku and in general circulation in North America through New Yorker Films. A young salaried office worker is bored with both his job and his wife. He has a slight affair with the office flirt; he and his wife quarrel. Later he accepts a transfer to the country. She goes to him and they agree to start again.

Early Spring. *1956. Keiko Kishi and Ryo Ikebe*

Early Spring. *Ryo Keiko Kish*

This film, the story of which recalls *The Flavor of Green Tea over Rice* and *An Introduction to Marriage,* is a late look at an earlier milieu, that of the office worker. Ozu himself called it an *"interi-no-nagaya-mono,"* which one might explain as a *kihachi-mono* with an "intellectual" in the leading role; loosely, then, a film with a hero at odds with his environment.[70] Sixth in the *Kinema Jumpo* polls that year, it represented something of an experiment for Ozu.

"Although I hadn't made a white-collar story for a long time, I wanted to show the life of a man with such a job—his happiness over graduation and finally becoming a member of society, his hopes for the future gradually dissolving, his realizing that, even though he has worked for years, he has accomplished nothing. By showing his life over a period of time I wanted to bring out what you might call the pathos of such a life. It is the longest of my postwar films, but I tried to avoid anything that would be dramatic and to collect only casual scenes of everyday life, hoping in doing so that the audience would feel the sadness of this kind of life."

The picture also took more time to make than most Ozu films. It took eighty-seven days just to write the script. "They kidded me at the company saying I'd better call the film *Raishun* (Next Spring); actually the title, *Early Spring,* refers to young people just starting out, that time of life. People seem to understand this kind of symbolism —and, besides, President Kido [of Shochiku] is very fussy about titles." [71]

Tokyo Twilight. *1957. Setsuko Hara and Ineko Arima*

Tokyo Twilight(*Tokyo Boshoku*). 1957. Shochiku/Ofuna. Script by Ozu and Kogo Noda. Photographed by Yuharu Atsuta. With Setsuko Hara, Isuzu Yamada, Ineko Arima, Chishu Ryu, Masami Taura, Kinzo Shin, Nobuo Nakamura, Haruko Sugiyama, Teiji Takahashi, Fujio Suga, et al. 141 min. Released April 30, 1957. Script and original negative in existence; prints at Shochiku. A father lives alone with his two daughters. The elder has left her husband and returned with her child. The younger is having an affair that results in an abortion. The daughters discover that their mother, whom they thought dead, is staying nearby, having left their father years before to live with another man. The discovery shatters them. The younger girl finally kills herself, the elder returns to her husband. The father is left alone.

Tokyo Twilight. *Ineko Arima, Setsuko Hara, Ozu*

Before this film was released Ozu said: "Recently there has been increasingly severe criticism of the *Ofuna-cho* [home drama] flavor in films. But the traditions of *Ofuna-cho* are the result of thirty years. They are not going to fall in one morning. I believe that the true flavor of the *Ofuna-cho* will be found in this film." [72] And so it is. The picture is one of Ozu's most melodramatic (in our sense, not his), with confrontation-suicides and the like. The idea of a missing parent dramatically reappearing, a favorite melodramatic device, was used by Ozu several times (in both versions of *Floating Weeds,* for example) but such excesses as suicide were rare for him. Still, Ozu's melodrama appears austere indeed by comparison with anyone else's, and sections of the film were salvaged by extraordinarily good dialogue.

241

The picture was Ozu's last black-and-white film. Of it, the director wrote: "Many people have found this picture to be about the wild behavior of the daughter, but I think the emphasis lies on the younger generation only as foil for the older." [73]

Equinox Flower (*Higanbana*). Shochiku / Kamata. Script by Ozu and Kogo Noda, after a novel by Ton Satomi. Photographed by Yuharu Atsuta. With Shin Saburi, Kinuyo Tanaka, Ineko Arima, Keiji Sada, Chieko Naniwa, Fujiko Yamamoto, Chishu Ryu, Nobuo Nakamura, Teiji Takahashi, Fumio Watanabe, Yoshiko Kuga, Miyuki Kuwano, et al. 118 min. Released September 7, 1958. Script and original negative in existence; prints at Shochiku and in general circulation in North America through New Yorker Films. A daughter wishes to marry the man of her choice, but her father objects. Her mother understands her feelings, however, as does her friend from Kyoto. Eventually the father is won over.

Equinox Flower. *1958. Kinuyo Tanaka and Shin Saburi*

Equinox Flower. *Ozu, Kinuyo Tanaka, Shin Saburi*

From *Tokyo Twilight* on, Ozu became more interested in the younger generation, or at least those members of it who were in rebellion. The traditional daughter in *Late Spring* is quite different from the modern girls in these later films, yet, as Ozu said:

In this film I am, I suppose, more sympathetic with the parents. All the recent movies seem to deny their values and to approve the behavior of the young. . . . In this film the daughters seem modern enough, but really they are traditional. The father seems to be sensible enough and he gives good advice to other people, but when it comes to his own problems he says one thing and means another; . . . he has raised his daughter and he worries about her marriage. She went and got engaged without telling him. He knows that her choice was good, but because he was neglected he feels somewhat injured and yet cannot totally oppose the marriage. It is this tension in the father that I wanted to show in the film.[74]

The film consequently contains some implicit criticism of the Japanese family system, but no denigration of it. Ozu never subjected the family system to the ironic treatment he gave, say, the social system. The completed film is so far from taking sides that it is impossible to call older or younger generation good or bad. It is a balanced picture of Japanese family life, made with loving irony.

This was Ozu's first color film. A dozen years earlier he had written, "Color is all right once in a while, but if you see it all the time it's like eating *tendon* [fried shrimp, fish, etc., over rice] —you get fed up with it." [75] He now said "I felt I'd regret it later if I didn't do it now," and the critics who had objected to the unreality of the sets in earlier films (too clean, too neat, not naturalistic enough) found new cause for complaint with a color system (Agfacolor) that rendered all things too pretty. Ozu, by contrast, liked his color effects from the first. ("Even when I was using black and white I was always interested in tone and mood, so it isn't too difficult to work with color. Red turns out magnificently on Agfa.") [76] He had none of the misgivings that went with his early sound films. (Though one must add that it was the company and not Ozu who decided the film would be in color, to do justice to Fujiko Yamamoto's famous beauty.) He said he felt that color made his "compositions" more interesting. He never, however, had any good words for any of the various-sized "scope" screens. "I have not seen CinemaScope," he wrote in 1958, "but I did see Vista-Vision—and I got fed up in the middle of *This is Cinerama*." [77] *Kinema Jumpo* Third Prize.

Good Morning (*Ohayo*). Shochiku/ Ofuna. Script by Ozu and Kogo Noda. Photographed by Yuharu Atsuta. With Chishu Ryu, Kuniko Miyake, Yoshiko Kuga, Keiji Sada, Koji Shidara, Masahiko Shimazu, Haruko Sugimura, Toyo Takahashi, Teruko Nagaoka, Eijiro Tono, Sadako Sawamura, et al. 94 min. Released May 12, 1959. Script

Good Morning. *1959. Masahiko Shimazu, Chishu Ryu, Koji Shidara, Kuniko Miyake*

243

and original negative in existence; prints at Shochiku and in general circulation in North America through Audio/Brandon Films. Two little boys live with their parents in a suburban Tokyo housing development. A misunderstanding among the neighbor ladies is innocently compounded by the two boys. After an argument with their parents (they want a television set and their father refuses to buy one), they are told to shut up. Taking their parents at their word they shut up completely, not speaking to anyone, even the neighbors. These ladies, finding that the customary morning greeting (*ohayo*) goes unanswered, at once assume the boys' mother is angry with them, and a neighborhood quarrel begins. Finally, the father relents, the television is bought, the boys answer the neighbor ladies politely, and all ends happily.

"I had this story in mind for a long time," Ozu said, "and I wanted to make it though I knew it would be difficult. I mentioned it a meeting of the Directors' Guild and they all seemed interested, so I told them that any of them was free to make it, but no one tried so I did it myself. At first I thought of this story as being more quiet and sober. After a while I thought I might have a money-maker here, so I made it funnier. Well, I guess what I mean is that I wanted more people to see and enjoy the film." [78] He also said, characteristically: "I would have been annoyed if people had said I now only made serious films because I'd just won the Academy of Fine Arts Prize." Hence perhaps the overabundant farting in this picture. [79]

Ozu himself never mentioned the film's close resemblance to *I Was Born, But . . . .* The two boys in the 1932 film question the assumptions the world entertains about bosses and workers, the two in the 1959 picture question the basis of all social conversation; in the first film the boys go on a hunger strike, in the second a silence strike; in both films they come around in the end. There are, between the two pictures, many differences, of course (and some resemblances to *Early Summer* as well). Easy good humor takes the place of irony, and the later film is one of the director's most approachable. It was also the first in a series of three "remakes."

Floating Weeds (*Ukigusa*). Daiei. Script by Ozu and Kogo Noda, based on the 1934 Ikeda script. Photographed by Kazuo Miyagawa. With Ganjiro Nakamura, Haruko Sugimura, Machiko Kyo, Ayako Wakao, Hiroshi Kawaguchi, Koji Mitsui, Mutsuko Sakura, Mantaro Ushio, Haruo Tanaka, et al. 119 min. Released November 17,1959. Script and original negative in existence; prints with Daiei estate and in circulation in North America through Audio/Brandon Films. A small theatrical troupe revisits a remote island town after some years' absence. The aging leading actor is particularly anxious to stop because he had had a son by one of the local women and wants to see him again. Though he has returned from time to time, his trips have been so infrequent that the boy thinks the

actor is his uncle. This visit, however, leads to complications. The leading lady is the actor's mistress and resents the boy's mother. Then the son falls in love with one of the younger girls in the troupe. Eventually she decides to stay with the son, the troupe fails, and the actor returns to his mistress.

Floating Weeds. *1959. Haruo Tanaka, Mantaro Ushio, Koji Mitsui, Mutsuko Sakura*

Floating Weeds. *Ozu on location at Shijima*

"Many years ago," wrote Ozu, "I made a silent version of this film [*A Story of Floating Weeds*]. Now I wanted to make it again up in the snow country of Hokuriku, so I did this new script with Noda [it was called *The Ham Actor* (*Daikon Yakusha*)], but that year there wasn't much snow so I couldn't use the locations I had in mind in Takado and Sado." [80] Consequently, he decided to film the picture in the Kii peninsula, the location being the island of Shijima in Wakayama. Ozu made the picture for a company new to him. Daiei had earlier asked Ozu to make a film, but his Shochiku contract required a film a year and he usually had no time left over for other projects. He had finished *Good Morning* early, however, won Shochiku's agreement, and moved for a season to the new company.

"Though this is a contemporary film," said Ozu, "in mood it really belongs to the Meiji period. It could have been filmed that way, too, but that would have meant going to all the trouble of getting the costumes, the manners, and so on, just right." [81] Almost alone among Japanese directors, Ozu never made a costume picture (except for his debut film), though, as we have seen, he once intended to. "I would

245

really like to make a *jidai-geki*," he once said, mentioning that the novelist Jiro Osaragi was always urging him to make one. *Floating Weeds* gives some indication of what such a film would have been like in Ozu's hands: it would have been much like his contemporary films.

The finished *Floating Weeds* is a remake and a close one. Ozu's series of remakes argues neither slackening of interest nor diminution in ability. Rather, since all Ozu's pictures have somewhat similar stories, since similar scenes occur again and again, something like a remake seems inevitable. There are significant differences, however, between *Floating Weeds* and its predecessor. The 1934 picture has the troupe going by train to a small town in the mountainous north of Japan, while the 1959 film has them going by boat to a small port in the Wakayama Peninsula in the south. The bits of theatrical performance seen are different, though they are equally delicious in their lovingly observed badness. There are in the 1934 version some camera movements that were discarded in the remake. And of course the earlier picture was silent, the later picture sound. But by and large, externally, the films are identical. There are even identical scenes, such as the fight between the leader of the troupe and his leading lady mistress in the rain. Koji Mitsui is in the cast of both pictures: in the 1934 film he plays the son; a quarter of a century later he plays one of the older actors in the troupe.

The main difference is internal. The earlier version is the more bitter. Toward the end of his life Ozu mellowed, and one does not see or feel the pain of the once again abandoned mother in the 1959 picture. To be sure Haruko Sugimura is by no means happy about further betrayal, but she has become philosophical. Choko Iida, in the earlier film, shows us a bleak despair rarely seen in Ozu's later work. In 1934 Ozu felt deeply and personally the wrong that life inflicts. Twenty-five years later he felt just as deeply, but perhaps less personally. The first version, on the other hand, is spring-like in its comedy; the second has an autumnal sadness about it.

Certainly, the 1959 film is the most physically beautiful of all of Ozu's pictures. It was photographed by Kazuo Miyagawa, one of Japan's greatest cinematographers (*Rashomon, Yojimbo, Ugetsu, Enjo, Kagi*). "Miyagawa," wrote Ozu, "went to lots of trouble and experimented a good deal with this film. I began to understand just what a color picture is. For example, you must give the right kind of lighting to a certain color to make it look on film the way it does to the eye. If you shoot two different colors with the same lighting, one of them won't come out, and so you have to decide from the beginning which color you don't want." "About this time," he added, "CinemaScope was getting popular. I wanted to have nothing to do with it, and consequently I shot more close-ups and used shorter shots." Having reacted against the long shots and long scenes of the new screen, he discovered that "this film must have more cuts in it than any other recent Japanese movie." [82]

Late Autumn (*Akibiyori*). Shochiku/ Ofuna. Script by Ozu and Kogo Noda, after the novel by Ton Satomi. Photographed by Yuharu Atsuta. With Setsuko Hara, Yoko Tsukasa, Chishu Ryu, Mariko Okada, Keiji Sada, Shin Saburi, Miyuki Kuwano, Nobuo Nakamura, Kuniko Miyake, Yuriko Tashiro, Ryuji Kita, Shinichiro Mikami, Shima Iwashita, et al. 125 min. Released November 13, 1960. Script and original negative in existence; prints at Shochiku and in general circulation in North America through New Yorker Films. A young girl lives with her mother. Though she has had opportunities to marry, she refused, preferring to stay at home. The widowed mother, however, feels that her daughter is sacrificing herself and attempts to find her a suitable husband. The daughter opposes this until she comes to believe, mistakenly, that her mother is motivated by a desire to remarry. The mother goes back to their apartment and begins her life alone.

Late Autumn. 1960. Ryuji Kita, Nobuo Nakamura, Shin Saburi

Ozu and Kogo Noda at Chigasaki during the writing of **Late Autumn**

This, the third of Ozu's "remakes" (and winner of fifth place in that year's *Kinema Jumpo* polls), is a version of *Late Spring*. Both feature Setsuko Hara; in the earlier film she had played the daughter, now she plays the parent. The major change is Ozu's substituting of mother for father. Minor changes include the substitution of a number of the widow's late husband's friends, all men, for the aunt who in the earlier picture helps to find a likely young man for the daughter. These friends (seen again in *An Autumn Afternoon*) are Ozu's schoolboys grown old. They are still mischievous, even malicious, but still, in their way, innocent. And again there is a change of tone. There is an elegiac sadness in *Late Autumn* and, perhaps in consequence, some relaxation of the extraordinary objectivity that so distinguishes *Late Spring*.

Of this 1960 film Ozu has written:

People sometimes complicate the simplest things. Life, which seems complex, suddenly reveals itself as very simple—and I wanted to show that in this film. There was something else, too. It is easy to show drama on film; the actors laugh or cry, but this is only explanation. A director can really show what he wants without resorting to an appeal to the emotions. I want to make people feel without resorting to drama. I've been trying to do this ever since *The Brothers and Sisters of the Toda Family,* but it is very difficult. Here [in *Late Autumn*] I think I was fairly successful, but still the results are far from perfect.[83]

The End of Summer (*Kohayagawa-ke no Aki*). Toho. Script by Ozu and Kogo Noda. Photographed by Asakazu Nakai. With Ganjiro Nakamura, Setsuko Hara, Yoko Tsukasa, Michiyo Aratama, Yumi Shirakawa, Reiko Dan, Chieko Naniwa, Keiju Kobayashi, Daisuke Kato, Akira Takarada, Haruko Sugimura, Hisaya Morishige, Chishu Ryu, Yuko Mochizuki, et al. 103 min. Released October 29, 1961. Script and original negative in existence; prints at Toho and in general circulation in North America through New Yorker Films. An older man has had three daughters by his wife, one by a former mistress. The eldest daughter is widowed but getting ready to remarry; the second is married and her husband runs the family business, a sake plant; the third has already had her husband picked out by the family. When the father decides to take up with his former mistress, the daughters are upset. In the midst of this the father has a heart attack, and later dies.

Ozu directing Ganjiro Nakamura in **The End of Summer**

BIOGRAPHICAL FILMOGRAPHY

The End of Summer. *1961. Ganjiro Nakamura, Keiju Kobayashi, Michiyo Aratama*

As in *The Brothers and Sisters of the Toda Family,* Ozu here creates a picture about an entire family, enriching the several strands of his story with many anecdotes. The film is unusually rich, even for Ozu, in character vignettes. At the same time, it is one of the director's bleakest films. Despite the setting, the season, the lushness of the production that Toho allowed Ozu, there is little of the golden, autumnal atmosphere of *Late Autumn,* which went before, or *An Autumn Afternoon,* which followed. Kogo Noda remembered that the idea for the film came from a story they heard from a girl they knew, about a father who one day collapsed with a heart attack. The family all gathered and overnight he got well. From this slender beginning (incorporated in the finished film), the film grew. "From early February in 1961 we shut ourselves up at Tateshina (in Nagano) and worked on the scenario for *Kohayagawa-ke no Aki* [lit. The Autumn of the Kohayagawa Family]. Fewer guests than usual, so less drunken merrymaking and dancing. For this reason the work proceeded fast, and the manuscript was finished on April 21." [84]

The film begins in the lightest manner. One expects a comedy, consummately well-done, the kind of picture Ozu was making during the thirties. The surface is mundane, marvelously so, but with almost no hint of the depths we are later to view. With humor, with affection, we are willingly led deeper and deeper until we are faced with death.

And death triumphs. It is shown in the most direct and uncompromising manner, with the funeral bed, cremation, a smoking chimney. At the end the family moves on, goes home; only the crows remain. It is perhaps the only Ozu picture in which there is no spiritual survivor. One of Ozu's most beautiful films, it is one of his most disturbing.

An Autumn Afternoon (*Samma no Aji*). Shochiku/Ofuna. Script by Ozu and Kogo Noda. Photographed by Yuharu Atsuta. With Shima Iwashita, Shinichiro Mikami, Keiji Sada, Mariko Okada, Nobuo Nakamura, Chishu Ryu, Kuniko Miyake, Ryuji Kita, Eijiro Tono, Teruo Yoshida, Noburo Nakamura, Michiyo Tamaki, Haruko Sugimura, Daisuke Kato, Kyoko Kishida, Toyo Takahashi, et al. 112 min. Released November 18, 1962. Script and original negative in existence; prints at Shochiku and in general circulation in North America through New Yorker Films. A company auditor, widowed and getting on in years, lives with his son and daughter and has as friends a few men his own age. From one of them he hears of the marriage of yet another friend's daughter. This sets him thinking about his own daughter. He decides that she should marry, and eventually arranges it with a young man recommended by his friends. The event goes off as planned. Again he meets with his friends. They all drink together once more, and he realizes that he is getting old, and that he is alone.

An Autumn Afternoon. *1962. Kyoko Kishida, Keiji Sada, Chishu Ryu*

An Autumn Afternoon. *Kyoko Kishida, Keiji Sada, Chishu Ryu, Ozu*

About this film Kogo Noda wrote:

"While he was shooting *Kohayagawa,* Shochiku was already after him for the title of his next film. So he decided on this one [*Samma no Aji,* lit. The Taste of Mackerel]; only he did not intend to show any *samma,* only to have the whole feeling of the film that was suggested by this title.

During the writing of this script Ozu's mother died. It was during February 1962, and we were at Tateshina working. She had been in bed with neuralgia since the end of the year and wasn't doing well. We both [i.e., Noda and his wife] urged Ozu to go home, but he said, "It's still all right, she won't die yet." He seemed to have the firmest faith that she wouldn't die until she was eighty-eight, which would have been that May. But then she died.

250

After he had returned to Sarashina after the funeral, I found the following written in his diary:

Down in the valley it is already spring
Clouds of cherry blossoms;
But here, the sluggish eye, the taste of mackerel—
The blossoms are melancholy
And the flavor of sake becomes bitter." [85]

Ozu's last film, this is also his simplest. The ingredients are familiar. The story recalls *Late Autumn* and *Late Spring;* the colors are subdued; the viewing angle is invariable. Nothing is wanting, nothing is extraneous. At the same time there is an extraordinary intensification of mood in this picture. It is autumn again, but now it is deep autumn. Winter was always near, but now it will be tomorrow. At the same time Ozu's regard was never kinder, never wiser. There is a mellowness about this picture which is stronger than nostalgia.

Kogo Noda has left an account of Ozu's last days:

"That winter (i.e., 1963) we were working on *Daikon to Ninjin* (Radishes and Carrots, filmed in 1964 by Minoru Shibuya), and Ozu went back to Kamakura since he was writing a TV script for NHK [*Class Dismissed* (Seishun Hokago)]. When he returned to Tateshina in March, he seemed tired. He asked my wife to look at his neck, the right side of it. It was swollen, but not red, and neither of us imagined for a moment that this terrible thing was to take his life.

He himself wasn't worried. Even when he went back to Tokyo to have it looked at, he called us from a bar and seemed pretty drunk. It wasn't until April 10 that he went to see specialists in Osaka and entered the hospital. After the operation and the cobalt treatment, it started to hurt him, and even Ozu, who was so able to bear pain, could hardly stand it.

But then this got better, too, and on July 1 he left the hospital and went for convalescence to the Nakanishi *ryokan* at Yugawara. He invited us to come and stay, too, and seemed cheerful. "It will be about August when I can get back to Tateshina; by September 23 I'll be working again." But after he had returned home to Kamakura his shoulder started, and on October 12 he entered the Ochanomizu Hospital.

Until the last moment I continued to hope for a miracle, but finally Room 17 on the eighth floor became his last resting place. December 12 was his birthday and also the day of his *kanreki* [celebration of the sixtieth birthday]. Keiji Sada and his wife came with a *chan-chan-*

ko [a brightly colored vest often given on this occasion; when sixty is reached, one returns to the garments of childhood] with the Ozu family crest on it. They were too late. It was laid on his body.

Ozu used to say when we talked about death that he wanted to die of a stroke or something, to die without any pain. But, and my eyes burn when I think of it, he had to suffer much." [86]

Ozu died of cancer on the evening of his sixtieth birthday. His ashes were buried at the temple of Engaku in Kita-Kamakura, near the place he had spent much of his adult life.

His tombstone bears the single character for *mu*—an aesthetic word, a philosophical term, one which is usually translated as "nothingness" but which suggests the nothing that, in Zen philosophy, is everything.

Ozu on the set of **An Autumn Afternoon**

NOTES

PREFACE

1. Akira Iwasaki. Untitled essay on Ozu, published (in English) by Sho-chiku as advance publicity for *Late Autumn*, 1960.

2. According to legend the low angle demanded continual sacrifices from Ozu's helpers. It was claimed (wrongly) that lying flat on his stomach on cold floors and colder fields caused ailments that forced Ozu's first cameraman, Hideo Shigehara, to leave the profession; it was also claimed that his later cameraman, Yushun Atsuta, lasted so long only because he was blessed with an exceptionally strong stomach.

INTRODUCTION

1. Films in which the home predominates are: *That Night's Wife, Until the Day We Meet Again, Woman of Tokyo, A Mother Ought to Be Loved, The Only Son, The Brothers and Sisters of the Toda Family, There Was a Father, A Hen in the Wind, Late Spring, The Munekata Sisters, Early Summer, The Flavor of Green Tea over Rice, Tokyo Story, Tokyo Twilight, Equinox Flower, Good Morning, Late Autumn, The End of Summer, An Autumn Afternoon*, etc. Those in which school predominates are: *Dreams of Youth, Fighting Friends, I Graduated, But . . . , Walk Cheerfully, I Flunked, But . . . , The Lady and the Beard, Where Are the Dreams of Youth?, Tokyo Chorus*, etc. Those in which the office predominates are: *The Life of an Office Worker, Early Spring*, etc., and, in Ozu's opinion, *I Was Born, But. . . .*

2. Exceptions are the early comedies and such films as *Passing Fancy, What Did the Lady Forget?, The Flavor of Green Tea over Rice*, etc.

3. Examples are: *Late Spring, Early Summer, Tokyo Twilight, Late Autumn, An Autumn Afternoon*, etc.

253

4. Examples are: *I Graduated, But* . . . , *The Only Son, The Brothers and Sisters of the Toda Family*, etc.

5. Examples are: *There Was a Father, Tokyo Story, The End of Summer*, etc.

6. Akira Iwasaki, "Ozu to Nihon no Eiga" (Ozu and the Japanese Film), in *Kinema Jumpo Tokushu*, February 10, 1964.

7. To cite only the most striking instance: at the end of *Tokyo Story*, the younger sister says, "Isn't life disappointing?" The sister-in-law, with a smile, replies, "Yes, it is."

8. Such proletarian families are seen in *Tokyo Chorus, Passing Fancy*, etc.; the last such family appears in *The Record of a Tenement Gentleman*.

9. Ozu gave the following explanation for the differences in his later pictures to the critics Shinbi Iida and Akira Iwasaki: "You begin climbing the mountain when you're young; then at a certain height you discover a new pathway, so you go down and take it. This type of person is called a late-bloomer. I took one path and when I was almost to the summit I had a strong feeling that I should take another path. But I can't start all over again from the bottom." "A Talk with Ozu," *Kinema Jumpo*, June, 1958.

10. W. H. Auden, "Forgotten Laughter, Forgotten Prayer," *New York Times*, February 2, 1971.

11. "Ozu has actually described only the relations between parents and children . . . and we see their happiness and their sorrow and realize that this is the basis of Ozu's concept of man." Tadao Sato, *Ozu Yasujiro no Geijutsu* [The Art of Yasujiro Ozu] (Tokyo: Asahi Shimbunsha, 1971).

12. Examples are: *Woman of Tokyo, Passing Fancy, A Story of Floating Weeds, The Only Son, The Brothers and Sisters of the Toda Family, There Was a Father, Late Spring, Tokyo Twilight, Floating Weeds, An Autumn Afternoon*, etc.

13. Examples are: *A Couple on the Move, Body Beautiful, Wife Lost, An Introduction to Marriage, An Inn in Tokyo, What Did the Lady Forget?, A Hen in the Wind, The Flavor of Green Tea over Rice*, etc.

14. Examples are: *A Straightforward Boy, Young Miss, I Was Born, But* . . . , *Passing Fancy, The Flavor of Green Tea over Rice, Tokyo Twilight, Equinox Flower, Good Morning*, etc.

15. A distinction between story and plot is useful. A story is "a narrative of events arranged in their time-sequence. A plot is also a narrative of events, the emphasis falling on causality. 'The king died and then the queen died,' is a story. 'The king died, and then the queen died of grief,' is a plot." E. M. Forster, *Aspects of the Novel* (London: Arnold, 1927).

16. Quoted by Akira Iwasaki in untitled essay on Ozu published by Shochiku as advance publicity.

17. "I also like whales," he once said, talking about his predilections, "and I like brass—and I collect all kinds of patent medicines." Conversation with Yasujiro Ozu, 1959.

18. Examples are given in the Biographical Filmography.

19. *Ozu Yasujiro—Hito to Shigoto* [Yasujiro Ozu: The Man and His Work] (Tokyo: Banyusha, 1972).

20. Ozu expressed himself on this subject as follows: "What do I mean by character? Well, in a word, humanness. If you don't convey humanness, your work is worthless. This is the purpose of all art. In a film, emotion without humanness is a defect. A person who is perfect at facial expression is not necessarily able to express humanness. In fact, the expression of emotion often hinders the expression of humanness. Knowing how to control emotion and knowing how to express humanness with this control— that is the job of a director." "Humanness and Technique," *Kinema Jumpo,* December, 1953.

SCRIPT

1. "Ozu Jitaku o Kataru" [Ozu on Ozu], *Kinema Jumpo Tokushu,* February 10, 1964.

2. *Ibid.*

3. We know that one scene in *There Was a Father*—in which the young man places the container holding his father's ashes on the luggage rack above him on the train ride home—was taken directly from Ozu's life because of the fuss he made when critics attacked it. Hostile critics called the scene disgraceful: a dutiful son would have held the ashes all the way home. Ozu retorted: "My mother and I took my father's ashes to Mt. Koya by night train and we got sleepy, and if we'd kept them in our laps they might have fallen off. After all, the rack is the cleanest place in the train, and so far as I was concerned the best place." Recounted by Kogo Noda, "Yasujiro Ozu to iu Otoko" [A Man Called Ozu], in *Ibid.*

4. *Ibid.*

5. The diaries, for example, mention Ozu's desire to make a film about an ex-soldier and his difficulties. This became *Early Spring,* made long after the end of the war, at a time when ex-soldiers' difficulties were nominal. Nonetheless, in the film, Ozu brought together wartime buddies and used much of what he had learned in visiting bereaved families.

6. *Ozu Yasujiro—Hito to Shigoto* [Yasujiro Ozu: The Man and His Work] (Tokyo: Banyusha, 1972).

7. Noda's daughter Reiko noted in the diary during the work on *The End of Summer* that the producers (Toho) had called from Tokyo to inquire about the script's progress. Ozu had been reassuring. Reiko comments that if the producers had known how much drinking and chatting was going on, they would have had ample cause for worry.

8. There are exceptions, of course; e.g., Yeh Tung's perversely small-minded review of *Good Morning* in *Film Quarterly,* Winter 1965–66.

9. Interview cited in n. 1.

10. Interview cited in n. 3.

11. *Ozu Yasujiro—Hito to Shigoto.*

12. His drinking also accounted for his finally settling at Tateshina as a permanent scriptwriting place. Ozu had been to the Noda house there and liked it, and one New Year's as Noda and his wife were preparing to go there Ozu's mother came calling: " 'Yasujiro is drinking from morning to evening and I'm afraid he'll ruin his health. So if you should be going to the villa for New Year's [a traditional drinking time in Japan], please take him along but don't tell him I asked you to—if he hears that I did he'll be very angry.' (We took him and neither my wife nor myself ever told Ozu why.)" Recounted by Noda in interview cited in n. 3.

13. *Ibid.*

14. Interview cited in n. 1.

15. Interview cited in n. 3.

16. Interview cited in n. 1.

17. Tadao Sato, *Ozu Yasujiro no Geijutsu* [The Art of Yasujiro Ozu] (Tokyo: Asahi Shimbunsha, 1971).

18. All references to dialogue in this chapter include its place within the English subtitle list; this dialogue occurs at reel 4, line 57.

19. Noda's notes for *Radishes and Carrots*, in *Ozu Yasujiro—Hito to Shigoto*.

20. Senichi Hisamitsu, *The Vocabulary of Japanese Literary Aesthetics* (Tokyo: Center for East Asian Cultural Studies, 1963).

21. Ozu also had little faith that foreigners could appreciate his work: "They don't understand—that's why they say it is Zen or something like that." To which Shinbi Iida, the critic with whom he was speaking, added, "Yes, they make everything enigmatic." "A Talk with Ozu," *Kinema Jumpo*, June, 1958.

22. Conversation with Nobuo Nakamura, 1968.

23. *Ibid.*

24. Kogo Noda, comments in *Ozu Yasujiro no Sekai* [The World of Yasujiro Ozu], (Japan Victor Album SJV 1140 1-M, 1972), side 4, band 1.

25. Chishu Ryu, "Yasujiro Ozu," *Sight and Sound*, Spring, 1964.

SHOOTING

1. There are notable exceptions: the riverside scene in *The End of Summer;* and similar scenes (bird's eye view) in *Floating Weeds* and *Early Summer*. Ozu himself thought the angle became higher in his later films. So he told Tomo Shimokawara, who attributed the change to a change in living style among the Japanese—more chairs and fewer tatami mats and *zabuton* pillows. *Ozu Yasujiro—Hito to Shigoto* [Yasujiro Ozu: The Man and His Work] (Tokyo: Banyusha, 1972).

2. Quoted in Paul Schrader's *Transcendental Style in Film: Ozu, Bresson, Dreyer* (Berkeley and Los Angeles: University of California Press, 1972).

3. For the definitions in these paragraphs, I am indebted to the works of Jean Debrix.

4. The tracking shot is, of course, often used by directors to decorate a long talking scene, the dolly in Pasolini's *Acattone* being one celebrated example.

5. There are many examples of the dolly-in for interest; famous examples of the dolly-out to suggest tragic disassociation and helplessness occur in the final scenes of René Clement's *Jeux Interdits* and André Cayette's *L'Oeil pour l'Oeil,* etc.

6. A famous analogous example occurs in *La Jetée* of Chris Marker, a short film made entirely of still photographs except for one scene, in which we see the heroine's eyelashes fluttering. The effect is overwhelming.

7. Quoted in Schrader, *Transcendental Style in Film.*

8. One of the best-known examples occurs at the end of Antonioni's *L'Avventura,* where the two characters are placed so that the scenery (a distant and dormant volcano, a modern, windowless building) comments upon them.

9. Conversations between Yoda and Leonard Schrader.

10. Atsuta's article in *Kinema Jumpo Tokushu,* February 10, 1964.

11. Tadao Sato, *Ozu Yasujiro no Geijutsu* [The Art of Yasujiro Ozu] (Tokyo: Asahi Shimbunsha, 1971).

12. *Ozu—Hito to Shigoto.*

13. Later directors, however, have learned to use this aspect of the Japanese house; examples are Ichikawa's *Bonchi* and Yoshishige Yoshida's *Eros Plus Massacre.*

14. *Ozu—Hito to Shigoto.*

15. Chishu Ryu in *Ozu Yasujiro no Sekai* [The World of Yasujiro wozu], (Japan Victor Album SJV 1140 1-M, 1972), side 2, band 1.

16. Conversation with Masahiro Shinoda, 1971.

17. Chishu Ryu in *Ozu Yasujiro no Sekai,* side 2, band 1.

18. Conversation with Setsuko Hara, 1962.

19. Conversation with Yoko Tsukasa, 1968.

20. Daizo Hata, Ozu's sometime still man, asked Tomo Shimogawara if he didn't think Ozu's compositions brought to mind the kind of photos that won contests in the 1920's. Hata said that Ozu's interest in pictorial composition originated with the purchase of a Leica, early in his career. He also revealed that Ozu was a still-photo enthusiast, and used to develop his own prints and send them off to photo contests. *Ozu—Hito to Shigoto.*

21. Schrader, *Transcendental Style in Film.*

22. An architect told Tadao Sato that Japanese rooms, small ones at any rate, are not made for people sitting across from each other, but for people sitting side by side or on either side of a corner. *Ozu—Hito to Shigoto.*

23. Sato, *Ozu Yasujiro no Geijutsu.*

24. Schrader, *Transcendental Style in Film.*

25. This scene has also been commented upon by Sato and Schrader.

26. Shin Saburi in *Ozu Yasujiro no Sekai*, side 1, band 3.

27. Yasujiro Ozu in *ibid.*, side 1, band 4.

28. Chishu Ryu, "Ozu to Watakushi" [Ozu and I], *Kinema Jumpo*, June, 1958.

29. Chishu Ryu, "Yasujiro Ozu," *Sight and Sound*, Spring, 1964.

30. Chishu Ryu, "Ozu to Watakushi."

31. *Ibid.*

32. Conversation with Nobuo Nakamura, 1968.

33. Chieko Higashiyama, in *Ozu Yasujiro—Hito to Shigoto*.

34. Choko Iida, *ibid.*

35. Ganjiro Nakamura, *ibid.*

36. Chishu Ryu, *ibid.*

37. Choko Iida, *ibid.*

38. Mitsuko Yoshikawa, *ibid.*

39. Chishu Ryu, *ibid.*

40. *Ibid.*

41. Chieko Higashiyama, *ibid.*

42. Sato, *Ozu Yasujiro no Geijutsu.*

43. Ozu's idea of good acting was "a great scene in *The Little Foxes* where Bette Davis is standing beside her dying husband and making tea . . . no facial expression or anything—just making tea without any emotion. The only thing you can hear is the click of the cup and saucer." Ozu, "Humanness and Technique," *Kinema Jumpo*, December, 1953.

44. Chishu Ryu, "Ozu to Watakushi."

45. Sato, *Ozu Yasujiro.*

46. Noda, "Ozu to iu otoko," *Kinema Jumpo Tokushu*, February 10, 1964.

47. Chishu Ryu, "Ozu to Watakushi."

48. Sato, *Ozu Yasujiro.*

49. Conversation with Kinuyo Tanaka, 1965.

50. Sato, *Ozu Yasujiro.*

51. *Ibid.*

52. *Ibid.*

53. Jane Austen mentions several battles in *Persuasion* and names "Buonaparté" once in a letter of 1813. Ozu mentions the China War once, in *The Brothers and Sisters of the Toda Family*, but makes many references to it in the 1938–39 "War Diaries," and in the list of projects (see Biographical Filmography) that he announced, perhaps not altogether seriously, for the later war years.

54. Conversation with Nobuo Nakamura, 1968.

55. Conversation with Leonard Schrader, 1972.

56. There are different ways of being disconcerted. When Oliver Hardy looks into the camera, i.e. at us, after yet another example of Stan Laurel's stupidity, we are delighted at being made an accomplice (particularly by a

man who will shortly reveal himself as even more stupid) and surprised at this obvious violation of the convention that we are invisible to the actor. When the extras in Fellini's *Satyricon* turn to look at us, we are made uneasy at these visions from a past to whom we are obviously visible; if we feel delight, it is at the audacity of the director. When Peter Finch turns to us at the end of *Sunday, Bloody Sunday,* we are disconcerted (the director's breaking the convention means that it was inoperative throughout the film, and we were visible all during it), and any pleasure we feel is derived from our realization that the director has chosen to end the film by destroying a convention, and, of course, the gratitude we feel at being looked at in the eyes and addressed directly. In all these cases and many more, the effect of the full-face shot is disconcerting and strong because it is so rarely used. When used continually, as it is in Ozu's films, the shot soon ceases to disconcert: it is accepted as a new convention.

57. Ozu was not, however, looking for expression. "Skill at facial expression isn't enough. An actor who is good at making sad and happy faces—that is, an actor who has complete control of his facial muscles—is never sufficient. In fact those things are rather easy to do. . . . But I don't care whether an actor can express emotion well or not. To me the important thing is character, to catch the humanness." As an example Ozu chose a scene from John Ford: "Look at Henry Fonda in *My Darling Clementine:* motionless and expressionless—there is the greatness of John Ford. Fonda sits in a chair with his legs propped up on a pillar and a satisfied smile on his face—I really envy that rapport between Ford and Fonda." Ozu, "Humanness and Technique."

EDITING

1. They are used most noticeably in the films of Antonioni: the long shot of the sea and the rocks in *L'Avventura* at the point when it becomes apparent that the missing girl will not be found; the empty scenes during the final coda of *L'Eclipse,* etc. For their use in Eastern art see the discussion of *mu* in Paul Schrader, *Transcendental Style in Film: Ozu, Bresson, Dreyer* (Berkeley and Los Angeles: University of California Press, 1972).

2. Will Peterson, "Stone Garden," in *The World of Zen* (New York: Vintage, 1960).

3. Schrader, *Transcendental Style in Film.*

4. Tadao Sato, *Ozu Yasujiro no Geijutsu* [The Art of Yasujiro Ozu] (Tokyo: Asahi Shimbunsha, 1971).

5. *Ibid.*

6. *Ibid.*

7. *Ibid.*

8. Morishige, in *Ozu Yasujiro no Sekai* [The World of Yasujiro Ozu], (Japan Victor Album SJV-1140 1-M, 1972), side 4, band 2.

9. Sato, *Ozu Yasujiro no Geijutsu.*

10. *Ibid.*

11. For example, in *There Was a Father*, the father's kneeling in the opening scene is interrupted by a cut between two shots of the same action taken from different camera placements; and the activities of the workmen in *The Brothers and Sisters of the Toda Family*, are both fragmented and connected by one shot's showing half an action, the second shot's completing it.

12. Ozu's characters, like Antonioni's, live in this present and have no history. Ozu's purposeful failure to mention the all-important dead mother in *Late Spring* is just as astonishing, and just as right, as Antonioni's apparent lack of curiosity as to what happened to Anna in *L'Avventura*. And when a person dies in Ozu's world, which is often, he or she is merely and instantly *gone*. There are no ghosts in Ozu as there are in Resnais and Bergman. The past barely exists in Ozu. *Tokyo Story* is, indeed, about the natural advisability of forgetting the dead (daughter-in-law forgets dead husband; old man will forget dead wife), just as much as *L'Avventura* is about the horror Claudia and Sandro feel at forgetting Anna. The difference is that Ozu's people accept this from the beginning; Monica Vitti (in both *L'Avventura* and *L'Eclipse*) must "learn" to accept—she does not know the truth. The length of her education is the length of the film. Too, as we have seen, Ozu would not be concerned with a tableau at the end that faced Sandro with a blank wall and Claudia with a dormant or dead volcano.

CONCLUSION

1. For example, the classic unit of early cinema (long shot, medium shot, close-up), was originally occasioned by film so lacking in definition that one had to move forward to see what the character was doing. Today's finegrained film makes such primitive techniques unnecessary.

2. Donald Richie, *The Master's Book of Ikebana* (Tokyo: Weatherhill/Bijutu Shuppan-sha, 1966).

3. Jacques Maritain, *Religion and Culture* (1930); quoted in Paul Schrader, *Transcendental Style in Film: Ozu, Bresson, Dreyer* (Berkeley and Los Angeles: University of California Press, 1972).

4. *Ibid.*

5. Conversation with Ozu, 1959.

6. "Complaints about Films," *Bungei Shunju*, 1959; quoted in *Ozu Yasujiro—Hito to Shigoto* [Yasujiro Ozu: The Man and His Work] (Tokyo: Banyusha, 1972).

7. For example: "Much as I am impressed by the prodigiousness and virtuosity of Ozu's artistic rigor, I cannot suppress the feeling that Ozu's restrictive camera technique yields diminishing emotional returns in that by relentlessly transfiguring ordinary life it ends up by disfiguring it." Andrew Sarris, *Village Voice* (New York), May 4, 1972.

8. "A Talk with Ozu," *Kinema Jumpo*, June, 1958.

9. Kenzo Tange, *Katsura*, second edition (Tokyo and New Haven: Zokeisha/Yale University Press, 1972).

BIOGRAPHICAL FILMOGRAPHY

1. Tadao Sato, *Ozu Yasujiro no Geijutsu* [The Art of Yasujiro Ozu] (Tokyo: Asahi Shimbunsha, 1971).
2. Kogo Noda, "Ozu to iu Otoko" [A Man Called Ozu], *Kinema Jumpo Tokushu*, February 10, 1964.
3. Sato, *Ozu Yasujiro no Geijutsu.*
4. Noda, "Ozu to iu Otoko."
5. *Ibid.*
6. Sato, *Ozu Yasujiro.*
7. *Ibid.*
8. Conversation with Noboru Nakamura, 1969.
9. Max Tessier, *Yasujiro Ozu.* Anthologie due Cinéma, Juillet-Octobre, 1971.
10. Sato, *Ozu Yasujiro.*
11. "How I Became a Director," in Ozu, *Watashi no Shonen Jidai* [My Young Days], (Tokyo: Makishoten, 1954).
12. Sato, *Ozu Yasujiro.*
13. "Ozu Jitaku o Kataru" [Ozu on Ozu], *Kinema Jumpo*, June, 1958.
14. Noda, "Ozu to iu Otoko."
15. Conversation with Kiyohiko Ushihara, 1967.
16. Sato, *Ozu Yasujiro.*
17. A typical example occurs in *The End of Summer.* The old father is dying, the family is gathered about, pious remarks are heard. He recovers, and his first act, completed with a waggish wave at the surprised survivors, is to go to the toilet.
18. *Ibid.*
19. *Ibid.*
20. Conversation with Shiro Kido, 1963.
21. Sato, *Ozu Yasujiro.*
22. *Ozu Yasujiro—Hito to Shigoto* [Yasujiro Ozu: The Man and His Work] (Tokyo: Banyusha, 1972).
23. From a letter to Shiyo Oki and Yozo Yoshida, October 3, 1927, quoted in *ibid.*
24. *Ibid.*
25. *Ibid.*
26. *Ibid.*
27. *Ibid.*
28. With the home continuing (until recently) as the major social unit in Japan, it is difficult for a Japanese to understand that a term such as "home drama" can be perjorative, even though he recognizes the excesses of the genre. Ozu's feelings about the form, his acceptance of it despite its redundancies, is illustrated by an anecdote from the end of his life. As he

lay dying he was visited by Shiro Kido, of Shochiku. In pain, Ozu turned to Kido and, indicating the hospital, the bed, his own dying self, he smiled and said, "Well, it seems to be home drama to the last."

29. Conversation with Chishu Ryu, 1963.
30. *Ozu Yasujiro—Hito to Shigoto.*
31. Conversation with Kiyohiko Ushihara.
32. *Ozu Yasujiro—Hito to Shigoto.*
33. "Ozu Jitaku o Kataru" [Ozu on Ozu], *Kinema Jumpo,* June 1958.
34. *Ibid.*
35. *Ozu Yasujiro—Hito to Shigoto.*
36. "Ozu Jitaku o Kataru."
37. *Ibid.*
38. *Ibid.*
39. Sato, *Ozu Yasujiro.*
40. Noda, "Ozu to iu Otoko."
41. Matsuo Kishi, "Yasujiro Ozu no Issho" [The Life of Yasujiro Ozu], *Scenario* (Tokyo), February, 1964.
42. *Ozu Yasujiro—Hito to Shigoto.*
43. Noda, "Ozu to iu Otoko."
44. *Ibid.*
45. *Ozu—Hito to Shigoto.*
46. "Ozu Jitaku o Kataru."
47. *Ibid.*
48. *Ibid.*
49. "Ozu Jitaku o Kataru."
50. *Chuo Koron,* October, 1940.
51. *Ibid.*
52. *Ibid.*
53. Conversation with Akira Kurosawa, ca. 1959.
54. Conversation with Masahiro Shinoda, 1970.
55. Ozu, "One Year is Too Short." *Shin Eiga,* January, 1943.
56. *Ozu Yasujiro—Hito to Shigoto.*
57. *Star* (Tokyo), March, 1946.
58. Conversation with Kimisaburo Yoshimura, ca. 1960.
59. "Ozu Jitaku o Kataru."
60. Conversation with Noël Burch, 1972.
61. *Ozu Yasujiro—Hito to Shigoto.*
62. "Ozu Jitaku o Kataru."
63. *Ibid.*
64. *Ibid.*
65. *Ozu Yasujiro—Hito to Shigoto.*
66. "Ozu Jitaku o Kataru."
67. *Ozu Yasujiro—Hito to Shigoto.*
68. "Ozu Jitaku o Kataru."
69. From Yasujiro Ozu's acceptance speech, *Kinema Jumpo,* 1954.

70. *Ozu Yasujiro—Hito to Shigoto.*
71. "Ozu Jitaku o Kataru."
72. Ozu, program note for *Tokyo Twilight* (Shochiku, 1957).
73. *Ibid.*
74. "Ozu Jitaku o Kataru."
75. *Star* (Tokyo), March, 1946.
76. "Ozu Jitaku o Kataru."
77. *Ibid.*
78. *Ibid.*
79. *Ozu Yasujiro—Hito to Shigoto.*
80. From "Ozu Jitaku o Kataru," *Kinema Jumpo,* February, 1964.
81. *Ibid.*
82. *Ibid.*
83. Publicity statement for Shochiku, 1960.
84. "Ozu to iu Otoko."
85. *Ibid.*
86. *Ibid.*

BIBLIOGRAPHY

WRITINGS BY AND
CONVERSATIONS WITH OZU

Diaries; excerpts published in *Ozu Yasujiro—Hito to Shigoto.**
"Kogo Noda," *Eiga Hyoron,* Special Issue, June, 1933.
Discussion with Ozu on the film star, *Star* (Tokyo), October, 1935.
"Ofuna Kigeki." Skits and scenes written for the stage by Ozu, Noda, and others, ca. 1935–45. Unpublished. Shochiku Archives.
Program Notes. Hokakuza Theater, Tokyo, January 15–23, 1943.
"One Year is Too Short," *Shin Eiga,* January, 1943.
"American Films I Saw in the South" (interview), *Star,* March, 1946.
"Abusing the Star System," *Kinema Jumpo,* April, 1949. Translated in "Ozu Spectrum," *Cinema,* and in Schrader and Nakamura, eds., *Masters of the Japanese Film.*
"How I Became a Director," in compilation volume *Watashi no Shonen Jidai* [My Young Days]. Tokyo: Makishoten, 1954.
"Humanness and Technique," *Kinema Jumpo,* December, 1953. Translated in *Masters of the Japanese Film.*
"Complaints about Films," *Bungei Shunju,* 1959.
"Ozu Jitaku o Kataru" [Ozu on Ozu], *Kinema Jumpo,* June, 1958 (Part I), and February, 1964 (Part II). Translated in *Cinema* (Summer, 1970, Summer, 1971, Winter, 1972–3), and in *Masters of the Japanese Film.*

* There are fourteen volumes of diaries extant: 1933–35, 1936, in English-made Quick-Ref Diaries; 1938–39, so-called "War Diaries," Hakubunkan Pocket Diaries; 1952, Letters Diary; 1955, *Kinema Jumpo* Film Diary; 1962, Mitsui Bank Diary; 1954, 1959–61, 1963, Nihon Eiga Kantoku Kyokai Diary.

265

O Z U

"A Talk with Ozu," *Kinema Jumpo,* June, 1958. Translated in "Ozu Spectrum," *Cinema,* and in *Masters of the Japanese Film.* Taped interview with Ozu and Kogo Noda. Tokyo: Nippon Hoso Kyokai (NHK), ca. 1958. Excerpts recorded in *Ozu Yasujiro no Sekai* by Japan Victor. Remainder in vaults of NHK.

BOOKS, PAMPHLETS, AND SPECIAL MAGAZINE
ISSUES DEVOTED TO OZU

Ozu Yasujiro—Hito to Shigoto [Yasujiro Ozu: The Man and His Work]. Jun Satomi, Tomo Shimogawara, Shizuo Yamauchi, et al. eds. Tokyo: Banyusha, 1972.
Ozu Yasujiro—Hito to Geijutsu [Yasujiro Ozu: His Nature and Work]. *Kinema Jumpo Tokushu.* February 10, 1964.
Yasujiro Ozu. Program notes. Danske Filmmuseum, Copenhagen, November, 1963.
Yasujiro Ozu. Program notes. Nederland Filmmuseum, Amsterdam, September, 1963.
Filme von Yasujiro Ozu. Cinestudio OHTHW, Vienna, January 13–18, 1964.
Ozu. Program notes. National Film Theatre, London: August–November, 1963.
Ozu Yasujiro Eiga no Tokushu [Yasujiro Ozu Retrospective]. Program notes. The National Museum of Modern Art, Tokyo, December, 1965–January, 1966.
Richie, Donald. *Five Pictures of Yasujiro Ozu.* Tokyo: Shochiku, 1962. Translated into Japanese in *Ozu Yasujiro—Hito to Shigoto.*
Sato, Tadao. *Ozu Yasujiro no Geijutsu* [The Art of Yasujiro Ozu]. Tokyo: Asahi Shimbunsha, 1971. Sections translated into English in the *Japan Independent Film Bulletin,* Shibata K.K., 1966.
Tessier, Max. *Yasujiro Ozu.* Anthologie du Cinéma. Juillet–Octobre, 1971. Avant Scène du Cinéma, Paris.

BOOKS AND MAGAZINES WITH
SECTIONS DEVOTED TO OZU

Anderson, Joseph, and Donald Richie. *The Japanese Film: Art and Industry.* Tokyo and Rutland, Vt.: Tuttle, 1959. New York: Grove Press, 1960.
Burch, Noël. *Theory of Film Practice.* New York and Washington: Praeger, 1973.
Kinema Jumpo, June, 1958.
"Ozu Spectrum," *Cinema,* Summer, 1970.
Richie, Donald. *The Japanese Movie: An Illustrated History.* Tokyo and Palo Alto, Calif.: Kodansha, 1966.

BIBLIOGRAPHY

————. *Japanese Cinema: Film Style & National Character*. New York: Doubleday/Anchor, 1971.

Schrader, Leonard, and Haruji Nakamura, eds. *Masters of Japanese Film*. Tokyo and New York: Weatherhill, in press.

Schrader, Paul. *Transcendental Style in Film: Ozu, Bresson, Dreyer*. Berkeley and Los Angeles: University of California Press, 1972.

ARTICLES ON OZU AND
SELECTED REVIEWS

Anonymous. "Yasujiro Ozu," *Film*, Summer, 1963.

Byron, Stuart. "Late Spring," *The Real Paper*, Boston, February 28, 1973.

————. "Right Angles in the Circle" (*Late Spring*), *Village Voice*, New York, August 17, 1972.

————. "The Decline of Consciousness One" (*End of Summer*), *Village Voice*, January 21, 1972.

Child, James. "Humanity and Love Japanese Style," *New Haven Register*, June 19, 1972.

Clark, John. "Spatial Aspects of Ozu's Films." Unpublished ms.

Cocks, Jay. "An Autumn Afternoon," *Time*, June 4, 1973.

Cowie, Peter, ed. "Twelve Japanese Directors, an Index," *International Film Guide*. New York: Barnes, 1965.

Delpt, Gert. "Das foldende Gesprach zwischen Donald Richie und Gert Delpt über den japanischen Regisseur Ozu" (conversation), July, 1963, Berlin. *Kino* (Berlin), 1963.

Farber, Manny. "Ozu," *Art Forum*, June, 1970.

Foery, Raymond. "The Assimilation of Ozu." Unpublished ms.

Gilliatt, Penelope. "Sometimes the Twain," *The New Yorker*, April 8, 1972.

Greenspun, Roger. "Mizoguchi and Ozu—Two Masters from Japan," *New York Times*, July 9, 1972.

Halberstadt, Michael. "Ozu's Protagonists: Ignorance, Sacrifice, Loneliness, Resignation, Happiness." Unpublished ms.

Hatch, Robert. "The Family of Ozu," *The Nation*, June 22, 1964.

Hyberger, Hy. "Ozu and the Family," *The Foreign Screen*, January 20, 1967.

Iwasaki, Akira. "The Japanese Cinema," *Film*, November–December, 1956.

————. Untitled essay on Ozu, published (in English) by Shochiku as advance publicity for *Late Autumn*, 1960.

————. "Ozu," *Film*, Summer, 1965.

Kauffmann, Stanley. "A Masterpiece" (*Tokyo Story*), *The New Republic*, March 18, 1972.

Kelly, Kevin. "Ozu's Golden Imprint." *Boston Evening Globe*, February 27, 1973.

267

Kishi, Matsuo. "Yasujiro Ozu no Issho" [The Life of Yasujiro Ozu], *Scenario* (Tokyo). February, 1964.

Koch, John. "Late Spring," *Boston Herald-American*, February 26, 1973.

Lawson, Sylvia. "An Autumn Afternoon," *The Nation*, July 27, 1964.

Lebovich, Sheelagh. "The Ozu Retrospective," *Japan Times*, February 26, 1972.

Leonard, Harold. "Tokyo Story," *Film Notes* (University of California, Los Angeles), April 8, 1956.

Levine, Martin. "Why the Film Buffs Go Wild over Japan's Ozu," *Newsday*, New York, February 16, 1973.

Magliozzi, Ronald. *"Tokyo Story:* The Philosophy of Ozu's Geometry." Unpublished ms.

Michener, Charles. "A Master from Japan" (*Tokyo Story*), *Newsweek*, March 27, 1972.

———. "A Father and Daughter" (*Late Spring*), *Newsweek*, July 31, 1972.

Miller, David. "The Poetry of *Tokyo Story*." Unpublished ms.

Milne, Tom. "Flavor of Green Tea over Rice," *Sight and Sound*, Autumn, 1963.

Mukherjee, Dilip. "Ozu and *Equinox Flower*," *Parichaya* (Calcutta), January, 1966.

Newstat, Elizabeth. "Ozu's Use of the Familiar Object." Unpublished ms.

Philippe, Jean-Claude. "Yasujiro Ozu," in *Dossiers du Cinéma: Cinéastes* No. 1. Paris: Casterman, 1971.

Richie, Donald. "The Later Films of Yasujiro Ozu," *Film Quarterly*, Fall, 1959.

———. "Ozu, Naruse, Toyoda, and the Japanese Tradition," *Eiga Hyron*, August, 1960.

———. "Yasujiro Ozu: The Syntax of his Films," *Film Quarterly*, Winter, 1963–64.

———. "Yasujiro Ozu: A Biographical Filmography," *Film Comment*, Spring, 1971.

———. "Notes for a Definition of the Japanese Film," *Performance*, Spring, 1972.

Rosenbaum, Jonathan. "Ozu," *Film Comment*. Summer, 1972.

Ryu, Chishu. "Ozu to Watakushi" [Ozu and I: Reflections on My Mentor], *Kinema Jumpo*, June, 1958. Translated in "Ozu Spectrum," *Cinema*.

———. "Yasujiro Ozu," *Sight and Sound*, Spring, 1964.

———. "Ozu," *World Cinema*, August 4, 1972.

Sadoul, Georges. "Un très grand réalisateur japonais est mort," *Les Lettres françaises*, December 19, 1963.

Schrader, Paul. Introduction to "Ozu Spectrum," *Cinema*.

Scott, Jonathan. "The Art of Ozu," *Rolling Stone*, April 13, 1972.

BIBLIOGRAPHY

Simon, John. "Clever Adequacy, Simple Greatness," *The New Leader*, March 20, 1972.

Wolf, Barbara. "Those Longueurs in Japanese Films," *The Nation*, August 30, 1971.

Wolfe, Charles. "Inside the Japanese Home: The Cinematic Architecture of Yasujiro Ozu," in *Projections* (Columbia University), 1973.

Zeaman, Marvin. "The Zen Artistry of Yasujiro Ozu: The Serene Poet of Japanese Cinema," *Film Journal*, Fall–Winter, 1972.

RECORDINGS

Ozu Yasujiro no Sekai [The World of Yasujiro Ozu]. Tokyo: Japan Victor, 1972. SJV-1140-1M (2 12″-LP discs). Produced by Kazuo Inoue, written by Toshio Shirai, in collaboration with the Chuo Ongaku Shuppan K.K. and Victor Shuppan K.K. Interviews with Ozu and Noda, as well as many actors and associates. Dialogue excerpts and music from the sound tracks of: *The Only Son, What Did the Lady Forget?, The Brothers and Sisters of the Toda Family, The Record of a Tenement Gentleman, Late Spring, Early Summer, Tokyo Story, Early Spring, Tokyo Twilight, Equinox Flower, Early Autumn, The End of Summer, An Autumn Afternoon.*

Ozu Yasujiro Meisaku Eiga Ongaku Shu [Ozu Yasujiro Memorial Album: Music from his Masterpieces]. Tokyo: Japan Crown, 1972. Stereo GW-5233 (1 12″-LP disc). Music by Kojun Saito. Played by the Rurijia Ensemble, conducted by Hiroshi Yoshizawa. Music from *An Autumn Afternoon, Late Autumn, Early Spring, Tokyo Story, Floating Weeds, Equinox Flower;* also the popular song "Sasereshiya" which appeared in several of Ozu's pictures, the music-box sounds used in *Late Spring*, etc., and the festival music used in both *Floating Weeds* and *Late Autumn*.

MEMORABILIA

Ozu, Yasujiro. Drawings. Fourteen color drawings, reproduced as supplement for *Ozu Yasujiro—Hito to Shigoto*.

———. Drawing. Sketch with calligraphic inscription, reproduced and distributed by Toho, as publicity for *The End of Summer*, 1961.

———. Drawing. Sketch reproduced on fishplates and distributed by Shochiku as publicity for *An Autumn Afternoon*, 1962.

INDEX

271

INDEX

DESIGN:	Bill Snyder
COPY-EDITING:	Muriel Bell
PROOFREADING:	Vail-Ballou Press, Inc.
LAYOUT:	Ernest Callenbach
IMPOSITION:	Vail-Ballou Press, Inc.
PRESSWORK:	Vail-Ballou Press, Inc.
BINDING:	Vail-Ballou Press, Inc.